VACATION TOWNS
OF CALIFORNIA

California Series

The Complete Gold Country Guidebook
The Complete Lake Tahoe Guidebook
The Complete Monterey Peninsula Guidebook
The Complete San Diego Guidebook
The Complete Wine Country Guidebook
Vacation Towns of California

Hawaii Series

The Complete Kauai Guidebook
The Complete Maui Guidebook
The Complete Oahu Guidebook
The Complete Big Island of Hawaii Guidebook

Outdoor Series

California Campers' Handbook
California State Parks Handbook

Adventure Series

An Adventurer's Guide to Humboldt County
An Adventurer's Guide to Mendocino County

Indian Chief Travel Guides are available from your local bookstore or Indian Chief Publishing House, P.O. Box 1814, Davis, California 95617.

VACATION TOWNS
of
CALIFORNIA

Published by Indian Chief Publishing House ™
Davis, California

Area Editor: **B. Sangwan**
Editorial Associate: **Phillippa Savage**
Photographs: **Monterey Peninsula**
Chamber of Commerce, B. Sangwan

ISBN 0-916841-65-0

Printed in the U.S.A.

CONTENTS

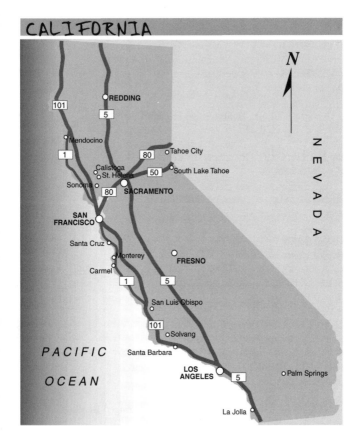

FOREWORD

California is one of the most desirable tourist destinations in the country, with more than three-quarters of all the tourist activity in the West centered in the state. California offers a variety that is both vast and astonishing—from sandy beaches and palm deserts to alpine settings, lush wine regions, and redwood forests—with good visitor facilities available throughout.

In *Vacation Towns of California* we have selected fourteen of the state's most exciting resort towns—Calistoga, Carmel, La Jolla, Mendocino, Monterey, Palm Springs, St. Helena, San Luis Obispo, Santa Barbara, Santa Cruz, Solvang, Sonoma, South Lake Tahoe and Tahoe City—which display a variety as diverse and interesting as California itself. In Santa Barbara, for instance, you will find one of the most amazing collections of old, Spanish architecture and some of the most beautiful, palm-fringed beaches; Santa Cruz, too is famous for its beaches and surf. Sonoma and St. Helena, of course, lie in the heart of the "wine country," with a flavor that is truly reflective of the good life of California. Monterey and Carmel are two picturesque little towns on California's Central Coast, which have long been havens for artists and writers. Mendocino, perched on a rocky bluff on the North Coast and frequently shrouded in fog, is perhaps most reminiscent of Cape Cod; while La Jolla, on the Southern California coast, has its distinct Mediterranean charm. Palm Springs, of course, is America's most famous desert resort, and a golf capital of sorts. And Tahoe City and South Lake Tahoe, situated in the High Sierra at an elevation of approximately 6,300 feet, are typical—and charming—alpine resorts.

Vacation Towns of California will introduce you to these and other towns, with information on all their major attractions and seasonal events, accommodations and restaurants, recreational facilities and other such special features as wineries, beaches, hot springs, casinos, ski resorts, art galleries, and more. Maps have also been provided, pinpointing hundreds of places of interest, and an index at the end of the book has been specially designed to enable you to access information simply and quickly.

We hope you enjoy the book and, with it, California's favorite vacation towns!

— Editors

CALISTOGA

Hot Springs of the West

 Calistoga is a small, colorful resort town situated at the northern end of the celebrated Napa Valley, famous for its mineral hot springs and mild climate, and now, increasingly, also for its wineries. It enjoys a picturesque setting near the base of Mount St. Helena, surrounded, almost completely, by preserved forest and lush, colorful vineyards. It also has good guest accommodations—including lodging at spa resorts—and abundant opportunities for outdoor enthusiasts, among them hiking, bicycling and soaring in gliders and hot air balloons.

 In order to reach Calistoga—lying approximately 55 miles northeast of San Francisco—it is necessary first to journey to the city of Napa at the southern end of the Napa Valley, either on Highway 101 north from San Francisco, and a combination of Highways 116 and 12; or by way of Interstate 80 east, and Highways 12 and 121 north. From Napa, again, you have a choice of routes, Highway 29 or the Silverado Trail, leading more or less directly to Calistoga.

DISCOVERING CALISTOGA

Calistoga is a place almost of pilgrimage, where health-seekers and holiday-makers alike go to reap the benefits of the area's chalybeate springs—as well as its volcanic ash, also noted for its curative powers—soaking in hot mineral pools and the equally invigorating mud baths. The town itself was originally founded by Sam Brannan, California's first millionaire, who established here in 1868 the first of the area's hot springs resorts, and named it "Calistoga" which, we are told, is derived from confusing the words, "California" and "Saratoga." In any case, there are no fewer than eight full-fledged hot springs spa resorts in this tiny town, offering visitors a wide range of health and beauty treatments, and all sorts of exotic baths—steam, mud, mineral, herbal, sulphur. Most of the resorts are located in the downtown area, on Lincoln Avenue and Washington and Lake streets, and Brannan's old resort—now Indian Hot Springs—situated just off Lincoln Avenue at the north end of town, is still open to the public.

Calistoga, notably, is also home to some of the nation's best known mineral water bottling companies. The Calistoga Mineral Water Company, for one, is located on Silverado Trail, bottling its sparkling water at the very source. Crystal Geyser, another well-known mineral water bottler, has its plant on Washington Street. Worth seeing too—and this is one of Calistoga's great spectacles—is the "Old Faithful" geyser on Tubbs Lane, just to the north of town. It is one of the area's oldest and most famous geysers, claimed to be among only three regularly erupting geysers in the world: it erupts approximately every 50 minutes, gushing forth in a fountain of boiling water and steam, some 60 feet or so directly into the air. There is a small picnic area at the site, and an admission fee is charged.

Downtown Calistoga also has something of interest. Its main street, Lincoln Avenue, is lined with many old and lovely buildings—both native-stone and clapboard structures—dating from the late 1800s and early 1900s, now housing modern shops, restaurants and one or two hotels. The loveliest of these is perhaps the Mount View Hotel, at the top end of Lincoln Avenue. It dates from the mid-1800s and has been splendidly restored to its former elegance. Across the street from the hotel is the old Calistoga Depot, also well worth visiting. It is said to be the oldest existing railroad depot in California, dating from 1868. It, too, now houses a charming little shopping arcade, with gift shops, a wine shop, delicatessen and a well-liked cafe. Alongside the depot, on the railroad tracks are a half-dozen old Southern Pacific rail cars, refurbished and converted, again, into unique shops, specializing in rare gifts and old-fashioned candy.

Just off Lincoln Avenue, a block or so east on Washington Street is the Sharpsteen Museum, another place of visitor interest. It is a small but unique museum, with some excellent displays of Calistoga's pioneer history, including three or four superb dioramas, one of which features Brannan's original hot springs resort and the town as it appeared in the 1860s. Adjoining the museum—and, in fact, with its entrance through the museum—is Brannan's old cottage, built in 1866

CALISTOGA

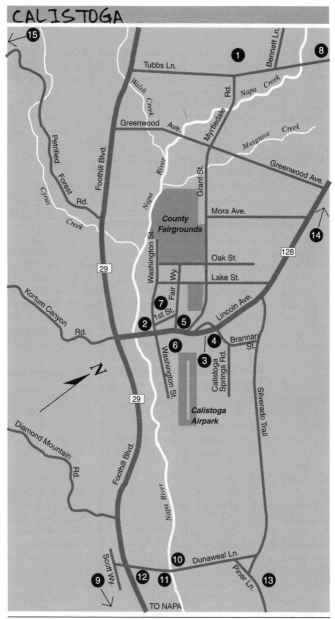

1. Old Faithful Geyser
2. Sharpsteen Museum
3. Old Calistoga Depot
4. Indian Hot Springs
5. Dr. Wilkinson's Hot Springs
6. Calistoga Spa Hot Springs
7. Roman Spa
8. Chateau Montelena
9. Schramsberg Vineyards
10. Clos Pegas
11. Sterling Vineyards
12. Stonegate Winery
13. Cuvaison Winery
14. Robert Louis Stevenson State Park
15. Petrified Forest

and now beautifully restored with original 19th-century furnishings and antiques. The museum and cottage are open on weekdays, 10 a.m.-4 p.m.

Calistoga also makes for an ideal base from which to explore the Napa Valley, with its famous old wine estates, just to the south. But first, in and around Calistoga itself there are a half-dozen or so well-known wineries which you should try to visit, some of them indeed quite historic. Just south of Calistoga, for instance, on a small side road off the highway (29), is the celebrated Schramsberg Vineyards, founded in 1862 by pioneer vintner Jacob Schram, and memorialized, in 1880, by noted author Robert Louis Stevenson in his book, *The Silverado Squatters*. Schramsberg makes bottle-fermented champagne primarily, and can be visited by prior appointment.

A little way from Schramsberg Vineyards, on Dunaweal Lane, which goes off the highway, eastward, are the Stonegate Winery and Sterling Vineyards, both with tourist interest. The latter is especially to be recommended to first-time visitors to the area, housed in a splendid, white Mediterranean-style building perched on a hilltop, overlooking valley vineyards. The only way up to the winery is by way of an aerial tram, which, again, has superb views of the valley. At the winery there is an excellent, self-guided tour of the winemaking facility, quite interesting to wine buffs who can study, at their own pace, the winemaking process. There is also a comfortable tasting room here, and a delightful patio with panoramic views, where you can sample Sterling wines. A gift-cum-wine shop on the premises retails Sterling wines, as well as wine-related books, gifts and other paraphernalia.

Also of interest, not far from Sterling Vineyards, located just to the north on Dunaweal Lane, is Clos Pegase, one of Napa Valley's newer but more prominent wineries, housed in a dramatic Greco-Roman, architect-designed stucco edifice, built in 1986 as a tribute to wine, art and mythology. The winery, in fact, is named for the mythological flying house, Pegasus, featured on its wine label. The winery is open to the public for wine tasting and sales, and tours of the facility can also be arranged.

Among other interesting wineries in the Calistoga area are the Robert Pecota Winery, just north of town, and Cuvaison which is situated at the top end of the Silverado Trail and housed in a lovely Spanish-style building. Chateau Montelana, also north of Calistoga, on a side road that dashes off Tubbs Lane, is housed in a picturesque, French chateau-style stone castle, overlooking the artificially-created, yet beautiful, Jade Lake, with its small, Oriental bridges and red, lacquered pavilions, and a real Chinese junk beached at one end of the lake. Chateau Montelana is also notable as the maker of the famous 1973 Chardonnay that won top honors at the "Paris Tasting" in 1976, launching California wines as among the finest in the world.

Besides touring wineries, Calistoga has several other activities to interest the visitor; among them, bicycling, with several scenic trails crisscrossing between valley vineyards, and hiking in the abounding state and national park lands. Calistoga also has a glider base from where you can take glider rides over the valley.

DETOURS

Two other places of note, quite close to Calistoga and worthy of a visit, are the Robert Louis Stevenson State Historic Park and the Petrified Forest. The first of these, located just north of Calistoga, off Highway 29, is a 4,000-acre state-run park, dedicated to the famous Scottish-born writer and containing in it the spectacular, 4,334-foot Mount St. Helena. Stevenson, it is told, spent his honeymoon in an abandoned old bunkhouse near the base of Mount St. Helena in the spring of 1880, gathering notes for his Napa Valley classic, *The Silverado Squatters*. The park offers good hiking possibilities, with one trail actually journeying to the summit of Mount St. Helena, from where splendid, all-round views can be enjoyed.

At the Petrified Forest, which lies six miles or so to the east of Calistoga on the Petrified Forest Road, one can view ancient, fallen redwoods—all turned to stone! The forest was first uprooted during the volcanic period, nearly six million years ago, and the fallen trees remained buried beneath the lava and volcanic ash over the next several centuries, until a few thousand years ago water and silica solution seeped through the ash and into the trees, turning them, over a period of time, into stone. Most of these petrified trees are now on display at the Petrified Forest, and there are, besides, a souvenir shop and picnic facilities here as well.

HOW TO GET THERE

Calistoga is situated in the upper Napa Valley, nearly 80 miles northeast of San Francisco. In order to reach it, follow *Highway 101* directly north from San Francisco to Novato (26 miles), then *Highways 37* and *121* northeast to the city of Napa, another 25 miles. From Napa, *Highway 29* leads more or less directly to Calistoga, some 27 miles northwest.

An alternative route is by way of *Interstate 80* east from San Francisco to Vallejo (31 miles), then *Highway 29* directly north to Napa, another 14 miles. From Napa, again, continue on *Highway 29* to arrive at Calistoga.

TOURIST INFORMATION

Calistoga Chamber of Commerce. Housed in the Old Depot, at 1458 Lincoln Ave., Calistoga; (707) 942-6333. Information on lodging, restaurants, spas and wineries; calendar of events. There is also a *Wine Country Bed & Breakfast Reservations* service in the Napa Valley area; call (707) 963-9114 for referrals and reservations.

ACCOMMODATIONS

Bed & Breakfast Inns

Brannan Cottage Inn. *$140-$215.* 109 Wapoo Ave.; (707) 942-4200. Award winning inn, housed in an historic cottage built by Sam Brannan in 1860. 6 guest rooms. Enchanting garden setting.

Culver's. *$140-$160.* 1805 Foothill Blvd.; (707) 942-4535. Beautifully restored 1875 Victorian home, now an historical landmark, situated within easy walking distance of shops and restaurants. 6 guest rooms, individually decorated with period furnishings; panoramic views of Mount St. Helena. Sitting room with fireplace; pool, spa, sauna.

The Elms. *$125-$185.* 1300 Cedar St.; (707) 942-9476. Elegant French-Victorian inn, built in 1871. 4 guest rooms, decorated with European antiques. Complimentary wine and cheese. Central location.

Larkmead Country Inn. *$138.* 1103 Larkmead St.; (707) 942-5360. Turn-of-the-century Victorian inn, surrounded by vineyards. 3 guest rooms, filled with antiques, Persian carpets and old paintings.

The Pink Mansion. *$135-$225.* 1415 Foothill Blvd.; (707) 942-0558. Charming 100-year-old Victorian mansion, nestled amid gardens on 3 wooded acres. 5 comfortable rooms with picture-postcard views of surrounding countryside. Also, heated indoor pool and game room. Gourmet breakfast.

Silver Rose Inn. *$155-$270.* 351 Rosedale Rd.; (707) 942-9581. Splendid setting among live oaks on a rocky outcropping overlooking Napa Valley vineyards. 4 guest rooms, with private baths and balconies. Pool, spa.

Trailside Inn. *$165-$185.* 4201 Silverado Trail; (707) 942-4106. Picturesque 1930s ranch house; 2 completely private suites, with private baths, living rooms with fireplaces, kitchenettes, and porches. Complimentary wine, and freshly-baked breads.

Zinfandel House. *$85-$110.* 1253 Tucker Rd.; (707) 942-0733. Country home in wooded setting, with commanding views of the Napa Valley. 2 beautifully furnished rooms; spacious deck. Country breakfast; complimentary wine.

Hotels and Motels

Calistoga Village Inn. *$65-$159.* 1880 Lincoln Ave.; (707) 942-0991. Newer inn and spa resort, offering rooms with TV and phone; some suites with whirlpools. Full range of spa services; also geothermal mineral swimming pools. Restaurant on premises.

Comfort Inn. *$75-$125.* 1865 Lincoln Ave.; (707) 942-9400/(800) 228-5150. 55 units, with TV and phones; heated pool, mineral water whirlpool, steamroom and sauna. Complimentary continental breakfast.

Hideaway Cottages. *$65-$125.* 1412 Fairway; (707) 942-4108. 17 vintage housekeeping cottages, with TV and air-conditioning. Jacuzzi and mineral-water pool for guests. No children.

Mount View Hotel. *$110-$200.* 1475 Lincoln Ave.; (707) 942-6877. Restored old hotel, with 24 rooms and 9 suites, all with private baths. Also pool, hot tub, restaurant and cocktail lounge; jazz music featured in restaurant on Sundays. Hotel rates include full breakfast.

Spa Resorts

(Note: Mud bath prices usually include blanket wrap, steam room and whirlpool bath.)

Calistoga Spa Hot Springs. 1006 Washington St.; (707) 942-6269. Family-style hot springs resort, with two outdoor hot mineral pools, one covered jet pool and one outdoor wading pool; also weight and workout rooms, and aerobic classes. Mud bath $44.00, with massage $70.00. 48 motel units on premises, with kitchenettes and air-conditioning; $87-$120.

Calistoga Village Inn and Spa. 1880 Lincoln Ave.; (707) 942-0991. Newer spa resort, offering accommodations and a full range of spa treatments. Geothermal mineral swimming pools. Mud bath $40.00; various treatment packages range in price from $65.00 to $150.00. Restaurant on premises.

Dr. Wilkinson's Hot Springs. 1507 Lincoln Ave.; (707) 942-4102. Well-known spa, with good accommodations. Offers two warm outdoor mineral pools, one large indoor mineral whirlpool, and a swimming pool. Mud bath $55.00, with massage $89.00. Accommodations include 37 air-conditioned motel units, some with kitchenettes; also some cottages; $109-$149.

Golden Haven Spa. 1713 Lake St.; (707) 942-6793. Facilities include a covered pool, hot mineral pools, an exercise room and sun deck. Mud bath $22.00, $35.00 with massage. Accommodations: 30 units, with air-conditioning; some kitchenettes, some private saunas and jacuzzis. $39-$79.

Indian Hot Springs. 1712 Lincoln Ave.; (707) 942-4913. Oldest spa resort in Calistoga, established in 1862. Facilities include an outdoor hot mineral pool and sulphur steam cabinet. Mud bath $50.00, with massage $70.00. Also, 17 rental cottages on grounds, with TV, full kitchens, and housekeeping facilities; $150-$180.

International Spa/Lavender Hill Spa. 1300 Washington St.; (707) 942-6122. Offer mineral water baths and also seaweed baths. Cost $55.00. Also a variety of other spa treatments. Pools and accommodations available at the adjoining Roman Spa.

Lincoln Avenue Spa. 1339 Lincoln Ave.; (707) 942-5296. Treatments offered here include mud wraps, herbal wraps, accupressure facelifts and foot reflexology. Cost for mud wrap with one-hour massage is $75.00. No accommodations.

Nance's Hot Springs. 1614 Lincoln Ave.; (707) 942- 6211. Family owned and operated spa resort, with hot mineral pool, whirlpool, hot sulphur and steam baths, and volcanic ash mud baths. Cost of mud bath $65.00 with half-hour massage, $85.00 with one-hour massage. Also available are 24 lodging units, with TV, air-conditioning, and kitchenettes; $60-$80.

Roman Spa. 1300 Washington St.; (707) 942-4441. Outdoor warm mineral pool and hot jacuzzi; also indoor hot mineral pool, Swedish sauna, and large swimming pool. Mud baths, massage and other spa treatments available at adjacent International Spa (see listing above). Accommodations include 51 modern units with air- conditioning, TV, and kitchenettes; also some cottages; $69-$179.

SEASONAL EVENTS

January. *Napa Valley Mustard Festival.* Valley-wide festivities highlighting the beauty, culture and agriculture of the Napa Valley. Events include food and wine tastings, and a marathon. For more information, call (707) 259-9020.

April. *Springfest.* Celebration of the arrival of spring held at the Napa County Fairgrounds in Calistoga. Music, food concessions, and beer sampling. (707) 942-5111.

July. *Napa County Fair.* Held at the Fairgrounds during the first week of the month. Activities include a carnival, horse show, wine show, exhibits and stage shows. *Fourth of July Celebrations.* Lincoln Ave. Colorful parade down the main street of town, followed by fireworks at the Fairgrounds. *Sharpsteen Annual Rummage Sale.* At the Sharpsteen Museum on Washington St.; also during the first week of the month. For more information on these events, contact the Calistoga Chamber of Commerce on (707) 942-6333.

October. *Calistoga Beer and Sausage Festival.* Sample dozens of varieties of beer and sausages at the fairgrounds. More information on (707) 942-6333.

PLACES OF INTEREST

The Sharpsteen Museum. 1311 Washington St.; (707) 942-5911. Unique small museum, founded by Disney producer Ben Sharpsteen. Displays are of items of local historical interest, and include a superb scale model diorama of Calistoga as it appeared in 1865; other dioramas feature the Chinese quarter of town, railroad depot, and the life of Robert Louis Stevenson. Also, adjoining the museum is the old Brannan Cottage, dating from the 1860s and now restored to its former glory; it, too, can be visited. The museum is open daily 10-4 in summer, 12-4 in winter; no admission fee, donations requested.

Robert Louis Stevenson State Park. Hwy. 29, 5 miles north of Calistoga; (707) 942-4575. Undeveloped 4,000-acre park, containing Mount St. Helena. Novelist Robert Louis Stevenson spent his honeymoon here in 1880, in a cottage at the base of Mount St. Helena. A hiking trail now journeys to the top of the mountain, with sweeping valley views to be enjoyed from the summit. There are no facilities available at park; bring your own water. Free admission.

The Old Calistoga Depot. 1458 Lincoln Ave.; (707) 942- 6332. Second oldest railroad depot in California, built in 1866. The Depot now houses a shopping arcade, with a restaurant and specialty shops; it also features a restored, 112-year-old passenger coach inside the arcade. Alongside the depot are six refurbished railcars, housing specialty shops featuring unique gifts and old-fashioned candy. Shops are open daily.

Old Faithful Geyser. 1299 Tubbs Lane (2 miles north of Calistoga, off Hwy. 128); (707) 942-6463. Oldest and most famous of Calistoga's geysers, and one of only three regularly erupting geysers in the world; erupts approximately every 40 minutes, in a fountain of boiling hot water and steam, some 60 feet directly into the air. Picnic area at site. Admission: $6.00/adults, $5.00/seniors, $2.00/children (ages 6-12). Open daily, 9-6 in summer and 9-5 in winter.

The Petrified Forest. Petrified Forest Road, 6 miles northwest of Calistoga; (707) 942-6667. View giant redwoods in an ancient forest, all uprooted during the volcanic period millions of years ago, and turned to stone. The largest of these, the "Queen of the Forest," measures 80 feet in length and 8 feet in diameter. Picnic area, and museum and gift shop on premises. Admission: $4.00/adults, $3,00/seniors (over 60) and juniors (ages 12-17), $2.00/children (ages 6-11). Open daily 10-5.

Pioneer Cemetery. Foothill Blvd.. Historic cemetery, with graves of early settlers; some headstones date from 1885.

Also see **Spa Resorts** under *Accommodations*.

WINERIES

Chateau Montelana. 1429 Tubbs Lane; (707) 942-5105. Winery housed in picturesque, native-stone castle dating from 1882, situated on a hillside overlooking beautiful Jade Lake. Producer of high-quality, Napa and Sonoma County varietal wines. Open for tasting and sales, daily 10-4; tours by appointment.

Clos Pegase. 1060 Dunaweal Lane; (707) 942-4981. Newer Napa Valley winery, housed in dramatic Greco-Roman, architect-designed stucco edifice, built in 1986 as a tribute to wine, art and mythology. The winery produces varietal wines. Tasting and sales 10.30-5 daily; tours by appointment.

Cuvaison Winery. 4550 Silverado Trail; (707) 942-6266. Elegant, white Spanish-style winery with landscaped grounds and picnic area. Owned by Swiss banking family. Tasting room open daily 10-4; tours by appointment.

Robert Pecota Winery. 3299 Bennett Lane; (707) 942- 6625. Small, owner-operated winery situated at the foot of Mount St. Helena, producing primarily varietal wines. Visitors by appointment only; call for hours.

Schramsberg Vineyards. 1400 Schramsberg Rd.; (707) 942-4558. Historic Napa cellars, established in 1862 by pioneer vintner Jacob Schram, and visited in 1880 by noted author Robert Louis Stevenson who wrote about in his book, *The Silverado Squatters*. Hillside setting; ancient ageing caves. Schramsberg specializes in fine *méthode champenoise* sparkling wines. Visitors by appointment.

Sterling Vineyards. 1111 Dunaweal Lane; (707) 942-3344. Spectacular, white Mediterranean-style winery, situated on a hill overlooking valley vineyards. Ride aerial tram up to the winery. Superb self-guided tour. Tasting room and patio, wine and gift shop. Open daily 10.30-4.30 (closed Mon. and Tues. in winter); tram fee: $6.00 adults, $3.00 children under 18.

Stonegate Winery. 1183 Dunaweal Lane; (707) 942-6500. Small, family owned and operated winery, founded in 1973. Tasting and sales 10.30-4 daily; tours by appointment.

RECREATION

Ballooning. *Calistoga Balloon Adventures,* (707) 942-6546. Scenic balloon flights over the upper Napa Valley, followed by champagne brunch; complimentary flight certificate and photo. Cost: $180.00 per person.

Bicycling. Calistoga, much like the rest of the Napa Valley, offers several opportunities to cyclists, leisurely exploring back roads, crisscrossing between vineyards. For bicycle rentals and service, contact *Palisades Mountain Sports,* 1330B Gerrard St. (off Washington St.); (707) 942-9687.

Golf. *Mount St. Helena Golf Course.* Located at the Fairgrounds; (707)

942-9966. 9-hole course, 2,700 yards, 34 Par; green fees: $12.00 weekdays, $18.00 weekends. Facilities include a clubhouse, coffee shop, rental of clubs and hand carts, pro shop, putting green, and practice fairway.

Tennis & Racquetball. *Monhoff Center,* cnr. Stevenson and Grant Sts.; (707) 942-2800. Facilities include 4 tennis courts, 2 indoor racquetball courts, and a jogging track; night lights.

Horseback Riding. *Oak Hill Stables,* 3485 Porter Creek Road, Santa Rosa (8 miles from Calistoga); (707) 528-6498. Horse rentals $20.00 per hour; breakfast rides $40.00 per person; dinner rides $45.00 per person.

RESTAURANTS

(Restaurant prices—based on full course dinner, excluding drinks, tax and tips—are categorized as follows: *Deluxe,* over $30; *Expensive,* $20-$30; *Moderate,* $10-$20; *Inexpensive,* under $10.)

Alex's. *Moderate-Expensive.* 1437 Lincoln Ave.; (707) 942-6868. House specialties include prime rib and seafood. Fresh fruit daiquiris. Open for breakfast, lunch and dinner daily.

All Seasons Market and Cafe. *Inexpensive-Moderate.* 1400 Lincoln Ave.; (707) 942-9111. Deli-cum-cafe, with a small restaurant, pastry shop, wine shop, delicatessen and market. Restaurant serves soups, sandwiches, salads, pate, and homemade croissants; also delicious pastries and ice cream. Napa Valley wines by the glass. Lunch daily; brunch and dinner on weekends.

Bosko's Ristorante. *Moderate.* 1364 Lincoln Ave.; (707) 942-9088. Delightful Italian restaurant, specializing in homemade pasta and Italian desserts. Espresso bar, wine bar. Casual atmosphere. Open for lunch and dinner daily.

Calistoga Inn. *Moderate.* 1250 Lincoln Ave.; (707) 942-4101. Seafood and continental specialties, served in a relaxed, turn-of-the-century atmosphere; menu changes daily. Garden patio for outdoor dining. Extensive wine list; full bar. Dinners from 5.30 p.m. daily; lunch in summer. Reservations required.

Catahoula Restaurant and Saloon. *Moderate-Expensive.* In the Mount View Hotel, 1475 Lincoln Ave.; (707) 942-2275. Southern-style cuisine, served in Art Deco-style dining room; some Cajun entrees. Extensive wine list, featuring Napa and Sonoma county wines. Open for dinner daily; breakfast and lunch on weekends.

The Cinnabar Restaurant and Cafe. *Moderate.* 1440 Lincoln Ave.; (707) 942-6989. Elegantly-furnished, established Calistoga restaurant serving omelettes, hot cakes, burgers and sandwiches; also fresh fish, broiled steaks, chicken and crepes. Wine by the glass, fresh fruit drinks and daiquiris; espresso bar. Open 7.30 a.m.-10 p.m. daily.

Hydro Bar & Grill. *Moderate-Expensive.* 1403 Lincoln Ave.; (707) 942-9777. Popular local restaurant serving steak, burgers and sandwiches. Also features beer from over 20 micro-breweries. Open for breakfast, lunch and dinner daily; also late night menu.

Pacifico Restaurante Mexicano. *Moderate.* 1237 Lincoln Ave.; (707) 942-4400. Features traditional and regional Mexican cuisine. Hand- shaken margaritas. Open for lunch and dinner daily; brunch on weekends.

SooYuan Restaurant. *Inexpensive.* 1345 Lincoln Ave.; (707) 942-9404. Mandarin and Szechuan cuisine. Open for lunch and dinner daily.

CARMEL-BY-THE-SEA

Shops, Galleries and English Charm

Carmel—pronounced, by the way, Car-*mel*, and meaning "at rest" —has the charm and gentility of an English village. It is small, rural, dignified, and yet a stunningly beautiful town, less than one mile square and situated on a splendid, forested coastal slope at the southern tip of the Monterey Peninsula—at the head of Carmel Bay—some 6 miles or so south of the city of Monterey itself. Its fame, of course, lies in its superb shopping district, where people from all over the country go—just to shop! There are also several fine restaurants here, and comfortable bed and breakfast accommodations.

Carmel lies approximately 120 miles south of San Francisco, reached more or less directly on Highway 1, or a combination of Highways 101, 152 and 1. From Monterey, an alternative route is the "17-Mile-Drive," world renowned, and infinitely scenic.

CARMEL-BY-THE-SEA

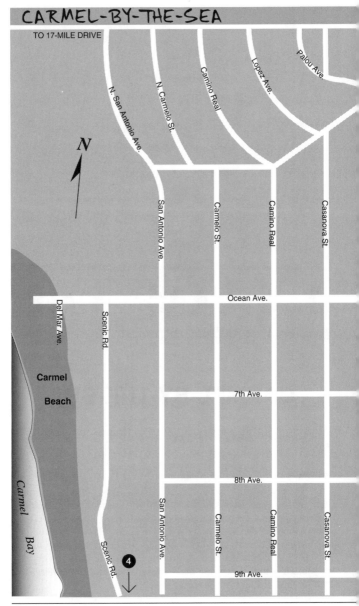

TO 17-MILE DRIVE

1. Carmel Mission
2. Carmel Plaza
3. Sunset Center
4. Tor House
5. Hog's Breath Inn
6. Tuck Box English Tea House
7. Carmel Art Association Galleries
8. The Weston Gallery
9. Photography West

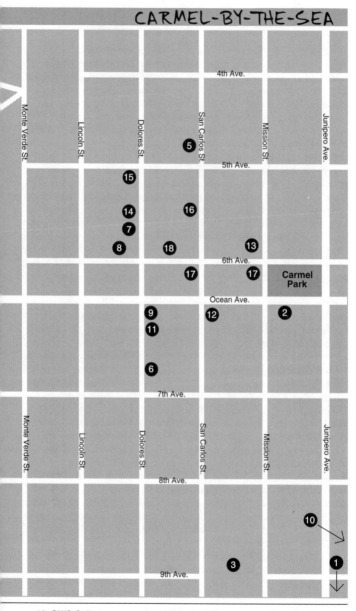

CARMEL-BY-THE-SEA

10. GWS Gallery
11. Bleich of Carmel
12. Hanson Gallery
13. Cottage Gallery

14. Highlands Gallery
15. Lindsey Gallery
16. Walter White Galleries

17. Zantman Galleries
18. Simic Galleries

DISCOVERING CARMEL

To say that Carmel is a fine place for shopping is to greatly understate the case. For here, within some four square blocks are clustered an astonishing 150 shops and more than 50 art galleries (not to mention at least 60 restaurants featuring almost every type of known cuisine)! The variety in the shopping is just as amazing: here you can buy everything from Gucci fashionwear to African tribal masks, from Charles Wysocki oils to Ansel Adams composites, from safari clothing to fine furs, from imported china and Wedgewood crystal to vegetable-dye Tibetan rugs and handcrafted, south-of-the-border pottery. Indeed, the shops here offer a startling variety, from locally-made gifts to handicrafts from far away lands, and art galleries display an equally wide spectrum of works, from those of resident artists to those of the internationally acclaimed, with prices ranging from modest to mind-boggling. But even more than the shopping possibilities, it is the shopping district itself that is most remarkable—rural, wooded and utterly charming, with shops tucked away among age-old shade trees which, on a larger perspective, are part of an unrestrained urban forest that requires four full-time city employees to maintain—a situation that owes something to a 1916 ordinance, banning the cutting of trees.

In any case, Ocean Avenue, quite lovely with its multifarious shade trees, shrubs and flower beds, is probably the town's most important street, with the majority of the chain and department stores situated along here, as well as the beautiful Carmel Plaza which has some thirty or so fine shops and restaurants—including such well-known names as Saks Fifth Avenue, I. Magnin and Banana Republic. Other streets in the shopping district include Dolores, San Carlos, Mission and Lincoln, and Fifth, Sixth and Seventh avenues. On Dolores, between Fifth and Sixth, lies Carmel's self-styled "Gallery Row," with more than a dozen art galleries to be found there, among them the Carmel Art Association Galleries, the most prestigious of all, where you can view the works of professional, local artists, displayed in eight different rooms, with exhibits changing every month. Also try to visit the Weston Gallery on Sixth, between Dolores and Lincoln streets, which has some original works of Ansel Adams and other noted 20th-century photographers; and south of Ocean Avenue on Dolores you can search out the Tuckbox English Tea House, housed in an enchanting little Doll House-style cottage, with a thatched roof and Tudor exterior.

On San Carlos Street, between Fifth and Sixth, is the Hog's Breath Inn, an essentially American-style restaurant, owned in part by actor Clint Eastwood, and now a favorite tourist haunt. Open for lunch and dinner, it has both courtyard and indoor dining, with fireplaces and a rustic, casual atmosphere. On the menu are such entrees as the Dirty Harry Burger, Enforcer Burger, Mysterious Misty and the Eiger Sandwich, reminiscent of Eastwood's most memorable films.

If you are in the area during the summer months (usually around July-August), try to attend Carmel's annual Bach Festival at the Sunset Center on San Carlos Street. It is one of the most notable classical music events on the Monterey Peninsula. Also, the small, open-air Forest Theater at the southeastern edge of town, schedules some theater performances in season; for a schedule call the theater at (831) 649-5561.

West of town, at the bottom end of Ocean Avenue lies the spectacular Carmel Beach, with white sand and foaming surf, and framed by dark, twisty Monterey cypresses. It is a popular place for strolling, picnicking and ocean viewing, although swimming is not particularly encouraged due to the shifting currents and the cold water. Just above the beach, northward, is one of the entrances to the fabled "17-Mile-Drive," which will take you through the scenic Del Monte Forest and the world-famous Pebble Beach; and to the south a mile-long scenic drive journeys along the head of Carmel Bay to lead to the Carmel Point State Beach, passing by, along the way, the picturesque, native-stone Tor House, formerly the home of California poet Robinson Jeffers, who built it with his own hands. Tours of the house are available by appointment, in small groups.

South of Carmel also, on a small rise, overlooking the Carmel River, is the Basilica San Carlos Borromeo del Rio Carmelo—or the Carmel Mission—originally built in 1770 in Monterey, and moved to its present site the following year, in 1771. The mission has a delightful courtyard, filled with poppies and other flowers, as in season, and a museum with displays of mission relics which include the original silver altar brought across by Father Junipero Serra, founder of the mission, from Baja California. Fathers Serra and Lasuen—each of whom founded nine California missions—and Father Crespi, are buried in the mission.

A little farther east in the Carmel Valley is the celebrated "Barnyard," a unique shopping complex with some 55 shops, galleries and restaurants—including the popular Thunderbird Bookshop and Cafe—housed in nine picturesque barns, and surrounded by lavish flower gardens. There are several other modern shops and shopping centers in the valley as well, quite close to the "Barnyard," and inland still are one or two wineries with visitor facilities, well worth a visit.

Another place of supreme interest, a mile or so south of Carmel Valley, situated along the coast, is the Point Lobos State Reserve—a 1,250-acre reserve containing indigenous coastal and inland habitat, with colonies of sealions and sea-otters and brown pelican breeding grounds. Point Lobos is also an excellent place for whale watching during the annual whale migration in November.

HOW TO GET THERE

Carmel is situated some 120 miles southeast of San Francisco, directly south of Monterey, at the head of Carmel Bay. Follow *Highway 101* south approximately 95 miles, then southwest on *Highways 156* and *1*, roughly 21 miles, to Monterey. From Monterey it is another 4 miles south on the coastal route, *Highway 1*, to Carmel.

TOURIST INFORMATION

Carmel Business Association. Cnr. San Carlos St. and 5th Ave., Carmel; (831) 624-2522. Carmel Gallery Guide and other tourist literature available. Also schedule of local events.

Carmel Valley Chamber of Commerce. 71 Carmel Valley Rd., Carmel Valley; (831) 659-4000. Tourist brochures and area maps; information on Carmel Valley wineries.

ACCOMMODATIONS

Bed & Breakfast Inns

Cobblestone Inn. *$95-$180.* 8th Ave. and Junipero St.; (831) 625-5222. Newer bed and breakfast inn with 24 beautifully furnished rooms; private baths, fireplaces, TV and phones. Afternoon tea; continental breakfast.

Green Lantern Inn. *$100-$225.* Casanova St. and 7th Ave.; (831) 624-4392. 19 remodelled rooms and cottages in 1926 inn. Private baths, some fireplaces. Garden setting; ocean views.

Happy Landing Inn. *$90-$165.* Monte Verde St. and 6th Ave.; (831) 624-7917. 7 comfortable rooms, with fireplaces and TV. Continental breakfast.

Monte Verde Inn. *$99-$155.* Monte Verde St. and Ocean Ave.; (831) 624-6046/(800) 328-7707. Delightful old inn with 10 rooms; some ocean views, some fireplaces; private baths, TV. Continental breakfast.

Sandpiper Inn At The Beach. *$125-$185.* 2408 Bay View Ave.; (831) 624-6433/(800) 633-6433 in California. 1930s inn, filled with antiques and fresh flowers, close to Carmel Bay. 15 rooms with private baths; some fireplaces. Complimentary sherry, continental breakfast.

Sea View Inn. *$80-$135.* Camino Real and 11th Ave.; (831) 624-8778. Bed and breakfast inn with 8 rooms. Continental breakfast, afternoon tea and wine and cheese.

Stonehouse Inn. *$110-$189.* Monte Verde St. and 8th Ave.; (831) 624-4569. 8 well-appointed rooms; hot tub. Wine and cheese in the evening.

Valley Lodge. *$99-$249.* Carmel Valley Rd. and Ford St., Carmel Valley; (831) 659-2261/(800) 641-4646. 31-room inn, featuring fireplaces in some of the rooms. Phones, TV, pool and hot tub; continental breakfast.

Hotels and Motels

Carmel Fireplace Inn. *$135-$200.* San Carlos St. and 4th Ave.; (831) 624-4862. 18 rooms, patio units, cottages and suites, some with fireplaces; also TV, refrigerators, and in-room coffee. Beautiful gardens; hot tub.

Carmel Mission Inn, Best Western. *$129-$189.* Hwy. 1 and Rio Rd.; (831) 624-1841/(800) 528-1234. 165 units; TV, phones, pool, hot tub and sauna. Restaurant on premises.

Carmel Studio Lodge. *$110-$180.* Junipero St. and 5th Ave.; (831) 624-8515. 19 units, with TV and phones; some kitchens. Also heated pool.

CarmelTownhouse Lodge. *$89-$145.* San Carlos St. and 5thAve.; (831) 624-1261. 28 units; TV, phones, pool.

Coachman's Inn. *$89-$145.* 7th Ave. and San Carlos St.; (831) 624-6421/(800) 336-6421. 30 units; TV, phones, spa; some kitchens.

Highlands Inn. *$225-$650.* 4 miles south of Carmel on Hwy. 1; (831) 624-3801/(800) 682-4811. Large, remodeled resort hotel, situated above the spectacular Big Sur coast. 146 units, including 43 rooms with fireplaces and decks, and 103 suites with kitchen, living room, bedroom, spa, fireplace and oceanview deck. Two restaurants on premises; also large outdoor pool.

La Playa Hotel. *$125-$350.* Camino Real and 8thAve.; (831) 624-6476/(800) 582-8900 in California. 3-story Spanish-style hotel, located two blocks from Carmel Beach. 75 units, featuring handcrafted furniture. Pool, gazebo, restaurant.

Lobos Lodge. *$110-$170.* Ocean Ave. and Monte Verde St.; (831) 624-3874. 27 units, with fireplaces, TV and phones. Continental breakfast.

Normandy Inn. *$145-$225.* OceanAve. and MonteVerde St.; (831) 624-3825/(800) 343-3825 in California. 48 rooms, cottages, suites, and apartments; some kitchens, and fireplaces; TV, phones, pool. Continental breakfast.

The Pine Inn. *$115-$250.* OceanAve., between Lincoln and MonteVerde Sts.; (831) 624-3851/(800) 228-3851. Century-old inn, with 49 rooms; TV, phones, restaurant and cocktail lounge.

Quail Lodge. *$275-$400.* 8205 Valley Greens Dr., Carmel Valley; (831) 624-1581/(800) 583-9516/(800) 682-9303 in California. 100 luxury units, many with fireplaces. The lodge also offers golf and tennis facilities, and a pool, spa and restaurant.

Stonepine. *$250-$650.* 150 E. Carmel Valley Rd., Carmel Valley; (831) 659-2245. Secluded hideaway; 12 units with fireplaces, TV and phones. Pool, spa; day transportation and airport transfers for hotel guests.

Sundial Lodge. *$95-$165.* Monte Verde St. and 7th Ave.; (831) 624-8578. 19 units, some with kitchens; TV, phones, continental breakfast.

Tally Ho Inn. *$125-$250.* Monte Verde St. and 6th Ave.; (831) 624-2232. 14 units, some with fireplaces; also TV, phones, and spa.

SEASONAL EVENTS

June. *Forest Theater.* 70-year-old outdoor theater, cnr. Mountain View Ave. and Santa Rita St. Schedules regular performances of Shakespeare, as well as repertory theater and musicals. Season runs from June through October. For program information and reservations, contact the theater at (831) 655-7529/626-1681.

July. *Carmel Bach Festival.* Usually held in mid-July, at the Sunset Center in downtown Carmel, with special performances at the Carmel Mission.

Renowned three-week-long festival; features recitals and classical music concerts, offered by world-famous musicians. Advance reservations required; (831) 624-1521.

September. *Sandcastle Contest.* At the Carmel Beach. 4th weekend. Popular annual event, with over 400 entrants creating elaborate sand structures, including profiles, castles and cars. Hosted by the American Institute of Architects. For exact dates and more information, call (831) 624-2522. *Carmel Shakespeare Festival.* 6-week-long festival held during September and October. Professional and local actors present a variety of Shakespearean plays, as well as special children's theater performances. Call (831) 622-0700 for tickets or other information.

PLACES OF INTEREST

Carmel Mission. Located on Rio Rd., off Hwy. 1.; (831) 624-3600. Second oldest of California's 21 Spanish missions, originally founded by Father Junipero Serra in Monterey in 1770, and moved to its present site, overlooking the Carmel River, in 1771. Mission museum features some excellent exhibits, including the original altar brought across by Father Serra from Baja California. Also view crypt inside mission, where Fathers Serra, Lasuen and Crespi are buried. Gift shop on premises. Open Mon.-Sat. 9.30-4.30; Sun. 10.30-4.30. Donations accepted.

The Barnyard. Unique shopping complex with some 55 specialty and import shops, art galleries, bakeries and restaurants—including the Thunderbird Bookshop and Cafe—housed in nine beautifully restored barns. Lavish flower gardens.

Tor House. Located on Carmel Point, between Stewart Way and Ocean View Ave., just south of Carmel Village. Picturesque, granite-stone house overlooking Carmel Bay, built by California poet Robinson Jeffers, between 1918-1930, as his home. Features a spectacular 40-foot tower—the Hawk Tower—which contains stones taken from the Great Wall of China, Pyramid of Cheops and Hadrian's Villa. Also view secret staircase in tower, and an ancient porthole between the second and third floors, reputed to have come from the ship on which Napoleon escaped from Elba in 1815. Tours of the house (for small groups only) are conducted on Fridays and Saturdays, 10-4; admission fee: $5.00. For reservations call (831) 624-1840.

Carmel Beach. Picture-perfect beach, with white sand and crashing surf, framed by gnarled Monterey cypresses. The beach is open to the public for picnicking and ocean walks; swimming is discouraged due to shifting currents.

17-Mile Drive. See *Places of Interest* in the *Monterey* section.

Point Lobos Reserve. 1 mile south of the Carmel River Bridge on Hwy. 1; (831) 624-4909. 1,250-acre state-owned coastal reserve, with sea lion and sea otter colonies and brown pelican breeding grounds. The reserve is also a good place for whale watching—in season. Picnic facilities available. Open daily 9- 5 (9-7 in summer); admission fee: $7.00 per car.

ART GALLERIES

Bleich of Carmel. On Dolores St. near Ocean Ave.; (831) 624-9447. Features works of American Impressionist George J. Bleich. Large selection of paintings depicting French scenes; also landscapes and seascapes of Carmel. Open daily 10.30-5.30.

Carmel Art Association Galleries. Dolores St., between 5th Ave. and 6th Ave. (831) 624-6176. 8-room gallery, exhibiting the finest of Carmel's professional artists. Paintings, sculpture, graphics. Regularly changing exhibits. Gallery open 10-5 daily.

Cottage Gallery at Carmel. Cnr. 6th Ave. and Mission St.; (831) 624-7888. Original paintings by renowned artists, among them Thomas Kinkade, Joyce Motazedi and K. Martell. The gallery is open 10-5 daily.

Hanson Gallery. Ocean Ave. at San Carlos; (831) 625-6142. Original oils, watercolors and limited edition serigraphs by renowned artists such as Picasso, Erte, Neiman and Pissaro. Open daily 10 a.m.-5 p.m.

Highlands Gallery. Dolores St., between 5th Ave. and 6th Ave.; (831) 624-0535. Features wood, stone and metal sculpture by recognized West Coast sculptors. Open 11 a.m.-4.30 p.m. daily.

Lindsey Gallery. Dolores St. at 5th Ave.; (831) 625-2233. Primarily paintings, featuring seascapes, landscapes, still life, harbor scenes, city scenes, rural Americana, and watercolors; some Western bronze sculpture. Open 10 a.m.-6 p.m. daily.

Photography West Gallery. Ocean Ave. and Dolores St.; (831) 625-1587. Exhibits by photographers who have lived and worked on the Monterey Peninsula, including such well known names as Ansel Adams, Weston and Bullock. Also photographic books, cards and posters. Open daily 11-5.

Simic-New Renaissance Galleries, Inc. Three locations on San Carlos St. and 6th Ave.; (831) 624-7522. Wide selection of seascapes by renowned artists; also Master Impressionists' works, and wood and bronze sculpture. Open daily 10-6.

Walter White Galleries. San Carlos St., between 5th Ave. and 6th Ave.; (831) 624-4957. Handblown art glass from Steven Corriea's California studio; also hardwood furniture, prints, paintings and paper works. Open 9.30-5.30 daily.

The Weston Gallery. 6th Ave., between Dolores and Lincoln Sts.; (831) 624-4453. Superb selection of original works by Paul Strand, Edward Weston, Ansel Adams, and other contemporary and 19th-century photographers. Hours: 11-5 Tues.-Sat., 12-5 Sun.

Zantman Art Galleries, Ltd. 6th Ave. near Mission St., and 6th Ave. near San Carlos St.; (831) 624-8314. Oldest gallery in town, established in 1959. Features paintings and sculpture by contemporary American artists, as well as selected European artists, mostly French. Open 10 a.m.-5 p.m. Mon.-Sat., 11 a.m.-5 p.m. Sun.

RECREATION

Golf. See *Golf Courses* in the *Monterey* section.

Tennis. Tennis facilities are available at the *Mission Tennis Ranch,* 26260 Dolores St., (831) 624- 4335; and the *Carmel Valley Racquet & Health Club,* 27300 Rancho San Carlos Rd., Carmel; (831) 624-2737.

Horseback Riding. *Pebble Beach Equestrian Center,* Portola Rd., Pebble Beach; (831) 624-2756/624-9821. Escorted trail rides; 30 miles of trails. Appointments only.

RESTAURANTS

(Restaurant prices—based on full course dinner, excluding drinks, tax and tips—are categorized as follows: *Deluxe,* over $30; *Expensive,* $20-$30; *Moderate,* $10-$20; *Inexpensive,* under $10.)

Anton & Michel. *Expensive.* In the Courtyard of the Fountains, Mission St. and 7th Ave.; (831) 624-2406. Continental cuisine; varied menu. House specialties include Scampi Marinara, Veal Oscar and Tournedos Rossini. California and French wines and champagnes. Cocktail lounge; elegant setting. Open for lunch and dinner daily.

The Covey. *Expensive-Deluxe.* At Quail Lodge, 8205 Valley Greens Dr.; (831) 624-1581. European cuisine, with emphasis on beef, poultry, and fresh local seafood. Varied wine list, featuring Monterey County, California and imported wines. Rustic, country atmosphere. Dinners from 6.40 p.m. daily; jackets required. Reservations.

Creme Carmel. *Expensive.* San Carlos St. near 7th Ave.; (831) 624-0444. Newer, well-regarded Carmel restaurant, specializing in California and French cuisine, and creative homemade desserts. Open for dinner daily.

The French Poodle. *Expensive.* Junipero St. and 5th Ave.; (831) 624-8643. Classic French cuisine; intimate setting. Restaurant established in 1961. Open for dinner; jackets required.

From Scratch. *Inexpensive-Moderate.* Located in the Barnyard shopping center; (831) 625-2448. Features homemade food prepared with the freshest ingredients. Country-style dining room; patio for outdoor dining. Open daily for breakfast, lunch and dinner; also Sunday brunch.

Hog's Breath Inn. *Moderate.* San Carlos St. and 5th Ave.; (831) 625-1044. Casual, English pub-style restaurant, owned by actor-director Clint Eastwood. Informal American fare, featuring such entrees as the Dirty Harry Burger, Mysterious Misty, Enforcer Burger and Eiger Sandwich! Dine in a rustic courtyard with fireplaces, or indoors. Open for lunch and dinner daily; brunch on Sundays.

Katy's Place. *Inexpensive-Moderate.* Mission St., between 5th and 6th Aves.; (831) 624-0199. Casual cafe, serving egg dishes, and soups, salads and sandwiches. Open for breakfast and lunch daily.

Pernille Restaurant. *Moderate.* San Carlos St. and 6th Ave.; (831) 624-6958. Italian restaurant, open for breakfast, lunch and dinner; also weekend brunch.

The Ridge Restaurant. *Expensive.* At the Robles Del Rio Lodge, 200 Punta Del Monte, Robles Del Rio; (831) 659-0170. Elegant restaurant, in spectacular setting, 1000 feet above Carmel Valley. Features California and French cuisine; excellent wine list. Open for lunch and dinner Tues.-Sun.; also Sunday brunch. Reservations recommended.

Rio Grill. *Moderate.* 101 Crossroads Blvd.; (831) 625-5436. Nouvelle California cuisine, with oak grill specialties. Seasonally changing menu; vintage wines by the glass. Cocktail lounge. Restaurant open for lunch and dinner daily.

Sans Souci. *Expensive.* Lincoln St., between 5th Ave. and 6th Ave.; (831) 624-6220. Gourmet French restaurant, with Parisian decor. Favorites here are Escargots, white veal, roasted quail and Coho salmon; also, delicious chocolate mousse. Extensive wine list, featuring French and California wines. Classical music. Dinners from 6 p.m., Thurs.-Tues.

Sassy's Bar and Grill. *Moderate.* At the Carmel Mission Inn, Hwy. 1 and Rio Rd.; (831) 624-3399. Continental cuisine; also buffet-style meals, and salad bar. Open for breakfast, lunch and dinner, and Sunday brunch.

The Terrace Grill. *Expensive.* At the La Playa Hotel, Camino Real and 8th Ave.; (831) 624-4010. Elegant dining room with expansive views; terrace for outdoor dining. Menu stresses fresh California seafood. Open for breakfast, lunch and dinner daily; also Sunday brunch.

Thunderbird Bookshop and Restaurant. *Moderate.* At The Barnyard; (831) 624-9414. Informal American fare. Casual setting; books to browse. Lunch daily, dinner Tues.-Sun.

LA JOLLA

"The Riviera of California"

La Jolla—pronounced "La Hoya," and meaning "jewel"—is a small, picturesque, Mediterranean-style town on the Southern California coast, nestled in the hills directly above La Jolla Cove, some 14 miles north of San Diego, and frequently referred to as the "Riviera of California." It is, quite typically, filled with Mediterranean and new wave California architecture, and trendy little shops, boutiques, galleries, cafes and restaurants, and luxury hotels and private clubs where the rich and famous mingle. It also has in it a handful of delightful, sun-drenched beaches, and one or two splendid parks, including the coastal Torrey Pines State Reserve just to the north. Besides which, there is a university here, the University of California, San Diego, sprawled on a mesa overlooking the Pacific Ocean.

La Jolla is situated approximately 105 miles south of Los Angeles, reached on Highway 5—or 405 and 5—and a short detour southwestward on La Jolla Village Drive and Torrey Pines Road. From San Diego, you can take Highway 5 north, some 8 miles, then Ardath Road and Torrey Pines Road west, directly into La Jolla. An alternative route from San Diego is by way of the coastal Mission and La Jolla boulevards northward, 8 miles.

DISCOVERING LA JOLLA

La Jolla is undoubtedly one of the most splendid of Southern California's coastal villages, steeped in glorious sunshine, and brimming over with Mediterranean charm. There are of course several places of interest in and around La Jolla, including beaches and parks, but the center of interest for any visitor to the area—and few would argue otherwise—has to be the village itself, at once costly and bohemian, filled with delightful little cafes, bistros and restaurants, and chic boutiques and art galleries, mostly concentrated in a small, one-square-mile section in the center of town, making it ideally suited to exploring on foot.

La Jolla's two principal streets are Prospect and Girard, which intersect each other near the northwest end of town, with most of the shops and restaurants located along these. On the latter, of course, you can search out a handful of colorful little sidewalk cafes and art galleries, and such well-known retail stores as Saks Fifth Avenue, Polo-Ralph Lauren, Laura Ashley and Banana Republic, among others; and on Prospect are several delightful oceanview restaurants—among them, George's at the Cove, Top O' the Cove, Alfredo's and El Crab Catcher—many of them strung along a section of the street known as Coast Walk. On Prospect Street, too, is La Jolla's landmark La Valencia Hotel, a striking, pink-stucco Mediterranean-style structure, with ornate, wrought-iron balconies and a Moorish tower, overlooking La Jolla Cove and the ocean. La Valencia, of course, is also a haven for visiting celebrities, socialites, and other well-heeled guests to La Jolla; it has 100 oceanview guest rooms and three quite popular restaurants.

From the downtown area, of course, Girard Avenue descends steeply to the palm-lined Coast Boulevard, along which lies the Ellen Browning Scripps Park, a public park, quite popular with walkers, joggers and ocean gazers; and directly below the park, and also of interest, is the picturesque La Jolla Cove, overhung by steep cliffs, and quite possibly La Jolla's foremost tourist attraction. The cove has a small, white-sand beach, a mile-long marine preserve, and a series of interesting little caves and tunnels. The La Jolla Cove also, we might add, is the site of La Jolla's annual Rough-Water Swim, claimed to be the largest such event in the country, held here in September, usually around the middle of the month.

North and south of La Jolla Cove are yet other places of interest. Southward, for instance, are the La Jolla Museum of Contemporary Art, located on Prospect Street, at the corner of Drape Avenue, and which houses one of the nation's finest collections of post-1950s art and design; and the well-liked Windansea Beach, one of the most popular surfing and swimming beaches in the area, situated just off Nautilus Street and La Jolla Boulevard, south a little way from the museum, and where you can also see some of Southern California's most lavish beachfront homes, including one or two designed by Frank Lloyd Wright and Irving Gill. Windansea Beach, by the way, was also the setting for Tom Wolfe's *The Pumphouse Gang*.

Northeastward from La Jolla Cove, of course, lie the La Jolla

LA JOLLA

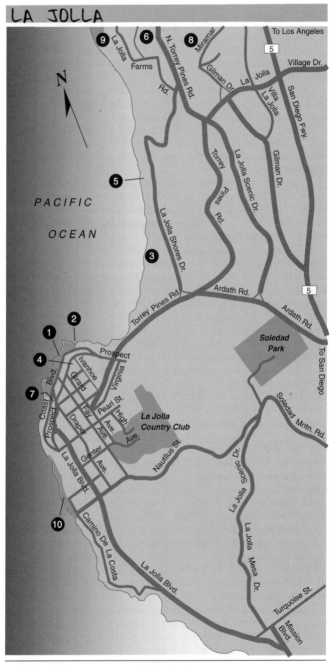

1. Scripps Park
2. La Jolla Cove
3. La Jolla Shores
4. La Valencia Hotel
5. Scripps Institute
6. Salk Institute
7. Museum of Art
8. University of California, San Diego
9. Torrey Pines State Park
10. Windansea Beach

Caves, located just off Coast Boulevard, and accessed from the La Jolla Caves and Shell Shop at 1325 Coast Boulevard, with a flight of some 130 steps leading down from the shop to the largest of the caves. The shop itself has photographs of the caves, and seashells, coral jewelry and La Jolla T-shirts for sale. It also charges a small admission fee for access to the cave.

Near at hand, too, are the La Jolla Shores—a coastal stretch extending from just north of the La Jolla Caves, northward a mile or so, and which has some good beaches and picnic areas, and superb views of the ocean. At the north end of the La Jolla Shores, also of interest, is the Scripps Pier, with one or two natural tidal pools located quite close to it, reached directly on the La Jolla Shores Drive; and immediately above the pier stands the Scripps Institute of Oceanography, a world-renowned oceanographic research center, with an excellent aquarium with 22 large tanks filled with some 300 species of saltwater fish and invertebrates from California, Mexico and the South Pacific. The aquarium also has a man-made outdoor tidal pool, stocked with a variety of indigenous sea creatures, including lobsters, crabs, starfish and sea anemones. The institute, in addition, offers films and lectures, of interest to marine life enthusiasts.

Northward from the Scripps institute there is yet something to interest the visitor to La Jolla. Directly above La Jolla Village Drive, at the corner of Torrey Pines Road, lies the University of California, San Diego, sprawled on hundreds of acres of lush, rolling hills, overlooking the Pacific Ocean. The campus was originally founded in 1959, and it now boasts an enrollment of over 15,000 students, and several architectural delights, notable among them the expansive Mandeville Auditorium, where the annual Summerfest series of music concerts and other special events are held.

Try to also see the Salk Institute, adjoining to the northwest of the university campus, just off North Torrey Pines Road. The world-famous medical research facility, which houses some 20 laboratories, conducting research in molecular and cellular biology and the neurosciences, was founded by the noted Dr. Jonas K. Salk. The center itself is housed in a unique, Louis Kahn-designed facility, and guided tours of it are conducted during scheduled hours on weekdays.

Farther still, immediately to the north of the Salk Institute, situated on clifftops overlooking the coast, is the Torrey Pines Glider Port, a good place to watch multicolored hang-gliders soar into the sky; and north of there lies the Torrey Pines State Park, a spectacular, 1,750-acre coastal reserve, with towering, 300-foot cliffs overlooking the ocean, stretching some 3 miles or so up the coast. The park has in it more than 5,000 ancient Torrey Pines—or *Pinus Torreyana*—a rare species of gnarled coastal pine that grows in only one other place in the world—the Santa Rosa Island, one of the Channel Islands, some 175 miles to the northwest. The park also has several scenic hiking trails, and picnic and beach areas.

HOW TO GET THERE

La Jolla is situated approximately 105 miles south of Los Angeles, or 14 miles north of San Diego. From Los Angeles it can be reached on *Highway 5*—or *405* and *5*—and a brief detour southwestward on *La Jolla Village Drive* and *Ardath Road*. From San Diego, follow *Highway 5* north, then *Ardath Road* and *Torrey Pines Road* west into La Jolla. An alternative route from San Diego is by way of the coastal Mission and *La Jolla boulevards* north, more or less directly into La Jolla.

TOURIST INFORMATION

La Jolla Town Council/Official Visitors Bureau. P.O. Box 1101, La Jolla, CA 92038; (619) 454-1444. Tourist information and brochures, including guide to La Jolla, with listings of area accommodations, restaurants, shopping, art galleries and places of interest; also free map of La Jolla.

San Diego Convention & Visitors Bureau. 1200 Third Ave., Suite 824, San Diego, CA 92101-4190; (619) 232-3101. Visitor information for San Diego, La Jolla, and other nearby places of interest. There is also an *International Visitor Information Center* located in the Horton Plaza Shopping Center in downtown San Diego, open daily 8.30-5, which offers a wealth of information to visitors to the area, in several different languages, including recorded visitor information; call the center at (619) 236-1212.

ACCOMMODATIONS

Andrea Villa Inn. *$85-$105.* 2402 Torrey Pines Rd.; (619) 459-3311. 50 units, with phones and TV; some kitchen units. Jacuzzi, sundeck, swimming pool and exercise room; complementary continental breakfast. Airport pick-up service. Located near beach.

The Bed & Breakfast Inn at La Jolla. *$85-$225.* 7753 Draper Ave.; (619) 456-2066. Delightful European-style inn with 16 individually-decorated guest rooms. Full breakfast.

Colonial Inn Hotel. *$125-$195.* 910 Prospect St.; (619) 454-2181/(800) 826-1278 in California. Restored turn-of-the-century hotel with 75 rooms with village or ocean views. TV, phones; pool, restaurant and lounge, and meeting rooms.

Embassy Suites Hotel—La Jolla. *$185-$275.* 4550 La Jolla Village Dr.; (619)453-0400/(800) EMBASSY. 335 suites with all amenities, including room service; also some kitchen units available. Complimentary beverages, full breakfast. Sauna, swimming pool, whirlpool, sundeck, exercise room, restaurant and meeting rooms. Handicapped facilities.

Empress Hotel of La Jolla. *$95-$225.* 7766 Fay Ave.; (619) 454-3001/(800) 525-6552. 73 units, including some suites with in-room spas; also kitchen units. Phones, TV, room service; complimentary continental breakfast. Spa, sauna, exercise room, restaurant and meeting rooms. Handicapped facilities; airport pick-up service.

Holiday Inn Express - La Jolla.. *$90-$140*. 6705 La Jolla Blvd.; (619) 454-7101/(800) 451-0358. 59 units, with TV, phones, and refrigerators; some ocean views. Kitchen units available. Swimming pool. Complimentary continental breakfast. Handicapped facilities. Located near beach.

Hotel La Jolla. *$129-$325*. 7955 La Jolla Shores Dr.; (619) 459-0261. 90 units, including some suites with in-room whirlpool spas; some ocean views. Also kitchen units available. Swimming pool, restaurant, cocktail lounge, and meeting rooms on premises. Airport pick-up service.

Hyatt Regency La Jolla at Aventine. *$169-$289*. 3777 La Jolla Village Dr.; (619) 552-1234/(800) 233-1234. Full-service 5-star hotel with 400 units and suites. Health club, spa, swimming pool, tennis courts, restaurants and meeting rooms. Handicapped facilities.

The Inn at La Jolla. *$69-$109*. 5440 La Jolla Blvd.; (619) 454-6121. 45 units, with phones and TV; also some kitchen units. Spa, swimming pool, and 9-hole putting green on premises.

Inn By The Sea. *$95+*. 7830 Faye Ave.; (619) 459-4461/(800) 462-9732/ (800) 526-4545 in California. 104 rooms and suites, with phones, TV, and room service; some ocean views. Swimming pool, sauna, whirlpool. Restaurant adjacent.

La Jolla Beach Travelodge. *$139-$189*. 6700 La Jolla Blvd.; (619)454-0716/(800) 255-3050. 44 units with ocean views. TV, phones; swimming pool and sundeck. Some kitchen units available.

La Jolla Cove Suites. *$89-$150*. 1155 Coast Blvd.; (619) 459-2621. 100 units, including suites, studios and kitchen units, all overlooking the ocean. Private balconies, solarium and sundeck; also swimming pool. Airport pick-up service; handicapped facilities.

La Jolla Travelodge. *$85+*. 1141 Silverado St.; (619) 454-0791/(800) 255-3050. 30 units, with phones and TV, and in-room coffee.

Radisson Hotel - La Jolla. *$155-$245*. 3299 Holiday Ct.; (619) 453-5500/(800) 854-2900. 200 rooms, including some kitchen units. TV, phones; swimming pool, restaurant, and meeting rooms. Airport pick-up service; handicapped facilities.

La Valencia Hotel. *$135-$250*. 1132 Prospect St.; (619) 454-0771/(800) 451-0772. La Jolla's best-known hotel, located in downtown, overlooking La Jolla Cove. Offers 100 well-appointed units, including suites with jacuzzis. Also swimming pool, sauna, restaurants, and meeting rooms on premises. Airport pick-up service.

Prospect Park Inn. *$79-$259*. 1110 Prospect Park St.; (619) 454-0133/ (800) 345-8577 in California. 25 units, with phones and TV; some private balconies with ocean views. Large sundeck, overlooking the ocean. Complimentary breakfast and afternoon tea. Kitchen units available.

Wyndham Garden Hotel. *$99-$199*. 5975 Lusk Blvd.; (619) 558-1818. 180 units; phones, TV, room service. Some kitchen units available. Also swimming pool, exercise room, and restaurant. Airport pick-up service; handicapped facilities.

Residence Inn by Marriott La Jolla. *$129-$165*. 8901 Gilman Dr.; (619) 587-1770/(800) 331-3131. 287 units with living room areas and full-sized, fully-equipped kitchens. Complimentary buffet breakfast, cocktails and hors d'oeuvres. Facilities include a swimming pool, restaurant and meeting rooms. Also handicapped facilities, and airport pick-up service.

San Diego Marriott—La Jolla. *$129-$285*. 4240 La Jolla Village Dr.; (619) 587-1414/(800) 228-9290. 360-room full-service hotel, with room service, concierge, and valet. Swimming pool, restaurant, cocktail lounges, meeting rooms, game room and health club on premises. Also handicapped facilities available.

Sands of La Jolla. *$45-$79*. 5417 La Jolla Blvd.; (619) 459-3336/(800)

367-6467. 39 units; TV, phones, refrigerators, in-room coffee; some ocean views. Swimming pool, sundeck. Kitchen units available.

Sea Lodge. *$115-$305.* 8110 Camino del Oro; (619) 459-8271/(800) 367-6467. 128 beachfront units; phones, TV, refrigerators, in-room coffee, room service. Restaurants and cocktail lounge, meeting rooms, tennis courts, and swimming pool. Handicapped facilities.

Sheraton Grande Torrey Pines. *$170-$350.* 10950 N. Torrey Pines Rd.; (619)558-1500/(800) 325-3535. Luxury hotel with 400 oceanview rooms with sitting areas and mini bars; concierge and butler on every floor. Also sports and business centers, meeting rooms, restaurant, swimming pool and golf course on premises. Handicapped facilities.

SEASONAL EVENTS

February. *Shearson Lehman Brothers Open.* Second weekend. PGA tournament, held at the Torrey Pines Golf Course in La Jolla. The event draws more than 100,000 spectators, and features a celebrity Pro-Am Day with national and local celebrities. For a schedule and more information, call (619) 281-4653.

March. *La Jolla Easter Hat Parade.* Popular annual event, held over the Easter weekend. Features a parade down Prospect and Girard streets, with participants donning all types of hats; prizes are awarded in various categories, such as "the most outrageous," "the most becoming," and the like. More information on (619) 454-2600/459-1571.

April. *Annual La Jolla Half Marathon.* Usually held during the third weekend of the month. Fourth largest half marathon in the country; begins at the Del Mar Fairgrounds and ends at La Jolla Cove Park, with superb views of the coastline enroute. (619) 272-8316. **Annual La Jolla Grand Prix.** 3rd Weekend. Monte Carlo-style bicycle race—one of the five largest in the U.S.—down the streets of La Jolla. Also features celebrity and wheelchair races, a product exposition, and a stunt show. (619) 232-7931.

June. *La Jolla Concerts by the Sea.* Outdoor concerts, staged at the La Jolla Cove on weekends, throughout the months of June, July and August. For a schedule of performances, call (619) 454-1314/699-2050. *Annual La Jolla Festival of the Arts.* Held at the La Jolla Country Day School; first weekend. Features well-known artists from across the country; also live entertainment, and a variety of international cuisine. (619) 456-1268/232-7655.

July. *La Jolla Independence Day Celebration.* Fourth of July celebrations, held at the La Jolla Cove. Includes a concert, and fireworks display. More information on (619) 454-1444.

August. *Annual Summerfest.* Usually held during the 3rd weekend of the month, at the Sherwood Auditorium in the La Jolla Museum of Contemporary Art and the Mandeville Auditorium at the University of California, San Diego. Offers more than 12 chamber music concerts, featuring world-famous musicians. For a schedule of performances, and more information, call (619) 297-3901.

September. *Annual La Jolla Rough-Water Swim.* At La Jolla Cove. 2nd Weekend. One of the largest rough-water swimming competitions in the country; begins at the La Jolla Cove, with participants swimming a mile out to sea. For more information, call (619) 456-2100.

December. *La Jolla Christmas Parade and Party.* First weekend. Annual Christmas parade, through downtown La Jolla, featuring marching bands and floats; begins at the corner of Torrey Pines Blvd. and Girard Street. The parade is followed by a party at the La Jolla Recreation Center, with a crafts fair, carnival rides and games, and food concessions. (619) 454-1314.

PLACES OF INTEREST

Ellen Browning Scripps Park. Situated off Coast Blvd., at the foot of Girard St. 5-acre coastal park, quite popular with residents and visitors alike. Offers a variety of recreational possibilities, including jogging, walking, and ocean-gazing. Of interest, too, is the *children's pool* at the south end of the park, where there is a sheltered beach and cove with shallow water. The park also has restrooms and barbecue facilities.

La Jolla Cove. Located directly below the Ellen Browning Scripps Park, off Coast Blvd. Small, sheltered cove, with a beach and a series of interesting little caves and tunnels, overhung by steep cliffs. The cove has a mile-long protected rough-water swimming area, with lifeguards, and preserved underwater marine life. The cove is also the site of several local events throughout the year, including the annual Rough-Water Swim in September, as well as the Fourth of July festivities.

Windansea Beach. Situated at the end of Nautilus St., off La Jolla Blvd., just south of La Jolla. This is one of the area's most popular surfing and swimming beaches, noted for its spectacular waves. The coastal stretch along here also showcases some of Southern California's loveliest and most luxurious beachfront homes, including one or two designed by Frank Lloyd Wright and Irving Gill. The beach, besides, was also the setting for Tom Wolfe's *The Pumphouse Gang*.

Scripps Institute of Oceanography. 8602 La Jolla Shores Dr.; (619) 534-6933/534-FISH. World-renowned oceanographic research center, with an excellent aquarium with 22 large tanks filled with some 300 species of saltwater fish and invertebrates from California, Mexico and the South Pacific. The aquarium also has a man-made outdoor tidal pool, stocked with a variety of indigenous sea creatures, including lobsters, crabs, starfish and sea anemones. The center, in addition, offers films and lectures, and has a bookstore on the premises. Nearby, too, are a handful of beach areas and a tidal pool, located at the La Jolla Shores, with walking paths leading from the aquarium down to the shore. Aquarium hours: 9-5 daily. Admission: $6.50 adults, $5.50 seniors, $4.50 students and juniors (13-17), $3.50 children (3-12).

La Jolla Museum of Contemporary Art. 700 Prospect St.; (619) 454-3541. Houses one of the nation's finest collections of post-1950s art and design. Also changing exhibits of contemporary art, including paintings, sculpture, photography and industrial design. Features lectures and films in its Sherwood Hall, as well as other special programs. Bookstore on premises, with an excellent selection of art books. Museum hours: 10-5 Tues.-Sat., 12-5 Sun. Admission fee: $4.00 adults, $2.00 students and seniors, children under 12 free; also free admission firstTuesday and Sunday of every month.

Salk Institute. 10010 N. Torrey Pines Rd.; (619) 453-4100. World-famous medical research facility, founded by the noted Dr. Jonas K. Salk. Houses some 20 laboratories, conducting research in molecular and cellular biology and the neurosciences. The center itself is housed in a unique Louis Kahn-designed facility. Guided architectural tours available, 11a.m. and 12 noon, Mon.-Fri. Call for reservations.

La Valencia Hotel. 1132 Prospect St. (cnr. Girard St.); (619) 454-0771. La Jolla's most famous, landmark hotel, located in the heart of town. The hotel is characteristic in its Mediterranean-style architecture, with pink stucco exterior, wrought-iron balconies, and a Moorish tower. It offers luxurious accommodations, with most rooms overlooking La Jolla Cove, and three superb restaurants, also with ocean views.

Mount Soledad. Highest hilltop in La Jolla, with an elevation of 822 feet, located at the northeastern end of La Jolla, and reached on Nautilus Street. Offers spectacular views of the city of San Diego, just to the south. Also features a large cross, erected on the peak, where Easter sunrise services are held every year.

La Jolla Caves. Located just off the Coast Blvd.; a trail and flight of stairs—with more than 130 steps—leads from the La Jolla Caves and Shell Shop at 1325 Coast Blvd., down to the largest of the caves, at the northern end of the La Jolla Cove. The shop itself has photographs of the caves, and seashells, coral jewelry, and La Jolla T-shirts. Small admission fee charged for access to the cave; shop phone, (619) 454-6080.

La Jolla Shores. Off La Jolla Shores Dr. Comprises the coastal stretch extending from just northeast of the La Jolla Cove, northward, approximately a mile, to the Scripps Institute of Oceanography. Offers some good beaches with scenic views, and picnic areas. Also located along here is the *Scripps Pier*, at the foot of El Paseo Grande (which goes off La Jolla Shores Dr.), close to which are one or two natural tidal pools.

Torrey Pines Glider Port. 10020 N. Torrey Pines Rd. Located at the south end of the Torrey Pines State Park, on the clifftops overlooking the coast. The glider port is a good place to watch colorful hang-gliders soar into the sky. There are also one or two hang gliding centers here, offering exhibition flights, lessons and rentals. (619) 452-9858.

University of California, San Diego. Cnr. Torrey Pines Rd. and Genessee Ave. This is one of the state's loveliest university campuses, originally founded in 1959, and sprawled over hundreds of acres of lush, rolling hills, just to the north of La Jolla, overlooking the Pacific Ocean. It has an enrollment of over 15,000 students, and several architectural delights, including the expansive Mandeville Auditorium where the annual Summerfest series of concerts and other musical performances are held. University phone, (619) 534-2230.

Torrey Pines State Park. Situated along N. Torrey Pines Rd. (Old Hwy. 101), just north of La Jolla. 1,750-acre scenic coastal preserve, with towering, 300-foot cliffs, overlooking beaches and the ocean. The park also has in it more than 5,000 ancient Torrey Pines—or *Pinus Torreyana*—a rare species of gnarled coastal pine that grows in only one other place in the world—the Santa Rosa Island, one of the Channel Islands, some 175 miles to the northwest. The park has several scenic hiking trails, guided walks, picnic facilities, and a beach. Park hours: 9 a.m. until sunset; parking fee: $6.00 per car.

RECREATION

Ballooning. *Skysurfer Balloon Co.,* 1221 Camino St., Del Mar, (619) 481-6800. Sunrise and sunset balloon flights along the coast. Cost: $135-$145.

Bicycling. *California Bicycle Inc.,* 633 Pearl St., La Jolla; (619) 454-0316. Bicycle rentals, sales and service.

Scuba Diving. There are several places for scuba diving along the La Jolla Coast; the ecological preserve at La Jolla Cove is especially popular with divers. For equipment rentals and diving information, contact *O.E. Express* (619) 434-6195, or *La Jolla Surf Systems,* (619) 456-2777.

Surfing. La Jolla is of course quite popular with surfers, with one or two of Southern California's best surfing beaches located in the area. For surfing enthusiasts, surfboards and wet-suits are available for both rental and sale from the following La Jolla surf shops: *La Jolla Surf Systems,* 2132 Avenida de la Playa, (619) 456-2777; *Mitch's Surf Shop,* 631 Pearl St., (619) 459-5933.

Hang Gliding. *Hang Gliding Center of Southern California;* located at the Torrey Pines Glider Port, at 10020 Torrey Pines Rd. Offers exhibition flights and lessons; open daily.

Tennis. *La Jolla Recreation Center,* 615 Prospect St., (619) 552-165/454-4434. 9 courts, 5 with lights.

Golf Courses. *Torrey Pines Golf Courses,* 11480 N. Torrey Pines Rd., (619) 570-1234. Offers two 18-hole courses; the North Course is par 72, 6,659 yards, and the South Course is par 72, 6,706 yards. Driving range, pro shop, restaurant.

RESTAURANTS

(Restaurant prices—based on full course dinner, excluding drinks, tax and tips—are categorized as follows: Deluxe, over $30; Expensive, $20-$30; Moderate, $10-$20; Inexpensive, under $10.)

Alfonso's of La Jolla. *Inexpensive.* 1251 Prospect St.; (619) 454-2232. Authentic Mexican cooking. Patio for outdoor dining. Lunch and dinner daily.

The Cottage. *Inexpensive.* 7702 Fay Ave.; (619) 454-0357. Casual restaurant and bakery. Menu selections include omelettes, Belgian waffles, sandwiches, salads, and fresh baked goods. Patio for outdoor dining. Open for breakfast and lunch daily.

Crab Catcher. *Moderate-Expensive.* 1298 Prospect; 454-9587. Well-known seafood restaurant, situated directly above La Jolla Cove, overlooking the coastline. Features an oyster bar, a variety of appetizers, and crab, shellfish, chicken and beef entrees. Tropical drinks, and champagne and wine by the glass. Patio for outdoor dining. Lunch and dinner daily, brunch on Sundays. Reservations advised.

Crescent Shores Grill at Hotel La Jolla. *Moderate.* 7955 La Jolla Shores Rd.; (619) 459-0261. Ocean views. Fresh seafood, prime rib, and pasta dishes. Extensive wine list. Open for breakfast, lunch and dinner; brunch on Sundays.

George's at the Cove. *Expensive.* 1250 Prospect St.; (619) 454-4244. Reputable La Jolla restaurant, located in the heart of the village, with views of La Jolla Cove. Features regional cuisine, with emphasis on seafood, poultry, pasta, beef, veal and lamb, prepared with the freshest ingredients; menu changes daily. Award-winning wine list. Open for lunch and dinner.

Hard Rock Cafe. *Moderate.* 909 Prospect St.; (619) 454-5101. Famous rock n' roll cafe, decorated with rock memorabilia. Features burgers, fish, ribs and chicken dishes. Patio for open-air dining. Open for lunch and dinner daily.

Jose's Courtroom. *Moderate.* 1037 Prospect; 454-1891. Established, 50-year-old restaurant. Features authentic Mexican food. House specialties include fish tacos, carne asada burritos, chicken fajitas and cheese enchiladas. Open for lunch Sun.-Thurs., dinner Fri.-Sat.

Marine Room. *Moderate.* 2000 Spindrift Dr.; (619) 459-7222. Oceanfront restaurant, established in 1941, located in the La Jolla Beach and Tennis Club. Offers primarily seafood, veal and chicken. California wines. Nightly dancing. Lunch and dinner; brunch on Sundays. Reservations suggested.

Milligan's. *Expensive.* 5786 La Jolla Blvd.; (619) 459-7311. American cuisine. Specialties include Southern Pan-Fried Chicken, prime rib, steaks, and fresh seafood. Live jazz on weekends. Open for lunch and dinner daily; also Sunday brunch.

Orchids—La Jolla Marriott. *Moderate.* 4240 La Jolla Village Dr.; (619)

587-1414. Elegant restaurant, specializing in Italian cuisine, with emphasis on fresh seafood and pasta dishes. Good selection of wines. Open for lunch Mon.-Fri., dinner Mon.-Sat.

Peking Palace III. *Moderate.* University Towne Center, 4405 La Jolla Village Dr.; (619) 452-7500. Well-liked Chinese restaurant, serving Mandarin and Szechuan dishes. House specialties include Peking duck, Hunan beef, sweet shrimp and scallops. Full service bar. Open for lunch and dinner.

Panda Country Restaurant. *Moderate.* 4150 Regents Park Row, Ste. 190; (619) 552-1345. Specializing in Mandarin and Szechuan cuisine primarily. Full bar. Lunch and dinner daily. Reservations suggested.

Sky Room—La Valencia Hotel. *Expensive.* 1132 Prospect St.; (619) 454-0771. Located on the 10th floor of the hotel, overlooking the ocean and La Jolla Cove. Gourmet French cuisine; romantic setting. Lunch Mon.-Fri., dinner Mon.-Sat.

Star of India Restaurant. *Moderate.* 1025 Prospect St.; (619) 459-3355. Established, upscale Indian restaurant, offering a good selection of Indian food, with a variety of curries, and kebabs and tandoori and vegetarian dishes. Also buffets; and beer and wine. Lunch and dinner daily. Reservations.

The Shores Restaurant—Sea Lodge. *Moderate.* 8110 Camino del Oro; (619) 456-5222. Award-winning oceanfront restaurant, specializing in seafood, seafood salads, and chicken and beef preparations. Cocktail lounge. Open for breakfast, lunch and dinner daily, and Sunday brunch.

Su Casa Seafood Grotto. *Moderate.* 6738 La Jolla Blvd.; 454-0369. Award-winning restaurant, specializing in fresh seafood and authentic Mexican dishes—all prepared without lard! Multi-flavored margaritas; entertainment. Casual atmosphere; decor features plants, aquariums and south-of-the-border antiques. Open for lunch and dinner daily.

The Spot. *Inexpensive.* 1005 Prospect St.; (619) 459-0800. A local favorite, serving primarily American fare, including burgers, sandwiches, steak, ribs, seafood, and pizza. Casual atmosphere; satellite TV. Open for lunch and dinner daily.

Top O'the Cove. *Expensive.* 1216 Prospect St.; (619) 454-7779. One of La Jolla's best-known and most romantic restaurants, offering superb views of La Jolla Cove, and lush decor. Features primarily Continental cuisine, with emphasis on veal, beef, poultry and seafood. Also dinner specials daily, and homemade pastry desserts. Extensive, award-winning wine list, with more than 1,000 selections. Open for lunch and dinner, and Sunday brunch. Reservations.

Yen's Wok on Pearl. *Inexpensive-Moderate.* 915 Pearl St.; (619) 456-1414. Gourmet oriental food, including Chinese, Japanese and Korean dishes. Sushi bar. Open for lunch and dinner daily.

MENDOCINO

"California's Cape Cod"

Mendocino is the most surprising of all California towns—a typical New England-style village, picturesquely perched on a rocky bluff jutting out into the sea—frequently to be seen shrouded in fog—overlooking, to its south, the sheltered coves at the mouth of the Big River. The town itself is cluttered with colorful little cottages and sea-worn Victorians, reminiscent of Cape Cod, housing quaint shops, galleries and inns. Its great attraction to tourists is of course its Down East looks, with typical weekend activities centering on shopping, browsing, walking, ocean viewing, and, in season, whale watching.

The best way to reach Mendocino—which lies about 115 miles north of San Francisco—is on Highway 1 directly north, journeying along the scenic North Coast for the most part. An alternative route is by way of Highway 101 to Cloverdale (70 miles), then northwestward on Highway 128, passing through the lovely, wine-growing Anderson Valley, to Mendocino.

DISCOVERING MENDOCINO

Mendocino is a former lumbering town, founded in the 1850s. It is, in fact, one of a series of such lumbering settlements to be established on the Mendocino Coast—all of them at the mouths of rivers which were critical to the transportation of logs from the inland forests to the sea, where waiting tug boats would then take the logs in tow and barge them down the coast to San Francisco and other coastal centers. After the lumbering, however, Mendocino, like the other towns, fell into decline, until in the 1950s it was rediscovered by artists from San Francisco and the Bay Area who, inspired by its picturesque setting and isolation, began to revive the old town. It is now home to a colony of more than 200 artists and craftsmen who display and sell their work at local shops and galleries. Besides which, the area now also has an increasing number of vacation homes, and fine inns and restaurants to cater to the year-round tourist influx.

The town itself is really quite enjoyable and easy to walk around—small, compact, and with a handful of little streets dashing off merrily to intersect with one another. The two principal streets here are Main and Lansing, intersecting each other at right angles. Main Street faces south across a stretch of grassy headland, and has upon it, among others, the Mendocino Hotel, perhaps the most attractive of Mendocino's older buildings. It dates from 1878 and has been beautifully restored to its former elegance, with antique decor and a superb, garden-style restaurant. A little way to the east from the hotel are two other places of visitor interest—the Ford and Kelley houses, both open to the public, and the former now an interpretive center of sorts, with old photographs and relics from Mendocino's lumbering past and some interesting nature exhibits, including an elaborate display of seaweed.

Farther inland, still on the same street, stands the handsome, redwood Presbyterian Church of Mendocino, one of the most photographed of Mendocino's old buildings—frequently the focus of photographs of "Mendocino on the bluff." The church dates from 1859.

On Lansing Street are dozens of interesting little shops and art galleries, stocked with locally produced handicrafts and art, and interspersed with a rustic cafe or two, making this a suitable place to stroll and browse. The most dominant structure here is of course the old Masonic Hall, more or less midway up the street, large, white, and topped with a most unique roof sculpture—of Father Time braiding a maiden's hair. From here also, you can go west briefly on Little Lake Street—which branches off Lansing Street—to the Mendocino Art Center which, most residents will tell you, is *the* place to visit in town. Besides constantly changing exhibits of works of resident and visiting artists, the center has a large collection of paintings, serigraphs and prints by local artists, available for sale at very reasonable prices, many of them original works.

The Hill House "at Cabot Cove," splendidly situated on a small hill above town, is also well worth a visit. It has superb guest accommodations, and a well-liked restaurant and lounge, the upper floor of which is much to be recommended for whale watching during the

MENDOCINO

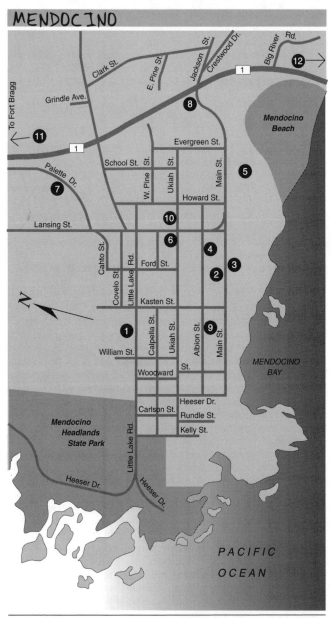

1. Mendocino Art Center
2. Mendocino Hotel
3. Ford House
4. Kelly House
5. Mendocino Presbyterian Church
6. Masonic Hall
7. The Hill House
8. Ruth Carlson Gallery
9. Zacha's Bay Window Gallery
10. Fine Line Gallery
11. Jughandle State Reserve
12. Van Damme State Reserve

annual whale migration in November. Nearby, too, is the Mendocino Headlands State Park, with good vista points and countless opportunities for ocean viewing.

Yet another place of interest, just to the south of town and nestled along the sheltered bay directly below the bluff, is the Mendocino Beach. It has good surf fishing and picnicking possibilities.

DETOURS

North and south of Mendocino are several other picturesque little coastal communities—villages, no more—most with a measure of tourist interest. Just 2 miles south, for instance, is Little River, notable for its charming Victorian inns, and which, together with Mendocino, makes up the "inn country" of the Mendocino Coast. South of Little River, a few miles, are Albion and Elk, the latter a good place for whale watching. Farther still, are Manchester, Point Arena, Anchor Bay, Gualala and Sea Ranch, all with spectacular ocean scenery. At Point Arena—which is some 35 miles south of Mendocino—there is an operating lighthouse which can be visited. Point Arena is also a good place for whale watching.

North of Mendocino, some 5 miles, is the tiny, weathered village of Caspar, another former lumbering settlement, but which now has only a handful of tumbledown structures, surrounded by rickety old fences and overgrown with brush and wildflowers, quite picturesque in spring. Close at hand, a mile or so up the road from Caspar is the Jughandle State Reserve, a place of supreme interest. It has in it the famous "Pygmy Forest," where fully matured trees stand only three or four feet off the ground—a unique natural phenomenon, which owes much to the peculiar disposition of soil and climatic conditions in that section of the forest. (Another good place to see a "Pygmy Forest" is the Van Damme State Park, just south of Mendocino, at Little River.)

North still, 6 or 7 miles, is Fort Bragg, the largest and most important town on the Mendocino Coast, with modern shops, motels, bed and breakfast inns, and some notable seaside restaurants. Fort Bragg was originally founded in 1857 as a military outpost, and one of the buildings from the original fort can still be viewed here, rescued and relocated on Franklin Street. The town's great glory, however, is its Skunk Train, a turn-of-the-century steam train which makes all-day trips through Mendocino's redwood groves to the town of Willits, some 40 miles inland. The Skunk depot has some 19th-century railroad buildings and an adjoining museum with several outdoor displays.

Directly below Fort Bragg, and also worth visiting, are the Mendocino Coast Botanical Gardens—with hundreds of species of North Coast plants and flowers, and a cafe of some interest—and Noyo Harbor, a small, working fishing village which also has one or two wharfside seafood restaurants, a gift and souvenir shop, and fishing charters in season.

Inland from Mendocino, too, some 25 miles on Highway 128, is the fertile, winegrowing Anderson Valley, which has in it a half-dozen or so small, family owned and operated wineries, including Husch Vineyards, Handley Cellars, Christine Woods Winery and Navarro Vineyards. Most of these have visitor facilities of some sort, and are well worth touring.

HOW TO GET THERE

Mendocino lies approximately 115 miles north of San Francisco. The best and most direct route to the town is by way of coastal *Highway 1*; this is also perhaps the most scenic. An alternative route is by way of *Highway 101* north, directly from San Francisco to Cloverdale, roughly 87 miles; then northwest on *Highway 128*, some 68 miles, to Mendocino.

TOURIST INFORMATION

Fort Bragg-Mendocino Coast Chamber of Commerce, 332 N. Main St., Fort Bragg; (707) 961-6300. Information on lodging, restaurants and art galleries, with maps to go by. Also calendar of events, and wineries information for nearby Anderson Valley.

ACCOMMODATIONS

Bed & Breakfast Inns

Agate Cove Inn. *$109-$250.* 11201 N. Lansing St.; (707) 937-0551. 10 rooms with ocean views and fireplaces; also some cottages in garden setting. Full country breakfast.

Blue Heron Inn. *$80-$95.* 390 Kasten St.; (707) 937-4323. 3 rooms with fireplaces and antiques, overlooking the ocean. Cafe on premises.

Brewery Gulch Inn. *$85-$135.* 9350 Hwy 1, Little River; (707) 937-4752. Old white farmhouse, built in the 1860s, and set amid two acres of gardens. 4 rooms and 1 suite, furnished with Victorian antiques, homemade quilts and down pillows. Full country breakfast, served in delightful common room, or in the garden. Ocean views.

Glendeven. *$98-$168.* 8221 N. Hwy. 1, Little River; (707) 937-0083. Beautiful Maine-style farmhouse built in 1867, set back, amid two acres of gardens, on a headland meadow overlooking Little River Bay. 9 antique-decorated rooms with ocean views. Private baths; some fireplaces. Breakfast comprises home-baked breads, fresh fruit and juice. Also a separate "barn" unit, which can accommodate up to six people, *$185-$275.*

Grey Whale Inn. *$88-$165.* 615 North Main St., Fort Bragg; (707) 964-0640. Weathered redwood inn, originally built in 1915 as a hospital, and converted to an inn in 1976. Features 14 guest rooms, most with private baths. Ocean views.

Headlands Inn. *$100-$195.* Cnr. Howard and Albion Sts.; (707) 937-4431. Small, 6-room inn, built in 1868. Fireplaces in most rooms; some ocean views.

Hill House Inn. *$145-$300.* 10701 Palette Dr.; (707) 937-0554. Delightful inn, situated on hilltop, overlooking the ocean. 44 well-appointed rooms, with fireplaces, TV, phones, and views. Lovely gardens; restaurant and cocktail lounge.

Joshua Grindle Inn. *$105-$195.* 44800 Little Lake Rd.; (707) 937-4143. Charming New England-style farmhouse, built in 1879. Features 9 rooms, some with ocean views and fireplaces. Full breakfast.

McCallum House Inn. *$100-$190.* 45020 Albion St.; (707) 937-0289. Housed in historic, 100-year-old mansion, decorated with antiques. 21 rooms and cottages; some private baths; also some woodburning stoves and fireplaces. Ocean views; restaurant and bar on premises. Continental breakfast.

Mendocino Hotel & Garden Cottages. *$55-$275.* 45080 Main St.; (707) 937-0511. Historic, 3-story hotel, with 50 antique-furnished rooms and suites, featuring down comforters; also 3 garden cottages. Most rooms have fireplaces or woodstoves; some offer bay views or garden views. The hotel also has a full-service restaurant and garden cafe.

Mendocino Village Inn. *$75-$175.* 44860 Main St.; (707) 937-0246. 1882 Queen Anne Victorian, with 12 individually decorated rooms. Many of the rooms have fireplaces; some ocean views and private garden entrances.

Rachel's Inn. *$96-$251.* 8200 N. Hwy. 1, Little River; (707) 937-0088. 9 rooms, some with fireplaces. Also ocean views.

Sea Rock Inn. *$85-$250.* 11101 N. Lansing St.; (707) 937-5517. 16 rooms with fireplaces and ocean views; also in-room TV. Continental breakfast.

Whitegate Inn. *$139-$229.* 499 Howard St.; (707) 937-4892. 1880s inn. 6 rooms, most with ocean views; some fireplaces.

Hotels and Resorts

Heritage House. *$125-$350.* 5200 N. Hwy. 1, Little River; (707) 937-5885. One of the best-known and most picturesque inns on the Mendocino Coast, overlooking the cove at Little River. 67 luxurious, individually decorated guest rooms, with fireplaces and ocean views. Restaurant and cocktail lounge on premises; restaurant features California country cuisine.

Little River Inn. *$90-$255.* N. Hwy. 1, Little River; (707) 937-5942/(800) 466-5683. Charming Victorian inn with a new annex and adjoining cottages, set amid landscaped grounds. 50 units, all with ocean views. Also restaurant and cocktail lounge, and 9- hole golf course for guests.

Stanford Inn By-The-Sea. *$215-$365.* Hwy. 1, Little River; (707) 937-5615. 23 antique-decorated rooms and suites with ocean views; most rooms also have fireplaces, TV, and phones.

SEASONAL EVENTS

March. *Whale Festival (Mendocino).* 3rd weekend of the month. Various events at Ford House, including whale watching, films, a barbecue and cioppino feed, wine tasting and music. For schedule and information, call (707) 961-6300. *Whale Festival (Fort Bragg).* Usually held during the 4th weekend of the month. Events include a parade, 10-kilometer whale run, whale watching tours, an arts and crafts show, wine tasting, and a variety of entertainment. (707) 961-6300.

May. *Rhododendron Show.* Fort Bragg. 1st weekend. Lavish flower show, featuring Rhododendrons. (707) 961-6300. *Historic House Tours.* One-hour guided walking tours of the town, highlighting Mendocino's Victorian architecture; conducted by the Mendocino Historical Research Group on Saturdays at 11 a.m. Call for more information; (707) 937-5791.

July. *World's Largest Salmon Barbecue.* Held at Noyo Fishing Village, usually during the Fourth of July weekend. Features entertainment and dancing, and barbecued salmon. (707) 964-2313. *Mendocino Music Festival.* 3rd week; at Mendocino. Series of outdoor orchestral and chamber music concerts, and opera and jazz, featuring internationally acclaimed artists and local musicians. Reservations required for all concerts; (707) 937-2044.

August. *Summer Arts & Crafts Show.* 1st weekend; at the Mendocino Art Center. Arts and crafts displays, food concessions, and entertainment. (707) 937-5818.

September. *Paul Bunyan Days Celebration.* Held at Fort Bragg, during Labor Day weekend. Logging show, parade, music, dancing, fuschia show, and various competitions. More information on (707) 961-6300. Mendocino Festival of Books. 3rd weekend; at the Mendocino Arts Center. Book fair, with booths, seminars and workshops for writers.

November. *Mushroom Festival and Mushroom Foray.* Held at the Ford House during the first week of the month. Events include slide show, display of edible mushrooms, demonstration of mushroom textile dyeing, and mushroom hunting expedition at Little River. (707) 937-5397.

December. *Mendocino Christmas Festival.* Three-week Christmas festival, featuring stage performances, dance series, Christmas carols, tours of Bed & Breakfast inns, lavish decorations and lights, parties, buffets, display of antique quilts, arts and crafts show highlighting work of local artisans, horse-drawn carriage rides, and more. For a complete schedule of events and more information, call (707) 961-6300.

Ongoing Event. *Mendocino Theatre Company.* At the Helen Schoeni Theatre in Mendocino. Live theater, featuring evening performances Thurs.-Sun., March-Nov. For a schedule of performances, and reservations, call (707) 937-4477.

PLACES OF INTEREST

Ford House. Located on the south side of Main St., between Lansing and Kasten Sts. Historic home, built in 1854 by pioneer lumber baron Jerome Bursley Ford. Now operated as an interpretive center by the California State Parks Department. Displays of exhibits depicting the history of Mendocino's logging industry, including old photographs; also indigenous wildlife exhibits, Pomo Indian artifacts, and works of local artists. Open 11-4 daily. (707) 937-5397.

Kelley House. On Albion St., near cnr. of Lansing St. Built in 1861 as the home of pioneer settler William Kelley, the house is now operated by Mendocino Historical Research, Inc. Contains a large collection of old photographs and research materials on local history and genealogical data, as well as exhibits of the area's logging and shipping history and the town's Victorian architecture. The Historical Research group also offers guided walking tours of the town on Saturdays at 11 a.m., April-Nov. The house is open 1-4 daily, June-Aug.; 1-4 Fri.-Mon., Sept.-May. Admission fee: $1.00. For more information, call (707) 937-5791.

Mendocino Presbyterian Church. Situated on Main St.; (707) 937-5441. Claimed to be the oldest Presbyterian Church in continuous operation in

California, dating from 1858. Focus of "Mendocino on the bluff" photographs.

Mendocino Art Center and Gallery. 45200 Little Lake St.; (707) 937-5818. Established in 1959 by resident artist Bill Zacha, the center offers classes in art, weaving and ceramics, conducted by professionals. It also has an art library, and an art gallery featuring works of regional and international artists and craftsmen. During the summer months, open-air concerts and art shows are held at the center. Open daily 10-5.

Point Arena Lighthouse and Museum. Historic lighthouse with 115-foot tower, located on the tip of a narrow peninsula just outside the town of Point Arena, 20 miles south of Mendocino, on Hwy. 1. Originally built in 1870, and rebuilt in 1908 as the first steel-reinforced lighthouse in the United States. View original Fresnel lens, and old Fog Signal Building, which now houses a small museum. Also, 3 cottages on grounds, available for vacation rentals. The lighthouse is open daily, 11- 2.30 (10-3.30 on weekends in summer). Admission fee: $3.00 adults, $1.00 for children. For cottage rentals, call (707) 882-2777.

Van Damme State Park. Located at Little River, just south of Mendocino. 1,826-acre park, with ferns and redwoods, meadows and beaches. Visit "pygmy forest" in southeastern part of park, where a soil deficiency has created a natural curiosity with fully-matured trees standing only a few feet tall! The park also offers camping, picnicking and hiking possibilities. Open daily, year-round; day-use fee: $5.00. (707) 937-5804.

Jughandle State Reserve. 8 miles north of Mendocino on Hwy. 1 (just north of Caspar). Hiking and picnicking; self-guided tour of a "pygmy forest." Also 4-hour ranger-guided nature hike to "pygmy forest." Open daily, year-round. Park information on (707) 937-5804.

Little River. Peaceful little village just south of Mendocino on Hwy. 1. Formerly a shipbuilding and lumbering town, Little River is now famous as the "Inn Country" of the Mendocino Coast, filled with dozens of superb bed and breakfast inns and delightful restaurants. Popular scuba-diving spot; also features a 9-hole golf course.

Russian Gulch State Park. 2 miles north of Mendocino on Hwy. 1. 1,122-acre park, with camping, picnicking, and a waterfall with a pool. Also blowhole at beach. (707) 937-5804.

Point Cabrillo Lighthouse. Near Caspar, 5 miles north of Mendocino. Limited public access.

Mendocino Coast Botanical Gardens. On Hwy. 1, just south of Fort Bragg; (707) 964-4352. 17-acre garden, filled with hundreds of species of plants and flowers which have adapted to the unique North Coast environment. Colorful displays of rhododendrons, fuschias and azaleas, March through October. Picnic facilities and coast access. Also retail nursery on premises, and a small, casual restaurant serving lunch. Open daily 9-5 May-Oct, 9-4 Nov.-Feb. Admission: $6.00 adults, $5.00 seniors, $3.00 students, $1.00 children.

Noyo Fishing Village. 1 mile south of Fort Bragg, off Hwy. 1. Colorful, working fishing harbor, claimed to be the largest port between Eureka and San Francisco. Boat charters available for fishing and whale-watching (in season). Also one or two souvenir shops and waterfront restaurants.

Caspar. 5 miles north of Mendocino on Hwy. 1. Tiny, sea-worn village, formerly a lumbering town and home to the Caspar Lumber Company which built the first railroad on the North Coast, in 1874, as well as the highest railroad trestle in North America. There is a sheltered, sandy cove here.

Fort Bragg. Located 10 miles north of Mendocino on Hwy. 1. Fort Bragg is the largest town on the Mendocino Coast, originally established in the 1850s as a military outpost. A surviving *Fort Building*, now housing displays depicting the history of the fort, can be seen at 430 N. Franklin St., open to the public Mon.-Fri. 9-5. Also visit the *Georgia Pacific Tree Nursery*, situated just off Main St., (707) 964-5651, which produces millions of seedlings used in various reforestation projects in the area; it is open to public tours during the summer months, weekdays 8.30-4.30. The *Guest House Museum* at 343 N. Main St. is another place of interest, featuring exhibits illustrating the history of the lumbering and shipping industries and the railroad in Fort Bragg; the museum is open 10.30-2.30 Tues.-Sun.; small admission fee. A highlight of any visit to Fort Bragg, however, has to be a ride on its turn-of-the-century *Skunk Train*, which makes half-day and full-day trips through majestic redwood forests, inland to Northspur and Willits (30 miles); cost of train ride: $25.00 adults/$13.00 children for full day, and $20.00 adults/$10.00 children for half day; reservations and information on (707) 964-6371. Fort Bragg also has some good waterfront restaurants, and bed and breakfast and motel accommodations.

ART GALLERIES

Ruth Carlson Gallery. Cnr. Hwy. 1 and Main St.; (707) 937-5154. Displays of works by professional local artists and craftsmen, including seascapes and landscapes by E. John Robinson. Gallery hours: 10-5 daily.

Fine Line Gallery. 16 Ukiah St.; (707) 937-4538. Specializing in regional paintings, prints, and photography; also ceramics, sculpture and jewelry. Open 11-5 weekdays, 10-5 weekends.

Zimmer Gallery. Cnr. Kasten and Ukiah Sts.; (707) 937- 5121. Gallery features paintings, furniture, jewelry and ceramics. Gallery hours: 10.30-5 daily.

Gallery Mendocino. 10351 Nichols Lane; (707) 937-0214. Art gallery-cum-frame shop, featuring works of local artists. Open 10.30-4.30 daily (except Tues.).

Highlight Gallery. 45052 Main St.; (707) 937-3132. Features decorative and fine arts; furniture, paintings, sculpture, ceramics, jewelry and textiles. Open daily 10-5.

Mendocino Art Center Gallery. 45200 Little Lake Rd.; (707) 937-5818. Open Mon.-Thurs. 10-4, Fri.-Sun. 10-5. Also see listing under *Places of Interest*.

Old Gold. Cnr. Albion and Lansing Sts.; (707) 937-5005. Jewelry and timepieces, both antique and contemporary. Hours: 10.30-5 daily.

Panache. 20400 Kasten St.; (707) 937-1234. Contemporary jewelry, sculptures and stained glass. Open daily 9.30-5.

Studio 2. 450 Main St.; (707) 937-4934. Handcrafted gold and silver jewelry; also mixed media work by local artists. Open daily 10-5.

Zacha's Bay Window Gallery. 560 Main St.; (707) 937-2505. Paintings, prints, pottery, sculpture and glass art by former members of the Art Center faculty. Open daily 10-5.

Artists' Studios. There are also several artists' studios in Mendocino which may be visited by appointment. The following are some of the better known. *Jim Bertram*, (707) 937-5182; paintings. *Hilda Pertha*, (707) 937-5605; paintings. *Ilja Tinfo*, (707) 937-4620; paintings. The *Mendocino Art Center* also organizes tours of artists' studios on weekends in the summer, with visits to nearly 45 different studios; for more information, call the center at (707) 937-5818.

RECREATION

Boating and Fishing. For boating and fishing enthusiasts, the place to visit is the Noyo Fishing Village, directly below Fort Bragg. It has boat rentals, sport fishing charters, whale watching cruises (in season), and a variety of other special charters and expeditions out to sea. Following are some of the charter operators in the area: *The Cavalier Fleet*, (707) 964-4550; *Tally Ho II*, (707) 964-2079; *Lady Irma II*, (707) 964-3854. Also, the *Noyo Fishing Center* arranges boat charters and excursions; (707) 964-7609.

Scuba Diving. *Sub-Surface Progression*, 18600 Hwy. 1, Fort Bragg; (707) 964-3793. Equipment rental, repairs, lessons.

Bicycling. *Catch A Canoe and Bicycles Too!* Cnr. Hwy. 1 and Comptche-Ukiah Rd.; (707) 937-0273; bicycle rentals and repairs. *Fort Bragg Cyclery,* 579 S. Franklin St., Fort Bragg; (707) 964-3509; bicycle rentals and repairs.

Horseback Riding. *Richochet Ridge Ranch*, 24201 N. Hwy. 1, Fort Bragg; (707) 964-7669. Offers escorted trail rides along the beach and through redwoods.

RESTAURANTS

(Restaurant prices—based on full course dinner, excluding drinks, tax and tips—are categorized as follows: *Deluxe*, over $30; *Expensive*, $20-$30; *Moderate*, $10-$20; *Inexpensive*, under $10.)

Bay View Cafe. *Moderate-Expensive*. 45040 Main St.; (707) 937-4197. Well-liked restaurant, overlooking Mendocino Bay. Fresh seafood and pasta dishes; also daily lunch specials. Large sundeck for whale watching. Open for breakfast on weekends, lunch daily, dinner Fri.-Tues. Reservations suggested.

Cafe Beaujolais. *Moderate*. 961 Ukiah St.; (707) 937-5614. Housed in a restored Victorian building, Cafe Beaujolais specializes in California cuisine prepared with the freshest ingredients. Open for breakfast and lunch daily, dinner Thurs.-Mon. in summer.

Chocolate Moosse. *Inexpensive-Moderate*. 390 Kasten St.; (707) 937-4323. Delicious desserts; also soups, salads and pates. Open 10 a.m.-9 p.m. daily.

Gardens Grill. *Inexpensive-Moderate*. At the Mendocino Coast Botanical Gardens, Fort Bragg. Casual cafe, serving soups, sandwiches, salads and burgers. Open for lunch Mon.-Sat., brunch on Sundays.

Heritage House. *Expensive-Deluxe*. 5200 N. Hwy. 1, Little River; (707) 937-5885. Well-known oceanview restaurant, housed in the picturesque Heritage House inn. Features primarily California country cuisine. Extensive wine list. Bar and cocktail lounge. Open for breakfast and dinner. Reservations advised.

Hill House Restaurant. *Expensive*. 10701 Pallette Dr.; (707) 937-0554. Elegant restaurant, featuring fresh seafood and New England cuisine. Spectacular ocean views. Open daily for dinner; also weekend brunch. Reservations advised.

Ledford House. *Expensive*. 3000 N. Hwy. 1, Albion; (707) 937-0282. Housed in charming 1860s farmhouse overlooking the ocean. Hearty country food, featuring several local California specialties. Extensive wine list. Dinners from 6 p.m. daily; also Sunday brunch.

McCallum House. *Expensive*. 45020 Albion St.; (707) 937-5763. Superb Continental restaurant, housed in restored Victorian mansion. Old stone fireplace, intimate setting; ocean and bay views. Dinner daily.

Mendocino Cafe. *Inexpensive-Moderate.* 10451 Lansing St., between Ukiah St. and Little Lake Rd.; (707) 937-2422. Homemade breads, cakes and pies; also soups, sandwiches and pizza. Open daily.

Mendocino Hotel. *Expensive.* 45080 Main St.; (707) 937-0511. California cuisine in historic Victorian-style dining room. Home baked specialties. Open for breakfast, lunch and dinner daily.

The Wharf Restaurant. *Moderate.* 780 N. Harbor Dr., Noyo Harbor; (707) 964-4283. Wharfside dining featuring fresh seafood and steaks. Also cocktails, entertainment and dancing. Open for lunch and dinner daily.

CANNERY ROW

MONTEREY

History, Golf and Steinbeck

Monterey is one of California's most attractive and well-cared-for towns, rich in history, with much still surviving from its colorful past, including scores of typical Monterey adobes and other handsome old buildings. The town is also, it must be said, an enormously popular tourist destination, with luxury hotels, gourmet restaurants, and a first class shopping district. Typically, tourist activities here include browsing, fishing, whale watching (in season), bicycling, and, best-loved of all, golf, with at least a dozen championship golf courses situated in and around town.

The town of Monterey is picturesquely situated along the southern end of Monterey Bay, some 125 miles south of San Francisco, adjoined to its west by the essentially Victorian town of Pacific Grove and to its south by world-famous Pebble Beach. It can be reached on Highway 101 south and a brief detour southwestward on Highway 1. Alternatively, you can follow Highway 1 directly south.

DISCOVERING MONTEREY

To discover Monterey is to discover an important part of California's past. It is one of California's oldest settlements—first sighted in 1542, discovered in 1602, and settled in 1770 by Franciscan monk, Father Junipero Serra—who founded here the second of California's twenty-one missions, which a year later, in 1771, was moved to nearby Carmel—and Captain Don Gaspar de Portola, Governor of Baja California, who built here the second of California's four presidios (now the site of the Defense Language Institute, West Coast Branch, near Pacific and Artillery streets). Monterey also, we might add, has been the capital of California under three different banners—Spanish (1770-1822), Mexican (1822-1846) and American (1846-1848)—with its history representing, to a great extent, the history of pre-Gold Rush California.

For history buffs, Monterey is indeed *the* place to visit. It has no fewer than forty most historic buildings—largely old adobes—dotted along its famed "path of history" in the Monterey State Historic Park, most of them rescued, restored and preserved through the efforts of the highly active Monterey History and Art Association. Most of these can be visited on a self-guided tour, either by walking round or driving, with good maps to go by. A fair number of these contain original 18th- and 19th-century furnishings, and delightful, well-kept gardens; while some are still in use, as city or park offices. The State Parks Department, by the way, also has guided tours of many of these old relics, available for a fee of around $1.00 each.

In any event, at the top of the tour are the Colton Hall (1847), notably the first public building of California's American period, and the site of the California Constitutional Convention in 1849; the Stevenson House, dating from the late 1830s, where Scottish writer Robert Louis Stevenson stayed briefly in 1879; the Royal Presidio Chapel (1794), believed to be the oldest existing structure in Monterey, still in use; and the Cooper-Molera Adobe, an excellent example of the Monterey-colonial architecture style, and quite possibly one of the largest walled-in complexes in Old Monterey—2½ acres. Two other outstanding examples of the "Monterey" style of architecture are the Larkin House—a two-story adobe surrounded on three sides by a balcony, dating from 1835—and Casa Soberanes, a beautifully kept private residence which is now also open to public tours. There are several other ancient and lovely buildings worth seeing here too, including dozens of Monterey-style adobes, well preserved, and from all three periods. Among the most notable are the splendidly restored Merritt House; the Casa del Oro, dating from the 1850s and formerly a gold depository; Casa Guiterrez, originally built in 1841 as a private residence; Casa Serrano, which houses Monterey's History and Art Association; California's First Theatre, dating from the 1840s, where theater groups still perform; and the Underwood-Brown, Vasquez, Alvarado and Fremont adobes, all quite lovely, and dating from the 1800s. (Most of these—and others—are further described in a brochure published by the Old Monterey Council, in cooperation with the

MONTEREY

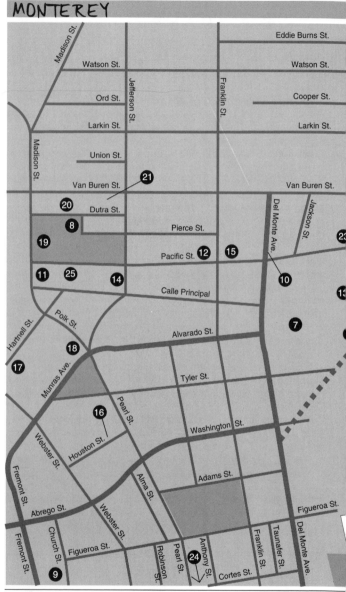

1. Monterey Bay Aquarium
2. Custon House
3. Pacific House
4. Fisherman's Wharf
5. Municipal Wharf
6. Coast Guard Wharf
7. Monterey Plaza Covention Center
8. Colton Hall
9. Royal Presidio Chapel
10. Casa Soberanes
11. Casa Guiterrez
12. Casa Serrano
13. Casa del Oro
14. Larkin House
15. Merritt House

MONTEREY

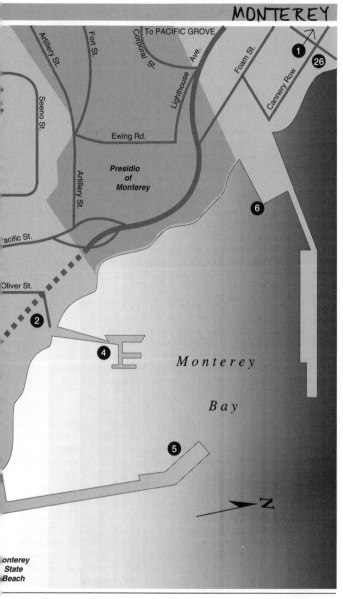

To PACIFIC GROVE

Artillery St.

Fort St.

Corporal St.

Lighthouse Ave.

Foam St.

Cannery Row

Seeno St.

Ewing Rd.

Artillery St.

Presidio of Monterey

acific St.

Oliver St.

Monterey

Bay

N

onterey State Beach

Monterey History and Art Association and the State Parks Department, available from the local Chamber of Commerce or the Art and History Association office.)

A highlight of Old Monterey, however, quite close to the waterfront and still on the "path of history," is the venerable old Custom House—a superb Monterey adobe, dating from 1797 and claimed to be the oldest government building on the West Coast. It is adjoined to its back by the equally historic Pacific House, which has a good museum and a pleasant little courtyard garden, and directly above which lies the Monterey Plaza Convention Center, a more modern structure, but quite in keeping with the Monterey flavor and architecture, and with a measure of tourist interest. The center has in it a 547-room luxury hotel, several fine shops, a convention facility with a seating capacity of around 1,500, and a delightful, brick-paved plaza with a statue of Gaspar de Portola, founder of Monterey.

Immediately below the Custom House, and overlooked by it, is the colorful old Fisherman's Wharf, with its lighthearted, haphazard jumble of gift and souvenir shops, kiosks, seafood restaurants and fish markets. It is an immensely popular tourist spot, both with adults and children, and a good place to spend an afternoon. Here you can stroll the piers, with their old, creaking boards, or feed the sea lions that lurk amid the pilings directly beneath the pier, frequently joined by brown pelicans—a common sight here—all scavenging for food. From here, also, you can take sportfishing trips out to sea, or enjoy whale watching cruises in season, usually in November. Nearby, at the Municipal Wharf, it is possible to watch fishing boats as they unload their catch of the day—salmon, cod, kingfish, herring, tuna, anchovies. In fact, seven fish processing plants share space at the end of the wharf, cleaning and packing fish. The wharf also has good pier fishing.

The great glory of Monterey yet, is its famed Cannery Row, lying just to the northwest of Fisherman's Wharf, stretching from the Coast Guard station in the east to more or less the outskirts of neighboring Pacific Grove. This, in fact, is the Cannery Row of John Steinbeck fame, romanticized in his classic of the same name—*Cannery Row*—as "a poem, a stink, a grating noise." Starting at the turn of the century, several sardine canning factories located along this row, peaking to over sixteen in the 1930s; and scores of bawdy, raucous fishermen, eccentrics, and other interesting characters were attracted here as well, many of whom Steinbeck encountered during his visit to the row, and who later became the inspiration for his novels, *Tortilla Flats* (1935), *Cannery Row* (1945) and *Sweet Thursday* (1945). Most of the canneries, of course, closed in the late 1940s, and have, in recent years, been remodeled and converted into colorful little arcades, with fine shops, galleries, restaurants and game parlors. A place of special interest here, housed in the old Monterey Canning Company building, is the Spirit of Monterey Wax Museum, where you can view many of Steinbeck's characters, including the marine biologist "Doc" Rickett, the most famous of all, and Lee Chong and Sam Mally.

Try to also visit the Monterey Bay Aquarium—quite possibly Monterey's greatest tourist attraction—located at the west end of

Cannery Row, at the site of the old Hovden Cannery. The aquarium was originally built in 1981, at a cost of around $40 million, and is believed to be one of the largest of its kind in the nation. It has in it a giant Kelp Forest Tank which rises two stories, opening up to the sky, as well as two or three other huge tanks containing native fish and invertebrates, several petting pools, an aquaculture laboratory, and countless marine exhibits, highlighting native sea life. There is also a gift shop on the premises.

Monterey has another distinction. It is famous the world over as the home of golf, with no fewer than a dozen superb golf courses in and around town, many of them championship courses which host professional golf tournaments year-round. Here, for instance, are the Pebble Beach Golf Course, situated just south of Monterey on the 17-Mile Drive, with its spectacular ocean vistas and a lodge of considerable repute; and the Cypress Point Golf Club, also located on the 17-Mile Drive, quite close to the Pebble Beach course, and renowned for its 16th green which can only be reached by driving over some 200 yards of open ocean! Among other notable courses here are Spyglass Hill, Del Monte—claimed to be the oldest golf course west of the Mississippi—and the Monterey Peninsula Country Club's two world-class courses which, before Spyglass Hill was built, were the site for the Bing Crosby National Pro-Am Tournament.

DETOURS

Monterey has two other places of supreme tourist interest, adjoining to its west and south. Pacific Grove, just to the west, is a picturesque little coastal town, abundant in brightly colored Victorian homes—quite in contrast to Monterey's Spanish-style adobes—and notable, too, as "Butterfly Town, USA," where millions of Monarch butterflies migrate for the winter. The butterflies can be seen—in season—in the Butterfly Park just to the northwest of town, hanging like dried leaves from the "butterfly trees." The town also hosts a Butterfly Parade in October each year, to celebrate the Monarch migration.

Pacific Grove's Victorians, of course, can be seen throughout town, especially concentrated on Lighthouse and Central avenues and along the waterfront. The finest of them all is perhaps The Centrella, a thoroughly enchanting bed and breakfast establishment, situated on Central Avenue; it dates from 1889 and was recently, in 1981, restored at a cost of around $1 million. Many of the town's other Victorians are also quite lovely, with their multicolored shutters and doors, and some actually date from over a century, to when the town was first founded, in 1875, as a Methodist seaside resort.

Pacific Grove also enjoys a beautiful coastline, with many miles of oceanside walks. Lover's Point Park, by the ocean at Pacific Avenue and Ocean View Boulevard, is especially popular with walkers and joggers. On the coast, too, is the Point Pinos Reserve, with an operating lighthouse—built in 1855 and believed to be the oldest continuously operating lighthouse on the West Coast—which can be visited on weekends. Also try to visit Pacific Grove's Natural History Museum on Central Avenue, which has displays of over 400 birds from Monterey County, and an excellent relief map of Monterey Bay, in which you can see the great chasm in the bay, plunging, in just a few files, from some 300 feet to over 8,400 feet!

South of Pacific Grove—and Monterey—lies the Del Monte Forest, which incorporates in it the fabled Pebble Beach—with its exclusive residential communities—and the 17-Mile Drive, an astonishingly scenic drive, billed as "the slowest way between Monterey and Carmel." There are three gates by which to enter upon the drive; two at Pacific Grove, and one at the south end, at Carmel. There is an admission charge for the drive, of around $7.00 per car, and a map pinpointing all the places of interest enroute is also available at the gate. Here you will see such well-known sights as the Lone Cypress, one of the most photographed of the Monterey Peninsula's landmarks; the storm- felled, splendid white Ghost Tree, with a legend all its own; the Bird and Seal rocks, where you can see countless sea gulls, black cormorants and other shore birds perched on the rocks, and sea otters, sea lions, and leopard and harbor seals lurking in the waters below; and the lovely Spanish Bay, Fanshell Beach and Point Joe, where ancient ships lie wrecked among the rocks just offshore. There are also a half-dozen or so superb, championship golf courses here, including the Cypress Point Golf Course and the Pebble Beach Golf Club, which has a notable lodge. Pebble Beach also has an equestrian center, with over 34 miles of bridle trails. Indeed, the 17-Mile-Drive and Pebble Beach are a worthwhile detour, not to be missed while in Monterey.

HOW TO GET THERE

Monterey is approximately 125 miles southeast of San Francisco, situated at the head of Monterey Bay. The best way to reach it is on the all-important *Highway 101*—with a brief detour southwestward on *Highways 156* and *1*. The scenic coastal route, Highway 1, also leads to Monterey.

Monterey also has a commercial airport, situated just outside the township on Highway 68. It is serviced by the following airlines: *United Airlines* (800) 241-6522; *US Air* (800) 428-4322; *Skywest* (800) 453-9417; *American Eagle* (800) 433-7300.

TOURIST INFORMATION

Monterey Peninsula Chamber of Commerce and Visitor & Convention Bureau. 380 Alvarado St., Monterey; (831) 649-1770. Tourist literature, including accommodation and restaurant listings, calendar of events, Old Monterey maps, and several free tourist publications. Monterey also has a *Restaurant Hotline* for restaurant information and reservations; (831) 372-DINE.

Pacific Grove Chamber of Commerce. Cnr. Central Ave. and Forest Ave., Pacific Grove; (831) 373-3304. Tourist brochures and listings of accommodations, restaurants, and places of interest; also "Butterfly Trees" map, and calendar of events.

ACCOMMODATIONS

Bed & Breakfast Inns

Centrella Hotel. *$135-$195.* 612 Central, Pacific Grove; (831) 372-3372. Award-winning Victorian inn, with 26 beautifully decorated rooms, including some attic suites and cottages; private baths, phones, TV, fireplaces, hot tub. Continental breakfast; complimentary wine and sherry.

Del Monte Beach Inn. *$50-$100.* 1110 Del Monte Ave.; (831) 649-4410. 18-room inn, housed in former boarding house for cannery workers, dating from 1925. Continental breakfast, comprising freshly-baked croissants, muffins and pastries, and fresh fruit and juices. No smoking.

Gosby House Inn. *$90-$160.* 643 Lighthouse Ave., Pacific Grove; (831) 375-1287. Turreted Victorian mansion; 22 rooms, 13 with fireplaces. Breakfast comprises homemade muffins, granola parfaits, fresh fruit and eggs; hors d'oeuvres in the afternoon.

The Jabberwock. *$105-$190.* 598 Laine St.; (831) 372-4777. Formerly a Dominican convent, the inn now offers 5 unique guest rooms. Spectacular ocean views from the third floor; milk and cookies by the fireplace in the living room in the evening.

Martine Inn. *$135-$245.* 255 Ocean View Blvd., Pacific Grove; (831) 373-3388. Elegant Victorian home, dating from 1899. 19 antique-filled rooms, private baths with clawfoot tubs and marble sinks; phones, fireplaces, spa. Spectacular bay views from front parlor.

The Merritt House. *$125-$220.* 386 Pacific St.; (831) 646-9686. 3 comfortable suites in historic adobe main house; 22 other rooms, located in newer buildings behind the main house. All rooms have private baths, fireplaces, phones and TVs, and are furnished with antiques and brass beds. Beautiful rose garden on premises. Continental breakfast.

Old Monterey Inn. *$200-$280.* 500 Martha St.; (831) 375-8284. English country house with beautiful gardens and oak trees. 10 rooms, all with private baths; some fireplaces, skylights, and stained glass windows. Full breakfast, served in bed, in the dining room, or on the patio. Also picnic baskets for guests, provided upon request.

The Old St. Angela Inn. *$100-$150.* 321 Central Ave., Pacific Grove; (831) 372-3246. Historic country home, built in 1910. 8 delightful rooms, decorated with pine antiques; some private baths. Solarium overlooking English garden. Afternoon wine and cheese; champagne breakfast. No children; no smoking.

Seven Gables Inn. *$155-$295.* 555 Ocean View Blvd., Pacific Grove; (831) 373-4341. 100-year-old Victorian mansion, located at the edge of Monterey Bay. 14 rooms with private baths; high tea; ocean views. No smoking.

Hotels and Motels

Best Western Monterey Inn. *$109-$139.* 825 Abrego St.; (831) 373-5345/(800) 528-1234. 79 rooms with phones and TV, some with fireplaces. Pool, hot tub.

Cannery Row Inn. *$99-$149.* 200 Foam St.; (831) 649-8550. 32 rooms, some fireplaces; phones, TV, spa.

Casa Munras Garden Hotel. *$115-$350.* 700 Munras Ave.; (831) 375-2411. 150 rooms; phones, TV, some fireplaces. Also restaurant and heated pool.

Cypress Tree Inn. *$89-$195.* 2227 Fremont St.; (831) 372-7586. 55 rooms, some with fireplaces; phones, TV. Hot tub and sauna.

Doubletree Hotel. *$150-$239.* 2 Portola Plaza; (831) 649-4511. One of Monterey's largest luxury hotels, with 374 well-appointed rooms. Tennis courts, pool, spa; gourmet restaurant.

Holiday Inn Resort of Monterey. *$125-$175.* 1000 Aguajito Rd.; (831) 373-6141. 203-room resort hotel. Facilities for guests include a swimming pool, spa, tennis courts, restaurant and cocktail lounge.

Hotel Pacific. *$199-$275.* 300 Pacific St.; (831) 373-5700. Luxury hotel with 104 rooms, most with fireplaces; also spa.

Hyatt Regency. *$155-$250.* 1 Old Golf Course Rd.; (831) 372-1234. 579-room resort hotel, with tennis courts, golf course, pool, hot tub and sauna; also gourmet restaurant and cocktail lounge. Many of the rooms have fireplaces.

Monterey Bay Inn. *$219-$350.* 242 Cannery Row; (831) 373-6242/(800) 424-6242. 47 rooms with private balconies; spectacular bay views. Also health club on premises, and hot tub, sauna, and special wash-down facilities for scuba divers. Complimentary continental breakfast.

Monterey Beach Hotel. *$109-$199.* 2600 Sand Dunes Dr.; (831) 394-3321. 196-room beachfront hotel, with pool, hot tub, and restaurant.

The Monterey Plaza. *$185-$295.* 400 Cannery Row; (831) 646-1700. 290 guest rooms, with ocean and bay views. The hotel also has a restaurant and cocktail lounge.

Monterey Marriott Hotel. *$199-$269.* Cnr. Del Monte Ave. and Calle Principal; (831) 649-4234. 5-star hotel, with 344 rooms; pool, restaurant and cocktail lounge.

The Lodge at Pebble Beach. *$350-$1500.* 17-Mile Drive, Pebble Beach; (831) 624-3811/(800) 654-9300. Luxury resort, located at the world-famous

Pebble Beach Golf Course. 161 well-appointed rooms, with phones, TV, wet bar and refrigerators; some fireplaces, and views. The Lodge also features 4 superb restaurants, a beach, heated pool and sauna, 13 tennis courts, and jogging and horseback riding facilities.

Sand Dollar Inn. *$80-$165.* 755 Abrego St.; (831) 372-7551/(800) 982-1986. 63 rooms, some with fireplaces; TV, phones; pool.

Victorian Inn. *$159-$299.* 487 Foam St.; (831) 373-8000/800 232-4141. 68 rooms, some fireplaces; TV, phones, hot tub.

Way Station Inn. *$89-$149.* 1200 Olmsted Rd.; (831) 372-2945. 46 rooms, with TV and phones. Fireplaces in some rooms; also restaurant on premises.

SEASONAL EVENTS

January. *Ben Hogan Pebble Beach Pro-Am Golf Tournament.* Held at the Spyglass Hill and Poppy Hills golf courses. Scheduled for the first week of the month. For more information, call (831) 649-8500. Also, the *Monterey Bay Symphony* offers a series of concerts, with performances in Monterey, Carmel and Salinas, throughout January, February, March, April and May. For information and schedule, call (831) 372-6276.

February. *AT&T Pebble Beach National Pro-Am Golf Tournament.* Held at the Pebble Beach, Cypress Point and Spyglass Hill golf courses, usually during the first week of the month. Popular event, attracting more than 100,000 fans and participants. Features famous professional players, among them Arnold Palmer, Jack Nicklaus and Lee Trevino. More information on (831) 541-9091.

March. *Dixieland Monterey.* Several nationally- and internationally-known jazz bands perform at various locations throughout Monterey. For locations and information on performers, call (831) 443-5260. *Monterey Wine Festival.* At the Monterey Conference Center. 3-day festival, with more than 200 California wineries participating. Wine-tasting, wine seminars. Phone (831) 656-9463.

April. *Wildflower Show.* Held at the Pacific Grove Museum of Natural History during the 3rd weekend of the month. The show features one of the finest exhibits of wildflowers in California. (831) 648-3116/373-3304.*Monterey Adobe Tour.* 4th weekend. Tours of Monterey's historic adobes; annual event. Reservations on (831) 372-2608.

May. *The Great Monterey Squid Festival.* Monterey County Fairgrounds; (831) 649-6544. Food, music, live entertainment, booths; squid prepared dozens of different ways.

June. *Monterey Bay Blues Festival.* At the Monterey Fairgrounds, Monterey. Well known national and regional blues musicians perform; also soul food. For information and reservations, call (831) 394-2652. *California State Amateur Golf Championship.* 3rd week of the month. Hosted by Pebble Beach, Spyglass Hill, Cypress Point, Del Monte and Carmel Valley Golf & Country Club courses. The tournament is now in its 78th year. For more information, call (831) 625-4653.

July. *Monterey National Horse Show.* At Monterey Fairgrounds during the 3rd week of the month. Well-established event, featuring show jumping, dressage and other equestrian events. For a schedule and more information, call (831) 372-1000.

August. *Monterey County Fair.* Monterey County Fairgrounds; 2nd week. Carnival, live entertainment, agricultural exhibits, wine show. More information on (831) 372-5863. *Annual Pebble Beach Concours d'Elegance.* Held at The Lodge at Pebble Beach during the 3rd weekend of the month. Antique car show, with more than 100 American and European classic cars on display. (831) 624-3811. *Annual Monterey Historic Automobile Races.* At Laguna Seca Raceway; 3rd weekend. Vintage car races, featuring over 150 restored automobiles of different vintages. Call the raceway for more information; (831) 648-5111.

September. *Monterey Jazz Festival.* Monterey Fairgrounds; 3rd weekend. Popular 3-day Jazz Festival, featuring such greats as Count Basie, Joe Williams, Art Blakey and Clark Terry. Also concerts by California High School All-Star Jazz Band. Advance reservations suggested; (831) 373-3366.

October. *Butterfly Parade.* In nearby Pacific Grove, also during the 2nd weekend of the month. Colorful parade through downtown Pacific Grove, celebrating the annual Monarch butterfly migration; creative costumes. (831) 646-6520.

December. *Festival of Trees.* Held at the Monterey Peninsula Museum of Art. A display of Christmas trees, each decorated with unique handmade ornaments. (831) 372-5477. Held during the first weekend of the month. *Christmas in the Adobes.* Public tours of many of Monterey's historic adobes, including some tours at night. Adobes are decorated for the holidays. (831) 649-7111.

PLACES OF INTEREST

Monterey Bay Aquarium. Located at the west end of Cannery Row. This is one of the largest aquariums in the country, and the chief attraction of Monterey, visited by an estimated 2.5 million tourists each year. The aquarium features a variety of superb marine exhibits, including a 90-foot-long recreation of a cross-section of Monterey Bay; a giant *kelp forest*, claimed to be the tallest aquarium exhibit in the United States, rising two full stories and containing 350,000 gallons of seawater; the spectacular Outer Bay Galleries, which features a million gallon indoor ocean, viewed through the world's largest window; and the *Marine Mammal Gallery*, which has life-sized displays of whales and other marine mammals. There are also several tidal and petting pools for children, and a large *Shorebird Aviary*, and a delightful two-level sea otter exhibit where visitors can watch playful sea otters dive, swim, and sun themselves. The aquarium also has vast decks with panoramic views of Monterey Bay; and gift and book shops on premises. Admission: $14.75 adults, $11.75 seniors and students, $6.00 children 3-12. Open daily 10-6 (9.30-6 during summer months and major holiday periods); closed Christmas day. For reservations and information, call (831) 648-4888.

Cannery Row. Historic, mile-long street, immortalized by John Steinbeck in his book of the same name, *Cannery Row.* The "row," which stretches from the Coast Guard Station in the east to the Monterey Bay Aquarium in the west, running along the bay, is lined with colorful old fish canneries. During the early 1900s, there were some 19 canneries situated along here, processing in excess of 235,000 tons of sardines annually. Most of the canneries closed in 1951, and several were destroyed by fire in the following years. The surviving canneries are now being restored and converted into fashionable little arcades, featuring fine shops and boutiques, restaurants and art galleries. For more information on Cannery Row, call (831) 373-1902.

Spirit of Monterey Wax Museum. 700 Cannery Row; (831) 375-3770. Housed in the old Monterey Canning Company building, the museum features life-sized wax exhibits of famous Cannery Row characters, among them the eccentric marine biologist "Doc" Rickett, and Sam Mally, Hazel, Mac and Lee Chong. Also wax models of other historical characters and scenes, including the building of the Monterey Mission. Open daily 9 a.m.-10 p.m. Admission fees: $4.95 adults, $3.95 students and seniors, $2.95 children.

Maritime Museum of Monterey and Stanton Center. 5 Custom House Plaza; (831) 375-2553. Nautical museum, housing an extensive collection of maritime artifacts, including hundreds of photographs, prints and paintings of ships, old steering wheels, compasses, bells, lanterns, navigation instruments, ship name boards, naval history books, old shipping records -- including a number of volumes of the old Lloyd's register -- and, most impressive of all, the old Fresnel Light from the Point Sur Lighthouse, dating from 1880. Also on display are scale models of Sebastian Vizcaino's ship, *San Diego*, Commodore Sloat's flagship, *Savannah*, and a restored captain's cabin. *Stanton Center*, which is part of the same complex, houses exhibits depicting the history of the sardine and whaling industries in Monterey, shipwrecks, and the history and culture of the Ohlone Indians. The museum and center are open daily, 10-5. Admission fee: $5.00 adults, $3.00 youth (13-18 years), $2.00 children (2-12 years), $4.00 seniors and disabled persons.

Monterey Peninsula Museum of Art at Civic Center. 559 Pacific St.; (831) 372-5477. Features seven galleries, housing permanent exhibits of international folk art, Asian art, California art, and photography. Also regularly changing exhibits, as well as special exhibits of early-day Monterey area artists. Open Wed.-Sat. 11-5, Sun. 1-4.

Monterey Peninsula Museum of Art at La Mirada. 720 Via Mirada; (831) 372-3689. Housed in a newer wing of the old, restored La Mirada adobe. The museum comprises four contemporary galleries, featuring both permanent and changing exhibitions. The premises also have spectacular rose and rhododendron gardens, and a picturesque stone wall. Open Thurs.-Sat. 11-5, Sun. 1-4.

Monterey Bay Sports Museum. 883 Lighthouse Ave., (831) 655-2363. Exhibits are of sports memorabilia, including a Babe Ruth display, as well as displays of heavyweight boxing champions. Also features an exhibit centered on the history of football, from the turn of the century to the present day. Open daily 10-6. Admission fee: $3.00 adults, $2.00 children.

San Carlos Beach. Located at the eastern end of Cannery Row. This is a recently-developed beach park, designed to provide easy access to scuba divers. There is also a grassy area here, with picnic tables.

Monterey State Historic Park (Monterey Path of History). The state park comprises mainly Old Monterey—a section extending from the waterfront south into downtown—where you can explore Monterey's rich history on a self-guided 3-mile tour of some 45 meticulously restored historic buildings, including many of the remaining adobes of Old Monterey. The tour can be joined at virtually any point along the route, and the State Parks Department also offers guided tours of many of these old relics, available for a fee of around $2.00 each. For more information on the buildings, tour times and admission fees, call the State Parks office at (831) 649-7118.

Highlights of the tour include the *Custom House,* dating from 1797 and claimed to be the oldest government building on the West Coast; the *Pacific House,* equally historic, and with a superb courtyard garden and museum; the *Stevenson House,* where, in 1879, noted author Robert Louis Stevenson stayed; *Colton Hall* (1847), which was the site of the first California Constitutional Convention in 1849; and the *Cooper-Molera Adobe,* an excellent example of the Monterey-colonial style of architecture. Other outstanding examples of Monterey-style adobes include *Casa Soberanes; Casa Guiterrez* (1841); *Casa Serrano,* where the Monterey History & Art Association has its offices; *Casa del Oro* (c.1850), which was once a gold depository; the *Fremont Adobe* (1840s) and the *Larkin House* (1835). Also worth visiting are the *First California Theatre,* built in the early 1840s, and where theater groups still perform; and the *Royal*

Presidio Chapel, said to be the oldest building in Monterey, dating from 1794.

Fisherman's Wharf. Colorful old wharf, with three or four seafood restaurants, specialty and gift shops, and fish markets. Stroll the weathered piers, and feed sea lions and pelicans. Also, sportfishing charters and whale-watching cruises are available from here. Nearby, at the *Municipal Wharf* you can watch fishing boats unload their catch of the day. The Municipal pier is also a good place for pier fishing.

Dennis the Menace Playground. Situated at the El Estero Lake Park, just off Pearl Street. Beautifully landscaped park, designed by Hank Ketcham, creator of "Dennis the Menace"; features imaginative mazes, slides and tunnels, and a stationary steam locomotive. Variety of play equipment, boat rentals, and picnic areas.

17-Mile Drive. Billed as "the slowest way between Carmel and Monterey," the 17-Mile Drive journeys through splendid groves of Monterey Pine and Gowen Cypress, and alongside ocean habitats of otters, seals and sealions. Points of interest include the famous *Lone Cypress,* one of the Monterey Peninsula's most photographed landmarks, and the storm-felled, splendid white *Ghost Tree.* Among others are the *Bird and Seal rocks,* where you can see countless shore birds perched on the rocks, and leopard and harbor seals in waters below. Also of interest are the lovely *Spanish Bay, Fanshell Beach,* and *Point Joe,* where ancient ships lie wrecked among rocks just offshore. There are also several picnic spots along the drive, and a half-dozen or so superb, championship golf courses, including the famed *Pebble Beach* and *Cypress Point* courses. *Pebble Beach* also has a lodge, and excellent shops and restaurants. There are four points of entry to the 17-Mile Drive, and the gate fee is $7.00 per car (which includes a map of the drive, pinpointing places of interest).

Pacific Grove. Small, picturesque seaside resort town, adjoining to the west of Monterey. Notable for its brightly colored Victorian homes, most of which can be viewed on Lighthouse and Central avenues, and famous, too, as "Butterfly Town, USA," where millions of Monarch butterflies migrate for the winter. The butterflies, of course, can be seen in the *Butterfly Park* just to the northwest of town. The town also has an excellent *Natural History Museum,* located on Central Avenue, which features displays of over 400 birds of Monterey County and a superb relief map illustrating the great chasm of Monterey Bay; museum hours are 10-5 Tues.-Sun., and information is available on (831) 372-4212. Among other points of interest here is the *Point Pinos Reserve* on the coast, which has an operating lighthouse—built in 1855 and believed to be the oldest continuously operating lighthouse on the West Coast—which can be visited on weekends, 1-4; for information, call (831) 372-4212.

Also see **Golf Courses**.

RECREATION

Boating and Fishing. Boating and fishing are popular leisure activities in the Monterey Bay area, with several operators offering a variety of sportfishing trips, boat charters and whale watching cruises. Prices usually range from around $19.00 to $45.00 for fishing trips, depending on the season and day of the week. For fishing trips, charters and excursions, contact any of the following: *Randy's Fishing Trips,* 66 Fisherman's Wharf, (831) 372-7440; *Sam's Fishing Fleet,* 84 Fisherman's Wharf, (831) 372-0577; *Monterey Sport Fishing,* 96 Fisherman's Wharf, (831) 372-2203; *Chris' Fishing Trips,* (831) 375-5951; *Olympus Sailing Charters,* 48 Fisherman's Wharf #1, (831) 647-1957; *Tom's Sportfishing,* Moss Landing, (831) 633-2564. Also, *Chardonnay Sailing Charters,* (831) 373-8664, offers sailing day excursions and sunset cruises aboard their 70 foot yacht.

Kayaking. *Adventures By The Sea,* 299 Cannery Row; (831) 372-1807. Offers kayaking trips along Monterey coast. *Monterey Bay Kayaks,* 693 Del Monte Ave.; (831) 373-5357. Kayak rentals, and 2-hour as well as half-day guided tours Of Elkhorn Slough.

Scuba Diving. *Aquarius Dive Shop;* two locations, at 2040 Del Monte Ave. and at 32 Cannery Row; (831) 375-1933/375-6605. Offers full line of equipment rentals, and air; also lessons. *Bamboo Reef,* 614 Lighthouse Ave. (831) 372-1685; diving lessons and equipment rentals.

Bicycling. *Adventures By The Sea,* (831) 372-1807; custom bicycling tours for groups, with catered meals. *Bay Bikes,* 640 Wave St., (831) 646-9090. Bike rentals; 10-speed bikes, mountain bikes and tandems; also guided tours. *Carmel Bicycle,* 7150 Carmel Valley Rd., (831) 625-2211. 12-speed bikes available. *Freewheeling Cycles,* 188 Webster St., Monterey, (831) 373-3855. Bike rentals; 10-speed bikes and mountain bikes.

Mopeds. *Monterey Moped Adventures,* 1250 Del Monte Ave.; (831) 373-2696. Single and double seater mopeds, tour maps, practice area; also picnic lunches available. Rates range from $10.00 an hour to $40.00 for a full day.

Hang Gliding. *Western Hang Gliders,* Reservation Rd. (off Hwy. 1), Marina; (831) 384-2622. Half-day flights, lessons, sales, repairs. Call for rates for flight instruction.

Horseback Riding. *Pebble Beach Equestrian Center,* Portola Rd., Pebble Beach; (831) 624-2756. Escorted trail rides; 30 miles of trails. Appointments only. *Monterey Bay Equestrian Center,* 19805 Pesante Rd., Salinas; (831) 663-5712. Horse rentals, and ocean rides; 250 acres of trails. Open daily, by appointment.

Tennis. Tennis facilities are available at the following locations in the area. *Monterey Tennis Center,* 401 Pearl St., Monterey, (831) 646-3881; lighted courts, lessons, pro shop. *Pacific Grove Municipal Courts,* 515 Juniper Ave., Pacific Grove, (831) 648-3130/648-3129; 5 courts. *Hyatt Regency Monterey Racquet Club,* 1 Old Golf Course Rd., Monterey, (831) 372-1234; 6 courts, open to the public; private lessons. Call for reservations. *The Inn at Spanish Bay Tennis Pavilion,* 17-Mile Drive, Pebble Beach, (831) 647-7500/(800) 654-9300; 8 courts; reservations required.

Tours. *A-One Chartered Limousine, Inc.,* (831) 889-2707. Group sightseeing tours of Cannery Row, 17-Mile Drive, Carmel, Big Sur and Hearst Castle. *California Heritage Tours,* 10 Custom House Plaza; (831) 373-6454. Half-day tours, daily at 1.30 p.m.; tour includes Old Monterey, Fisherman's Wharf, Cannery Row, Pacific Grove, 17-Mile Drive, Carmel Mission, and Carmel. *Otter-Mobile,* (831) 625-9782. Half-day tours of Pt. Lobos and Big Sur, the Hearst Castle, 17-Mile Drive, and the Monterey County wine country. Also, *Seacoast Safaris,* (831) 372-1288, and *Steinbeck Country Tours,* (831) 625-5107, offer tours of the Monterey Peninsula.

GOLF COURSES

Carmel Valley Ranch Golf Club. Carmel Valley Rd. (approximately 7 miles inland from Carmel); (831) 625-1010. Peter Dye-designed course, one of the newest in the area, completed in 1981. 18 holes. Private club, for members only.

Cypress Point Golf Course. 17-Mile Drive, Pebble Beach; (831) 624-3811/624-6611. One of the finest courses on the Monterey Peninsula, open to members only. A highlight of the course is its 16th hole, which can only be reached by driving 233 yards across open ocean. 18-hole course; 6,333 yards, par 72.

Del Monte Golf Course. Located adjacent to the Hyatt Regency Hotel in Monterey, at 1300 Sylvan Rd.; (831) 373-2700. Oldest course west of the Mississippi, designed by Charles Maud, and opened in 1897. 18 holes, 6,154 yards, par 72. Green fees: $75.00 ($93.00 with cart), twilight rate after 5 p.m., $15.00 ($33.00 with cart).

Laguna Seca Golf Club. Situated on York Road, off Hwy. 68; (831) 373-3701. Robert Trent designed 18-hole golf course; 6,162 yards, par 72. Green fees: $55.00, $30.00 twilight special (after 2 p.m.); golf carts: $28.00. Open to the general public.

Monterey Peninsula Country Club. Pebble Beach; (831) 373-1556. Private club, formerly the site of the Bing Crosby National Pro-Am Tournament. Features two 18-hole courses; *Dunes* and *Shore*. The *Dunes Course* is 6,246 yards, par 72; the *Shore Course* is 6,334 yards, par 70. Must be played with a member. Call the club for more information.

Pacific Grove City Golf Course. 77 Asilomar Ave., Pacific Grove; (831) 648-3177. 18-hole public course; 5,500 yards, par 70. Spectacular, all-round views, with 9 greens bordering on the ocean. Green fees: $25.00 Mon.-Thurs., $30.00 Fri.-Sun. and holidays; twilight rate (after 4 p.m.) $14.00. Carts optional. Restaurant, and driving range.

Pebble Beach Golf Links. Located adjacent to the Lodge at Pebble Beach, on the picturesque 17-Mile Drive; (800) 654-9300/(831) 624-3811/624-6611. One of the most popular courses in the area, and the site of the annual AT&T National Pro-Am Golf Tournament; originally built in 1919. 18 holes, 6,806 yards, par 72. Green fees: $245 for Lodge guests, $295.00 for non-guests, $320.00 with cart. Reservations may be made up to 18 months ahead.

Peter Hay Par 3 Golf Course. Located at The Lodge at Pebble Beach; (831) 624-3811. 9-hole course; green fees: $8.00 all day.

Quail Lodge Golf Club. 8000 Valley Greens Dr., Carmel Valley, 3 miles east of Hwy. 1; (831) 624-2770. Robert Graves-designed course, located at the 5-star Quail Lodge. 18 holes, 6,175 yards, par 71. Open to Quail Lodge guests and members of other private clubs. Green fees: $145.00, $115.00 to guests of Quail Lodge; twilight $75.00.

Rancho Canada Golf Club. On Carmel Valley Rd., 1 mile off Hwy. 1, Carmel Valley; (831) 624-0111. Situated beside the Carmel River, Rancho Canada offers two 18-hole championship courses, as well as a driving range. The *West Course* is 6,613 yards, par 72; the *East Course* is 6,434 yards, par 71. Green fees: West Course $70.00, $40.00 after 2 p.m.; East Course $55.00, $30.00 after 2 p.m.; cart rental $30.00.

The Links at Spanish Bay. Located at The Inn at Spanish Bay, at the northern end of Pebble Beach, along 17-Mile Drive; (831) 647-7500/(800) 654-9300. Newly-developed 18-hole course, modeled after the Irish and Scottish seaside courses; 6,357 yards, par 72. Green fees: $150.00 for Inn guests, $1655.00 for non-guests, $190.00 with cart.

Spyglass Hill Golf Course. Stevenson Dr. and Spyglass Hill Rd., Pebble Beach; (831) 624-6611/(800) 654-9300. Famous 18-hole championship course; a favorite of golf celebrities. 6,810 yards, par 72. Green fees: $175.00 for Lodge guest, $200.00 for non-guests, $225.00 with cart.

USNPS Golf Course. Located on Garden Rd., adjacent to Monterey County Fairgrounds; (831) 646-2167. 18-hole course; 5,480 yards, par 70. Open to active or retired members of the military, and guests of military personnel. Green fees: $20.00 weekdays, $25.00 weekends. Carts optional; rental $20.00.

RESTAURANTS

(Restaurant prices—based on full course dinner, excluding drinks, tax and tips—are categorized as follows: *Deluxe*, over $30; *Expensive*, $20-$30; *Moderate*, $10-$20; *Inexpensive*, under $10.)

Cafe Beach. *Expensive-Deluxe.* At the Monterey Beach Hotel, 2600 Sand Dunes Dr.; (831) 899-4544. Featuring aged beef, fresh pasta, and fresh seafood. Elegant setting; live entertainment. Open for breakfast, lunch and dinner daily.

California Grill. *Moderate-Expensive.* At the Doubletree Hotel, 2 Portola Plaza; (831) 649-4511. California cuisine, pasta, seafood, sandwiches; also soup and salad bar. Open for lunch 11-2 daily, dinner from 5.30 p.m.

Chef Lee's Mandarin House. *Moderate.* 2031 Fremont St.; (831) 375-9551. Mandarin cuisine. Open for lunch and dinner daily.

Clock Garden Restaurant. *Moderate-Expensive.* 565 Abrego St.; (831) 375-6100. Continental cuisine and fresh seafood; specialties include honey-glazed spareribs and shrimp fettucini. Patio for outdoor dining; full bar. Open for lunch and dinner daily; brunch on Sundays.

Club XIX. *Deluxe.* At The Lodge at Pebble Beach; (831) 624-3811. Gourmet luncheons, sandwiches and salads, served in outdoor patio in a Parisian cafe setting. Dinners feature French classic cuisine, served in elegant, intimate setting. Open daily; lunch 11.30 a.m.-4.30 p.m., dinner 6.30 p.m.-10 p.m.

Consuelo's. *Inexpensive-Moderate.* 361 Lighthouse Ave.; (831) 372-8111. Mexican restaurant, housed in two-story Victorian mansion built in 1886. Offers seafood and charbroiled specialties. Patio for outdoor dining. Open for lunch and dinner daily; brunch on Sundays.

The Cypress Room. *Expensive-Deluxe.* At The Lodge at Pebble Beach, 17-Mile Drive; (831) 624-3811. Contemporary California cuisine, prepared with the freshest ingredients. Restaurant overlooks Carmel Bay and the 18th green at the Pebble Beach golf course. Award-winning wine list, featuring primarily California wines. Open for breakfast, lunch and dinner daily; brunch on Sundays.

Domenico's. *Expensive-Deluxe.* No. 50 Fisherman's Wharf; (831) 372-3655. Lovely setting, overlooking the yacht harbor. Features fresh seafood entrees, grilled meat dishes, hand-rolled pasta, and oyster bar; also homemade ice cream. Excellent wine list. Lunch and dinner daily.

Ferrante's Restaurant & Bar. *Expensive.* At the Monterey Sheraton, 350 Calle Principal; (831) 649-4234. Creative Italian cooking; informal setting. Specialties include Focaccia bread, pasta dishes and fresh seafood. Spectacular bay views. Lunch and dinner daily; Sunday buffet brunch.

Fresh Cream Restaurant. *Expensive.* Heritage Harbor, Scott and Pacific Sts.; (831) 375-9798. Small, elegant French restaurant, offering traditional as well as nouvelle cuisine. House specialty is Rack of Lamb Dijon. Dinners from 6 p.m., Tues.-Sun.

Mike's Seafood Restaurant. *Moderate.* On Fisherman's Wharf; (831) 372-6153. Italian and American cuisine, with emphasis on seafood, chicken and beef preparations. Marina views, and sunroof cocktail lounge. Open for breakfast, lunch and dinner.

Monterey Joe's Ristorante. *Moderate.* 2149 N. Fremont St.; (831) 655-3355. Italian bistro-style restaurant, serving pasta, fresh seafood, wood-baked pizzas and Italian salads. Open for lunch Mon.-Fri., dinner daily.

The Peninsula Restaurant. *Expensive-Deluxe.* At the Hyatt Regency, 1 Old Golf Course Rd.; (831) 372-1234. California cuisine, with mesquite grill specialties and seafood and veal preparations. Restaurant overlooks the Del Monte Golf Course. Open daily for breakfast, lunch and dinner; brunch on Sundays.

Rappa's Seafood Restaurant. *Moderate-Expensive.* On Fisherman's

Wharf; (831) 372-7562. Fresh seafood, including calamari dishes. Views of the bay and fishing harbor. Lunch and dinner daily.

Red Snapper. *Moderate-Expensive.* Fisherman's Wharf; (831) 375-3113. Fresh local seafood, including crab and calamari; also steaks, pasta and chicken. Panoramic views of the yacht harbor; Cocktail lounge. Open for lunch and dinner daily. Reservations recommended.

Sardine Factory. *Expensive-Deluxe.* 701 Wave St.; (831) 373-3775. Superb, award-winning restaurant, featuring Old Monterey decor. Continental cuisine, with emphasis on fresh seafood and veal. Dinners from 4 p.m., Mon.-Sat.; also open Sundays, 2-10 p.m.

Schooner's Bistro on the Bay. *Moderate-Expensive.* At the Monterey Plaza Hotel, 400 Cannery Row; (831) 372-2628. Menu features homemade pasta, fresh seafood, and several grilled entrees. Open for lunch and dinner; reservations recommended.

Spadaro's Ristorante. *Expensive-Deluxe.* 650 Cannery Row; (831) 372-8881. Well-known Monterey restaurant, specializing in fine Italian cuisine. Entrees range from homemade pasta and Veal Parmigiana to succulent, charbroiled steaks and fresh seafood and shellfish. California wines; spectacular bay views. Open for lunch and dinner daily.

The Tap Room. *Moderate.* At The Lodge At Pebble Beach; (831) 624-3811. Casual English-style pub, serving light luncheons and dinners. Traditional American fare, as well as English meals. Full bar; large selection of beers. Open daily, 11.30 a.m.-10 p.m.

Triples. *Expensive.* 220 Olivier St.; (831) 372-4744. California cuisine. Located in historic home close to Fisherman's Wharf. Garden Patio for outdoor dining. Extensive wine list. Open for lunch Mon.-Fri., dinner Mon.-Sat. Reservations recommended.

Whaling Station Inn Restaurant. *Expensive.* 763 Wave St.; (831) 373-3778. Continental cuisine, with emphasis on fresh local seafood, mesquite-grilled over an open-hearth broiler, and succulent, savory steaks. Extensive wine list. Turn-of-the-century decor. Open for dinner 5-10.30.

Wharfside Restaurant. *Moderate-Expensive.* No. 60 Fisherman's Wharf; (831) 375-3956. Authentic Italian cuisine and fresh seafood, served in a delightful wharfside setting. Specialties include hand-rolled ravioli and pasta, and New England clam chowder; also delicious New York-style cheesecake and other homemade desserts. Open daily, 11 a.m.-10 p.m.

PALM SPRINGS

A Desert Resort

Palm Springs is America's most famous desert resort, situated in the Mojave Desert in Southern California, directly beneath the towering, 10,831-foot Mount San Jacinto. It is also, as its name suggests, a city of palms—with more than 4,000 of them!— and of celebrities, claiming among its residents such personalities as entertainer Bob Hope and former president Gerald Ford. The town, besides, has in it scores of luxury resort hotels, several fine restaurants and fashionable shops and boutiques, and a wealth of recreational facilities, for swimming, hiking bicycling, skiing (cross-country), horseback riding, tennis, and more. Palm Springs, in fact, boasts more than 30,000 swimming pools within its city limits, over 600 tennis courts, and no fewer than 90 golf courses located within a 25-mile radius of it.

Palm Springs is located roughly 100 miles east of Los Angeles, reached more or less directly on Interstate 10 and a short detour southeastward on Highway 111.

DISCOVERING PALM SPRINGS

Palm Springs lies in the heart of Southern California's rugged Coachella Valley, at the center of a growing community of desert resorts. Just to its east, for instance, is the satellite community of Cathedral City, and to the north, a little way, Desert Hot Springs. To the southeast, strung along Highway 111, are Rancho Mirage, with its myriad of restaurants; Palm Desert, which has in it the famed El Paseo Drive, a celebrated shopping district of sorts; and Indian Wells and La Quinta. To the southeast, too, at the intersection of Highway 111 and Interstate 10, is Indio, the "Date Capital of the World," with the town of Coachella just to the south of there. And farther to the northeast of Palm Springs, of course, some 55 miles distant, on Highway 62, lies Twentynine Palms, at the entrance to the idyllic Joshua Tree National Monument.

Palm Springs also, we might add, is a place abundant in natural and scenic beauty. It is surrounded, almost completely, by rugged, yet beautiful, mountains—the San Bernardino and Little San Bernardino mountains to the north and northeast, respectively, the Santa Rosa Mountains to the south, and the San Jacinto Mountain Range, with its towering Mount San Jacinto (elevation, 10,831 ft.), just to the west, providing in it perhaps one of the most dramatic meetings of mountains and desert in the world. There are, in addition, several picturesque old canyons all around Palm Springs—among them, the Chino Canyon in the west, above which you can journey on Palm Springs' aerial tramway; the lush Tahquitz Canyon, which provided the setting for "Shangri-La," in the movie, *Lost Horizon*, to the southwest; and Indian Canyons—the ancestral home of the Agua Caliente Indians (who, by the way, still own some 30,000 acres of land in the Palm Springs area, making them one of the wealthiest tribes in the nation)—just to the south, which has in it the palm-studded Palm Canyon and the equally lovely Murray and Andreas canyons, the latter with some interesting rock formations. Farther south, of course, is the Salton Sea, lying 234 feet below sea level, which once was a desert waste land, but which is now a recreation lake of sorts, with good boating, swimming, fishing, hiking, picnicking and camping possibilities, and a wildlife refuge at its southern end, with over 350 species of rare and unusual birds.

Palm Springs has several tourist attractions, especially for first-time visitors to the area, although a good place to begin your tour, we might suggest, is the Palm Springs Aerial Tramway, located just outside town, to the northwest, and reached by way of Tramway Road, which goes west off Highway 111. The tramway is really quite spectacular, built in the early 1960s, over a period of some 2 years, and claimed to be the longest single-span tramway in the world. Two 80-passenger tram cars journey from the desert floor, over the Chino Canyon, some 2½ miles—13,400 feet—more or less vertically to the mountain station, at an elevation of around 8,500 feet, from where you can enjoy good, all-round views of Palm Springs and the surrounding desert below, and, on clear days, also of Mount San Gorgonio to the north and the Salton Sea to the southeast. There is a restaurant and lounge

PALM SPRINGS

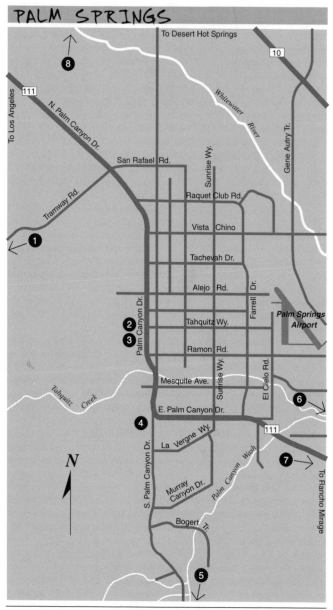

1. Palm Springs
   Aerial Tramway
2. Palm Springs
   Desert Museum
3. McCallum House
4. Moorten Botanical
   Gardens
5. Indian Canyons
6. Oasis Water Park
7. Living Desert
   Nature Preserve
8. Joshua Tree
   National Monument

located at the mountain station, also with superb mountain and desert views; besides which, the station offers access to the Mount San Jacinto State Park, which has excellent hiking, picnicking and camping possibilities, and cross-country skiing in the winter months. The tram operates daily between 10 a.m. and 8 p.m., with cable cars departing every half-hour.

In Palm Springs itself, the chief attraction, quite possibly, is Palm Canyon Drive, the town's main street, some 5 miles long, which runs through the heart of Palm Springs, north-south. It is lined with more than 1,800 palm trees, and dotted, quite consistently, with shops, boutiques, galleries and restaurants. Here you can visit such outstanding art galleries as the Palm Springs Fine Art Galleries, as well as explore the Desert Fashion Plaza, located more or less at a center point on Palm Canyon Drive, and which has in it, among others, the well-known Saks Fifth Avenue, I. Magnin, and Gucci's.

On Palm Canyon Drive, too, you can search out the historic McCallum House, which dates from 1885 and was formerly the home of Judge McCallum, and which is now preserved as a museum by the Palm Springs Historical Society, with displays of local historic interest. Try to also see the Cornelia White House, located adjacent to the McCallum House, and now also a museum. The Cornelia White House, dating from 1894 and built entirely from railroad ties, has in it several exhibits depicting Palm Springs' history, including such items as the town's first telephone. Both the McCallum and Cornelia White houses are open to public viewing.

Also of interest in Palm Springs is the Desert Museum, located on Museum Drive, just off Palm Canyon Drive. The museum is housed in an 85,000-square-foot architect-designed facility, situated on a 20-acre site, and it has in it permanent and changing exhibits of modern art and paintings of the American West, as well as natural science exhibits depicting the surrounding desert habitat. There is also a 450-seat performing arts theater on the premises, the Annenberg Theatre, with its associations to Frank Sinatra and Liza Minnelli, among others, who have, over the years, given concerts at the theater. The Annenberg Theatre now schedules chamber music, ballet performances, theater and film presentations.

Well worth visiting, too, is Ruddy's General Store Museum on South Palm Canyon Drive, where you can see an authentic, re-created, early 1900s general store, with more than 6,000 items and products from that period on display on the store shelves and counters; and Cabot's Old Indian Pueblo Museum, located on East Desert View Avenue in Desert Hot Springs, just to the north, and which is itself housed in a most interesting, four-story Indian Hopi-style building, with 150 windows of varying shapes, sizes and designs.

For nature buffs, of course, there are two places of supreme interest in the Palm Springs area. The first, the Living Desert Nature Reserve, a 1,200-acre wild animal park and botanical garden, is situated off Portola Avenue in Palm Desert, just to the southeast of Palm Springs; it features such wildlife as coyotes, bighorn sheep, Arabian oryx, eagles and other birds of prey, and indigenous reptiles, as well as over 1,500 varieties of desert flowers and plants, from eight different desert habitats. The second place of interest, the Moorten Botanical Gardens, located on South Palm Canyon Drive in Palm Springs, displays, in a 4-acre garden, some 3,000 varieties of desert plants from all over the world, including flowers, succulents and giant cacti. The gardens also feature birds and other wildlife in their natural habitats, and exhibits of Indian artifacts and wood, rock and crystal forms. Both the Moorten Botanical Gardens and the Living Desert are open to self-guided tours.

Yet another place of interest, much to be recommended to visitors to the area, is the Joshua Tree National Monument, some 55 miles northeast of Palm Springs, reached on Interstate 10 and Highway 62. The Joshua Tree National Monument is in fact a vast, 1240-square-mile desert sanctuary, where California's two great deserts—the high Mojave Desert and the low Colorado Desert—meet, offering in it some of the most unique desert scenery, with age-old palms and lavish displays of wildflowers in season. There is a Visitor Center at the park, and good campgrounds and picnic areas, as well as hiking and climbing possibilities. The park is open year-round.

HOW TO GET THERE

Palm Springs lies approximately 100 miles east of Los Angeles, reached more or less directly on *Interstate 10* and a short detour southeastward on *Highway 111*.

There is also a commercial airport in the Palm Springs area. The Palm Springs Regional Airport (airport phone, 619-323-8161) is located at 3400 East Tahquitz-McCallum Way, Palm Springs; it is serviced by *Alaska Airlines* (800) 426-0333, *America West* (800) 235-9292, *American Airlines* (800) 433-7300, *Canadian Airlines* (800) 426-7000, *Northwest Airlines* (800) 225-2525, *Sky West* (800) 453-9417, *TWA* (800) 221-2200, *United Airlines* (800) 241-6522, and *US Air* (800) 428-4322.

TOURIST INFORMATION

Palm Springs Desert Resorts Convention and Visitors Bureau. The Atrium, 69-930 Highway 111, Suite 201, Rancho Mirage, CA 92270; (760) 770-9000. Tourist information brochures, including accommodations guide with a map of the desert communities, and a guide to seasonal events and places of interest. There is also a toll-free reservation service available for accommodations in the Palm Springs area, at (800) 41-RELAX. Additionally, visitor information is available on the Visitors Bureau website, at *http://www.desertresorts.com*.

Chambers of Commerce. Palm Springs and the other surrounding desert resorts also maintain individual chambers of commerce, with useful visitor information available from these as well. The following are the area chambers of commerce: *Palm Springs Chamber of Commerce,* 190 West Amado Road, Palm Springs, CA 92262, (760) 325-1577; *Cathedral City Chamber of Commerce,* 68-703 Perez Road, Cathedral City, CA 92234, (760) 328-1213; *Desert Hot Springs Chamber of Commerce,* 13-560 Palm Drive, Desert Hot Springs, CA 92240, (760) 329-6403; *Rancho Mirage Chamber of Commerce,* 42-464 Ranch Mirage Lane, Rancho Mirage, CA 92270, (760) 568-9351; *Palm Desert Chamber of Commerce,* 72-990 Highway 111, Palm Desert, CA 92260, (760) 346-6111; *La Quinta Chamber of Commerce,* 51-351 Avenida Bermudas, La Quinta, CA 92253, (760) 564-3199; *Indio Chamber of Commerce,* 82-503 Highway 111, Indio, CA 92201, (760) 347-0676.

ACCOMMODATIONS

Best Western Inn at Palm Springs. *$49-$78 (summer); $88-$138 (winter).* 1633 S. Palm Canyon Dr.; (760) 325-9177/(800) 222-4678. 72 units, with phones and TV; some kitchen units. Swimming pool, therapeutic pool. Coffee shop on premises.

Courtyard by Marriott. *$39-$109 (summer); $64-$169 (winter).* 1300 Tahquiz Way; (800) 321-2211/ (760) 322-6100. 149 rooms with TV and phones. Swimming pool, spa, fitness center. Cocktail lounge and coffee shop on premises. Handicapped facilities.

Doubletree Resort Palm Springs. *$60-$125 (summer); $200-$250 (winter).* 67-967 Vista Chino Dr. (cnr. Landau Blvd.), Cathedral City; (800) 637-0577/(760) 322-7000. 289-unit full-service hotel, with concierge, restaurants, swimming pools, tennis courts, spa and health club, and meeting rooms; also 18-hole golf course on premises. Airport shuttle; handicapped facilities.

Embassy Suites, Palm Desert. *$69-$139 (summer); $169-$259 (winter).* 74-700 Hwy. 111, Palm Desert; (800) EMBASSY/(760) 340-6600. 198 units with TV and phones. Swimming pool, spa, fitness center and tennis courts. Cocktail lounge and restaurant. Handicapped facilities.

Estrella Inn. *$59-$195 (summer); $140-$300 (winter).* 415 S. Belardo St.; (800) 237-3687/(760) 320-4117. 70 units; TV, phones. Some kitchen units available. Pool, tennis court. Airport shuttle service.

Hampton Inn. *$45-$80 (summer); $60-$100 (winter).* 2000 N. Palm Canyon Dr.; (800) 732-7755/(760) 320-0555. 95 units, with phones and TV. Spa, pool. Handicapped facilities.

Holiday Inn. *$55-$80 (summer); $99-$145 (winter).* 155 South Belardo St.; (800) 622-9451/(760) 325-1301. 120 units; TV and phones; some kitchen units. Swimming and therapeutic pools; restaurants, cocktail lounge. Handicapped facilities. Airport shuttle service.

Howard Johnson Inn. *$42-$65 (summer); $50-$72 (winter).* 701 E. Palm Canyon Dr.; (800) 854-4345/(760) 320-2700. 205-room hotel. Phones, TV. Pool, spa, tennis courts. Coffee shop and cocktail lounge. Handicapped facilities.

Hyatt Regency Suites Palm Springs. *$79-$145 (summer); $165-$250 (winter).* 285 N. Palm Canyon Dr.; (800) 223-1234/(760) 322-9000. 194-room luxury hotel, with pool, sauna, spa, health club, restaurants and cocktail lounge, and meetings rooms on premises. Airport shuttle; handicapped facilities.

Ingleside Inn. *$71-$289 (summer); $95-$385 (winter).* 200 W. Ramon St.; (800) 772-6655/(760) 325-0046. 30 units; phones, TV. Pools and sauna; gourmet restaurant, and cocktail lounge. Handicapped facilities.

Marriott's Desert Springs Resort & Spa. *$110-$1000 (summer); $180-$1850 (winter).* 74855 Country Club Dr., Palm Desert; (800) 331-3112/(760) 341-2211. Five-star resort hotel; 884 rooms and suites. Facilities include swimming pools, sauna, spa, health club, tennis courts, restaurants and nightclubs, meeting rooms, and 36-hole golf course. Handicapped facilities.

Motel 6. *$33-$41 (summer); $34-$42 (winter).* 660 S. Palm Canyon Dr.; (760) 327-4200. 148 units, with phones and TV. Pool. Handicapped facilities.

Motel 6. *$33-$36 (summer); $33-$37 (winter).* 595 E. Palm Canyon Dr.; (760) 325-6129. 125-room motel. TV, phones; pool.

Oasis Villa Hotel. *$129+ (summer); $179+ (winter).* 4190 E. Palm Canyon Dr.; (800) 247-4664/(760) 328-1499. 64 units, with phones and TV; some kitchen units. Pool, sauna, tennis courts. Handicapped facilities.

Ocotillo Lodge. *$59-$99 (summer); $69-$139 (winter).* 1111 E. Palm Canyon Dr.; (760) 327-1141/(800) 777-1700. 124 units; TV and phones. Pool, spa and fitness center. Some kitchen units available. Handicapped facilities.

Palm Springs Hilton. *$70-$120 (summer); $155-$245 (winter).* 400 E. Tahquitz Way; (800) 522-6900/(760) 320-6868. 260-room full-service hotel, with concierge, restaurants and cocktail lounge, meeting rooms, swimming pool, spa and health club, and tennis courts. Airport pick-up service; handicapped facilities.

Palm Springs Marquis Hotel & Villas. *$89-$300 (summer); $169-$700 (winter).* 150 S. Indian Ave.; (800) 262-0186/(760) 322-2121. Full-service hotel, with 264 rooms and suites. Restaurants, meeting rooms, concierge; also swimming pools, spa and health club, and tennis courts. Airport pick-up service; handicapped facilities.

The Palms at Palm Springs. *$126-$209 (summer); $160-$265 (winter).* 572 N. Indian Ave.; (800) 753-7256/(760) 325-1111. 37 units with phones and TV. Pool, spa and fitness center; restaurant on premises.

Quality Inn-Palm Springs. *$39-$89 (summer); $79-$129 (winter).* 1269 E. Palm Canyon Dr.; (800) 472-4339/(760) 323-2775. 144 units; phones, TV. Pool, coffee shop, restaurant and cocktail lounge. Handicapped facilities.

The Racquet Club of Palm Springs. *$69-$99 (summer); $109-$395 (winter).* 2743 N. Indian Ave.; (800) 367-0946/(760) 325-1281. 72-unit hotel, with phones, TV, pools, sauna, health club, tennis courts, restaurant and cocktail lounge, and meeting rooms. Airport pick-up service; handicapped facilities.

Riviera Resort & Racquet Club. *$69-$99 (summer); $129-$169 (winter).* 1600 N. Indian Ave.; (760) 327-8311. 477 units; phones, TV, pools, tennis courts, coffee shop, restaurant and cocktail lounge. Handicapped facilities.

Ritz-Carlton Rancho Mirage. *$109-$299 (summer); $275-$2000 (winter).* 68-900 Frank Sinatra Dr., Rancho Mirage; (800) 241-3333/(760) 321-8282. Full-service luxury hotel with 239 rooms and suites. Pool, sauna, spa, health club, tennis courts, restaurants and meeting rooms. Airport shuttle; handicapped facilities.

Shilo Inn. *$68-$94 (summer); $100-$138 (winter).* 1875 N. Palm Canyon Dr.; (800) 222-2244/(760) 320-7676. 124 units; TV, phones, pool, sauna. Kitchen units available. Handicapped facilities.

Spa Hotel & Casino & Mineral Springs. *$59-$99 (summer); $139-$209 (winter).* 100 N. Indian Ave.; (760) 325-1461. 230 units; phones, TV, swimming and natural mineral water therapeutic pools; sauna and tennis courts. Indian gaming casino, restaurant and cocktail lounge. Handicapped facilities.

Super 8 Lodge. *$52-$62 (summer); $54-$74 (winter).* 1900 N. Palm Canyon Dr.; (800) 800-8000/(760) 322-3757. 61 units, with phones and TV. Pool.

Travelodge Palm Springs. *$35-$65 (summer); $55-$95 (winter).* 333 E. Palm Canyon Dr.; (800) 578-7878/(760) 327-1211. 158-unit motel. Phones, TV, pool. Handicapped facilities.

Vacation Inn Hotel. *$45-$60 (summer); $85-$108 (winter).* 74-715 Hwy. 111, Palm Desert; (800) 231-8675/(760) 340-4441. 130 units; phones, TV, pool, tennis courts. Some kitchen units available. Handicapped facilities.

Wyndham Palm Springs. *$69-$99 (summer); $159-$229 (winter).* 888 E. Tahquitz Way; (800) WYNDHAM/(760) 322-6000. 410-room hotel, with concierge, restaurants, meeting rooms, spa and health club, pool and tennis courts. Airport shuttle; handicapped facilities.

SEASONAL EVENTS

January. *Palm Springs International Film Festival.* 12-day festival, usually held during the middle of the month. Features over 120 new, highly-acclaimed American, Canadian and other international films. For a schedule and more information, call (800) 336-3546. *Bob Hope Chrysler Classic.* Third weekend. Popular annual golf tournament, held at various different locations in the Palm Springs area; attracts more than 100,000 spectators. More information on (760) 346-8184. *Southwest Arts Festival.* Riverside County Fairgrounds, Indio; (760) 347-0676. Work of 125 artists from southwestern United States is featured in a juried event. Food and entertainment.

February. *National Date Festival.* At Riverside County Fairgrounds, Indio. 10-day annual festival, originally begun in 1921. Celebrates the date harvest of Indio, the "Date Capital of the World." Events include livestock shows, camel and ostrich races, live entertainment, and a carnival. For more information, call (760) 863-8247. *Palm Springs Invitational Senior Olympics.* Scheduled for the second week of the month. More than 2,000 senior athletes compete in a variety of events, including track and field, swimming, golf, cycling, tennis, bowling and softball. (800) 323-5689.

March. *Nabisco Dinah Shore LPGA Championship.* Fourth weekend of the month. Held at the Mission Hills Country Club in Rancho Mirage. Features some of the world's best women golfers, as well as celebrities. (760) 324-4546. *Crossroads Renaissance Festival.* Downtown Palm Springs. Arts and crafts, costumes and live entertainment. (909) 943-5949. *La Quinta Village Faire.* At the Community Park in La Quinta (southeast of Palm Springs); third week. Features art and crafts, live entertainment, and food concessions. (760) 564-1244.

April. *Indian Heritage Festival.* Held at the Agua Caliente Cultural Museum, at the entrance to Palm Springs Indian Canyons during the third weekend of the month. This annual event features Indian dancing and storytelling, art exhibits, traditional games, music and food. (760) 778-1079. *Empire Balloon and Polo Festival.* Held at the Empire Polo Club in Indio. Features several polo games, and hot air ballooning. (760) 775-1715.

July. *Palm Springs International Short Film and Video Festival.* This mini version of the January Film Festival is the largest competitive showcase of international short films in North America. (760) 322-2930

October. *Tram Road Challenge.* Popular annual 6 kilometer race from the desert floor uphill to the Tramway station. (760) 325-1449.

November. *Palm Desert Golf Cart Parade.* Held during the first weekend of the month. Colorful parade down El Paseo in Palm Desert, featuring golf-cart floats, marching bands, clowns, drill teams, celebrities, and more. The parade is followed by a picnic and awards ceremony. (760) 346-6111.

December. *Annual Christmas Tree Lighting.* First weekend of month. Features a Christmas Tree lighting ceremony at the top of the Palm Springs Aerial

Tramway; also musical performance, celebrity appearances. For more information, call (760) 325-1449. *Lexus Celebrity Challenge.* Annual golf tournament featuring celebrities paired with Senior Tour pros. (760) 564-8700.

PLACES OF INTEREST

Palm Springs Aerial Tramway. 1 Tramway Rd. (west off Hwy. 111), Palm Springs. This is Palm Springs' foremost attraction, claimed to be the largest, single-span double-reversible aerial tramway in the world. It travels some 2½ miles—13,200 feet—in 14 minutes, over the Chino Canyon to the mountain station on Mt. San Jacinto, at an elevation 8,516 feet, offering spectacular views of the desert below. The mountain station has a restaurant and lounge, and offers access to the *Mt. San Jacinto State Park,* which has good camping, picnicking and hiking possibilities—with more than 54 miles of trails—and cross-country skiing in winter. Cable cars depart every half-hour, 10 a.m.-8 p.m. Mon.-Fri., 8 a.m.-8 p.m. Sat.-Sun. Tram fee: $17.65 adults, $11.65 children. Tramway phone, (760) 325-1449.

Indian Canyons. South Palm Canyon Dr., Palm Springs. Located on ancient Indian homelands, the canyons offer excellent picnicking, hiking and horseback riding possibilities. View palm-studded *Palm Canyon* and picturesque *Andreas* and *Murray canyons,* with their palm groves and scenic vistas; also pictographs and Indian grinding rocks. Indian trading post on premises. The canyons are open to the public Sept.-June, daily 8.30 a.m.-4.30 p.m.; admission fee: $6.00 adults, $3.50 seniors, $1.00 children. For more information, contact the Agua Caliente Tribal Council, 960 E. Tahquitz Way, Suite 106, Palm Springs, CA 92262; (760) 325-5673.

Palm Canyon Drive. Main Street of Palm Springs, some 5 miles long, running north-south, lined with more than 1,800 palms and dotted with chic boutiques, specialty shops, art galleries, and restaurants. A place of special interest here is the Desert Fashion Plaza, which has in it such well-known stores as Saks Fifth Avenue, I. Magnin and Gucci's.

McCallum House. 221 S. Palm Canyon Dr., Palm Springs; (760) 323-8297. Adobe home, built in 1885, formerly residence of Judge McCallum. Now houses a museum, with displays of local historical interest. Also visit the Cornelia White House, adjacent to the McCallum House, which dates from 1894 and is built entirely from railroad ties; it has on display such historic items as Palm Springs' first telephone. Open Oct.-May, Wed.-Sun. 12-3.

Palm Springs Desert Museum. 101 Museum Dr., Palm Springs; (760) 837-0777. The museum is housed in an 85,000-square-foot red-rock building located on a 20-acre facility. Features permanent and changing exhibits of modern art and paintings of the American West; also natural science exhibits depicting surrounding desert habitat. There is also a 450-seat performing arts theater on the premises, the *Annenberg Theatre,* which schedules ballet, chamber music and films. Museum hours: 10-4 Tues.-Fri., 10-5 Sat.-Sun., Oct.-May. Admission fee: $5.00 adults, $2.50 children.

Oasis Water Resort. 1500 S. Gene Autry Trail, Palm Springs; (760) 327-0499. Popular water park, featuring 29,000-square-foot wave pool for bodysurfing, a 500-foot whitewater river, and giant water slides. Open on weekends, Mar.-Oct.

Moorten Botanical Gardens. 1701 South Palm Canyon Dr., Palm Springs; (760) 327-6555. 4-acre garden, with self-guided nature trails leading past some 2,000 varieties of desert plants from all over the world, including flowers, succulents and giant cacti. Also view birds and other desert wildlife in their natural habitats, as well as displays of Indian artifacts and wood, rock, crystal and other mineral exhibits. The gardens are open 9-5 daily; admission fee: $2.00 adults, 75¢ children.

Ruddy's General Store Museum. 221 South Palm Canyon Dr., Palm Springs; (760) 327-2156. Museum comprises an authentic, re-created, early 1900s general store, with more than 6,000 items and products from that period on display on the store shelves. Open 10-4 Thurs.-Sun., Oct.-June; and weekends, 12-6, July-Sept.

The Living Desert Nature Reserve. 47-900 Portola Ave., Palm Desert; (760) 346-5694. 1,200-acre wild animal park and botanical garden. Features coyotes, bighorn sheep, Arabian oryx, eagles and other birds of prey, and desert reptiles. There are also over 1,500 varieties of desert flowers and plants on display here, from eight different desert habitats, and exhibits of Indian culture and geology. Picnic areas, and 6 miles of hiking trails. Open Sept.-June, 9-5 daily; admission fee: $5.00 adults, $4.00 seniors, $2.00 children.

Joshua Tree National Monument. 74485 National Monument Dr., Twentynine Palms (reached by way of I-10 and Hwy. 62, approximately 55 miles north of Palm Springs); (760) 367-7511. Scenic 850-square-mile reserve, where California's two great deserts — the low Colorado Desert and the high Mojave Desert — come together, offering some of the most unique desert scenery, with age-old palms and lavish displays of wildflowers in season. Visitor Center on premises; also good campgrounds and picnic areas. Open year-round.

Palm Springs Air Museum. 745 Gene Autry Trail, Palm Springs; (760) 778-6262. Houses one of the world's largest collections of World War II era airplanes. Displays highlight the history of aviation during the Second World War. Gift shop on premises. Open daily 10-5; admission fees $7.50 adults, $6.00 seniors and military personnel, $3.50 children.

Hot Springs Park. Cnr. 8th Street and Palm Drive, Desert Hot Springs; (760) 329-6411. New interpretive park with hot and cold water features, a grove demonstrating water use in the desert, and a man-made fault line. Free admission.

Oasis Date Gardens. Hwy. 111, Thermal; (760) 399-5665/(800) 827-8017. 250-acre date garden established in 1912. Features a palm arboretum, packing house, store and cafe. Tours daily.

Shields Date Gardens. 80225 Hwy. 111, Indio; (760) 347-0996/(800) 414-2555. Date garden, established in 1924. Offers tours of the gardens, and a selection of date shakes and date ice cream in the cafe.

Children's Discovery Museum. 71701 Gerald Ford Drive, Rancho Mirage; (760) 321-0602. A new, hands-on children's science and nature museum. Open Tues.-Sat. 10-5, Sun. 12-5. Admission: $3.00 per person.

RECREATION

Tours. *Celebrity Tours of Palm Springs,* 333 N. Palm Canyon Dr., Palm Springs, (760) 770-2700. Tours of celebrity homes in the area; also sight-seeing tours. *Classi Cab.* (760) 322-3111 (888) 644-TAXI. Offers city, celebrity and hiking tours. Also day trips to wineries. *Desert Adventures,* 73955 Alessandro Dr., Palm Desert, (760) 324-JEEP. Daily tours of Indian Canyons, the Santa Rosa Mountains, and the San Andreas Fault; group and individual tours. *Palm Springs International Transportation and Tours.* (760) 320-0044.

Hot Air Ballooning. *Dream Flight Balloons,* 42955 Conn St., Palm Desert Country Club, (760) 321-5154; hot-air balloon flights over the desert.

Scenic Flights. Scenic flights in the area are available through *Sailplane*

Enterprises, (800) 586-7627. Exciting sailplane rides over the desert and Palm Springs area.

Bicycling. The Palm Springs area has five designated bicycle trails, offering bicycling enthusiasts a good variety of terrain and scenery. For rentals and trail maps, contact any of the following: *Adventure Bike Tours,* (760) 328-0282; *Bighorn Bicycles,* (760) 325-3367

Dune Buggies. *Dune Off Road Rentals,* Palm Springs, (760) 325-0376.Rentals of off-road vehicles for ages 6 and up. $30.00 per hour. Lessons and safety equipment provided.

Horseback Riding. *Smoke Tree Stables,* 2500 Toledo Ave., Palm Springs, (760) 327-1372. Offers horse rentals, and horseback tours through nearby Indian Canyons.

Polo. Polo games, including celebrity tournaments, and horse shows and other special equestrian events are held at two facilities in the Palm Springs area— *Eldorado Polo Club* (760) 347-0907/(800) 525-7634 and *Empire Polo Club* (760) 342-2762. Call the clubs for information and schedule of events.

Golf. See *Golf Courses* section.

Tennis. There are over 600 tennis courts in the Palm Springs area, although most are private, at private clubs or resorts. The following, however, are open to the public—*Emerald Court Resort Hotel,* 69375 Ramon Rd., Cathedral City, (760) 324-4521; *The Tennis Center,* 1300 E. Baristo Rd., Palm Springs, (760) 320-0020; and *Marriott's Desert Springs Resort,* 74855 Country Club Dr., Palm Desert, (760) 341-2211.

Swimming. Most hotels, motels and resorts in the Palm Springs area have swimming pools for guests' use. There is also a public swimming pool available in the area, at *Hacienda Riviera Spa,* 67375 Hacienda Ave., Desert Hot Springs, (760) 329-7010; open daily 9-5 (except Tues.); all-day pool use fee: $4.00.

GOLF COURSES

Canyon South Golf Course. 897 Murray Canyon Dr., Palm Springs; (760) 327-2019. 18 holes, 6,205 yards, par 71; pro shop, snack bar. Green fee: $60.00 (cart included).

Date Palm Country Club. 36-200 Date Palm Dr., Cathedral City; (760) 328-1315. 18 holes, 3,083 yards, par 58; pro shop, snack bar. Green fee: $40.00 (with or without cart).

Desert Crest Country Club. 69-400 S. Country Club Dr., Desert Hot Springs; (760) 329-8711. 9 holes, 999 yards, par 27. Green fee: $10.00.

Desert Dunes Golf Club. 19-300 Palm Dr., Palm Springs; (760) 325-GOLF. 18 holes, 6,205 yards, par 72; pro shop, snack bar. Green fee: $110.00 (including cart).

Desert Falls Country Club. 1111 Desert Falls Parkway, Palm Desert; (760) 341-4020. 18 holes, 6,174 yards, par 72; pro shop, restaurant and snack bar. Green fee: $170.00 (including cart).

Desert Springs Resort (Marriott). 74-855 Country Club Dr., Palm Desert; (760) 341-1756. Palms Course is 18 holes, 6,143 yards, par 72. Valley Course is 18 holes, 6,003 yards, par 72. Pro shop, snack bar and restaurant. Green fee: $150.00 (including cart).

Desert Willow Golf Club. 38-500 Portola, Palm Desert; (760) 346-7060. 18 holes, 6,173 yards, par 72. Pro shop, restaurant and snack bar. Green fee: $155.00 (including cart).

Indian Palms Country Club. 48-630 Monroe St., Indio; (760) 347-2326. 18 holes, 6,403 yards, par 72; pro shop, restaurant and snack bar. Green fee: $65.00 (including cart).

Indian Springs Country Club. 46-080 Jefferson St., La Quinta; (760) 775-3360. 18 holes, 6,169 yards, par 71; pro shop. Green fee: $50.00 (including cart).

Indian Wells Golf Resort. 44-500 Indian Wells Lane, Indian Wells; (760) 346-4653. East Course is 18 holes, 6,232 yards, par 72. West Course is 6,157 yards, par 72. Pro shop, restaurant and snack bar. Green fee: $120.00 (including cart).

Indio Municipal Golf Club. 83-040 Avenue 42, Indio; (760) 347-9156. 18 holes, 3,004 yards, par 54; pro shop, snack bar. Green fee: $10.00 without cart, $15.00 with cart.

Ivey Ranch Country Club. 74-580 Varner Rd., Thousand Palms; (760) 343-2013. 9 holes, 2,632 yards, par 35; pro shop. Green fee: $35.00 (including cart).

Mesquite Country Club. 2700 E. Mesquite Ave., Palm Springs; (760) 325-GOLF. 18 holes, 5,944 yards, par 72; pro shop, restaurant and snack bar. Green fee: $85.00 (including cart).

Mission Lakes Country Club. 8484 Club House Blvd., Desert Hot Springs; (760) 329-8061. 18 holes, 6,396 yards, par 71; pro shop, restaurant and snack bar. Green fee: $75.00 (including cart).

Oasis Country Club. 42-300 Casbah Way, Palm Desert; (760) 345-2715. 18 holes, 3,118 yards, par 60; pro shop, restaurant and snack bar. Green fee: $40.00 without cart, $50.00 including cart.

Palm Desert Resort Country Club. 77-333 Country Club Dr., Palm Desert; (760) 345-2791. 18 holes, 6,288 yards, par 72; pro shop, restaurant and snack bar. Green fee: $75.00 (including cart).

Palm Springs Country Club. 2500 Whitewater Club Dr., Palm Springs; (760) 323-2628. 18 holes 5,885 yards, par 72; pro shop, restaurant and snack bar. Green fee: $50.00 (including cart).

Sands RV Country Club. 16-400 Bubbling Wells Rd., Desert Hot Springs; (760) 251-1173. 9 holes, 2,127 yards, par 32; pro shop. Green fee: $15.00.

Suncrest Country Club. 73-450 Country Club Dr., Palm Desert; (760) 340-2467. 9 holes, 2,250 yards, par 33; pro shop, snack bar. Green fee: $35.00 including cart, $26.00 without cart.

Tahquitz Creek Golf Resort. 1885 Golf Club Dr., Palm Springs; (760) 328-1005. Legends Course is 18 holes, 6,422 yards, par 72. Resort Course is 18 holes, 5,825 yards, par 72. Pro shop, snack bar. Green fee: Legend Course $60.00 with cart, $50.00 without cart; Resort Course $90.00 (including mandatory cart).

Tommy Jacob's Bel Air Greens. 1001 S. El Cielo Rd., Palm Springs; (760) 322-6062. 9 holes, 1,570 yards, par 32; restaurant. Green fee: $19.00 for first round, $12.00 to replay.

RESTAURANTS

(Restaurant prices—based on full course dinner, excluding drinks, tax and tips—are categorized as follows: *Deluxe*, over $30; *Expensive* $25-$30; *Moderate*, $10-$20; *Inexpensive*, under $10.)

Alfredo's. *Moderate.* 285 S. Palm Canyon Dr.; (760) 325-4060. Specializing in Italian cuisine. Menu features pasta dishes, pizza, chicken, ribs, veal and seafood. Full bar; patio for outdoor dining. Open for lunch and dinner.

Banducci's Bit of Italy. *Expensive.* 1260 S. Palm Canyon Dr.; (760) 325-2537. Family-style restaurant; authentic Italian cuisine. Patio for outdoor dining. Piano Bar. Open for dinner daily.

Elmer's Pancake and Steak House. *Inexpensive-Moderate.* 1030 E. Palm Canyon Dr.; (760) 327-8419. Offers more than 20 varieties of pancakes and waffles. Also seafood, steaks and poultry dishes; children's menu available. Open breakfast, lunch and dinner daily.

Fiesta Mexican Restaurant. *Moderate.* 35360 Date Palm Dr., Cathedral City; (760) 328-1660. Authentic Mexican food, including fajitas, mariscos and menudo. Family-style meals; cocktails. Lunch and dinner daily, breakfast on weekends.

Flower Drum. *Moderate.* 424 S. Indian Ave.; (760) 323-3020. Specializing in Hunan, Cantonese, Szechuan, Peking and Shanghai cuisines, with emphasis on fresh vegetables and seafood, all prepared without MSG. Nightly entertainment. Open for dinner daily.

Karla's Restaurant. *Inexpensive-Moderate.* 143 S. Farrell Dr.; (760) 327-1369. Casual restaurant, serving hamburgers, eggrolls, homemade date nut bread and corn bread, Belgian waffles, bran muffins, and fresh fruit salad. Also daily specials. Open for breakfast, lunch and dinner daily.

Kiyosaku. *Moderate.* 1563 S. Palm Canyon Dr.; (760) 327-6601. Tempura, sukiyaki and teriyaki; sushi bar. Also sweet plum wine. Open for lunch and dinner, Tues.-Sat.

Las Casuelas Original. *Moderate.* 368 N. Palm Canyon Dr.; (760) 325-3213. Popular Mexican restaurant, established in 1958. House specialties include carne asada and crab enchiladas; also multi-flavored margaritas. Patio for outdoor dining; live entertainment. Open for lunch and dinner daily. Reservations advised.

LeVallauris. *Expensive-Deluxe.* 385 W. Tahquitz Canyon Way; (760) 325-5059. Exclusive French restaurant, featuring nouvelle French cuisine. Piano bar. Lunch and dinner daily. Jackets required. Reservations.

Nate's Deli & Restaurant. *Inexpensive-Moderate.* 100 S. Indian Ave.; (760) 325-3506. Wide selection of sandwiches, corned beef and rye bread, and chicken. Patio for outdoor dining. Open for breakfast, lunch and dinner daily.

Riccio's. *Expensive.* 2155 N. Palm Canyon Dr.; (760) 325-2369. Well-regarded area restaurant, serving old-fashioned Italian food. Menu features fresh seafood, including live Maine lobster, and homemade pasta and bread and Italian cheesecake. Open for lunch and dinner. Reservations recommended.

Sorrentino's. *Expensive.* 1032 N. Palm Canyon Dr.; (760) 325-2944. Fresh seafood, including Maine lobster; also steak and pasta dishes. Open for dinner daily.

Tai Ping. *Moderate-Expensive.* 45299 Lupine Lane, Palm Desert; (760) 340-1836. Specializing in Cantonese, Mandarin, Hunan and Szechuan cuisine. Wide selection of Polynesian drinks. Cocktail lounge. Dinners from 5 p.m., Tues.-Sun.

Tony Roma's A Place For Ribs. *Moderate.* 73-155 Hwy. 111, Palm Desert; (760) 568-9911. House specialties include baby back ribs and barbecued chicken; also onion-ring loaf. Casual atmosphere; entertainment. Open for lunch and dinner daily.

ST. HELENA

"Heart of the Wine Country"

St. Helena is an elegant, if somewhat small town, lying at the very heart of the Napa Valley, world-famous wine growing region. It is backed by the picturesque Mayacamus Mountains, just to the west, and surrounded by scores of well-known Napa wineries, most of them with tourist interest. The town itself also has something of value, including a wine library, a museum dedicated to a famous writer, some fine shops and restaurants, and several superb bed and breakfast accommodations. The chief tourist pursuit here is of course visiting wineries, with some bicycling and hiking possibilities nearby as well.

The town of St. Helena lies approximately 55 miles northeast of San Francisco, reached by way of Highway 101 north and Highways 116 and 12 eastward to the city of Napa, then Highway 29 directly north to St. Helena. Journeying from the north, the town is accessible, again, on Highway 29, lying just 10 miles or so to the south of Calistoga.

DISCOVERING ST. HELENA

St. Helena is an historic wine town, founded in the 1850s by pioneer vintners. It has an especially charming main street, lined with antique street lamps dating from 1915, and several old and lovely native-stone buildings—also from the late 1800s and early 1900s. But its great glory—and few would argue otherwise—is the Napa Valley Wine Library, itself housed in the St. Helena Public Library building on Library and Adam streets, east off the main street. It has in it some 3,000 volumes on wine and wine-related subjects, believed to be one of the largest such collections of wine literature on the West Coast. The library also schedules wine appreciation seminars and an annual tasting for its members during the summer months, and is a sponsor of such notable wine events as the Napa Valley Wine Auction and the Napa Valley Wine Symposium.

Near at hand, also of interest, is the Silverado Museum, devoted to the life and works of celebrated Scottish writer Robert Louis Stevenson, who honeymooned at nearby Mount St. Helena in the spring of 1880, gathering, too, notes for his Napa Valley classic, *The Silverado Squatters*. The museum has over 7,800 items of Stevenson memorabilia, said to be one of the world's largest such collections of Stevensoniana. Included are some first editions of the author's books, original manuscripts and letters, paintings, photographs and sculptures of the author, and several of his personal and work related items. The museum was originally founded in 1969.

Besides the immediate town, however, St. Helena has much else to offer the visitor. There are, in fact, no fewer than 40 premium Napa wineries within easy driving distance of town, including such well-known estates as Beringer, Charles Krug, Hanns Kornell, Niebaum-Coppola, Markham and Louis M. Martini. Most of the wineries offer public tours, wine tasting and retail sales; a few—largely the smaller winemakers—require an appointment but are nevertheless eager to receive visitors. (See *Wineries* later in this chapter for hours, facilities and other relevant information.)

In any case, just north of the St. Helena township, on the main highway (29) is Beringer Vineyard's majestic Rhine House, easily the most photographed building in the Napa Valley. Originally built in 1876 as the home of Frederich Beringer, co-founder of the winery, the elegantly restored European-style mansion now houses one or two tasting rooms, with superb period decor, and a well-stocked gift and wine shop. The winery also has daily scheduled tours of its premises, which include a visit to Beringer's 1,000 feet or so of ancient limestone caves and tunnels, dug into the hillside by hand in about 1861, and where fine wines are now aged.

A little farther on, at the end of an avenue of splendid shade trees that line the highway, is the grand old Christian Brothers' Greystone Cellar, one of Napa Valley's most prominent landmarks, and also one of the region's most famous wineries until 1993, when it finally closed as a winemaking establishment. The winery's castle-like greystone building itself dates from 1889, originally built by mining magnate

ST. HELENA

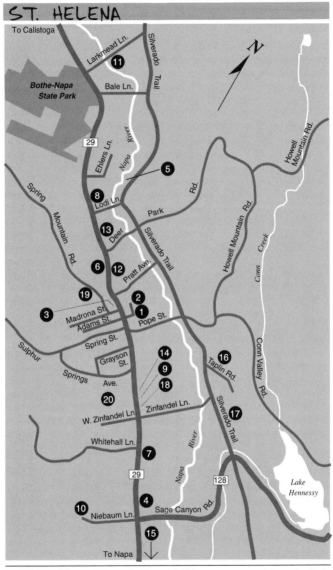

1. Silverado Museum
2. Napa Valley Wine Library
3. Beringer Rhine House
4. Beaulieu Vineyard
5. Casa Nuestra Winery
6. Culinary Institute of America
7. Franciscan Vineyards
8. Freemark Abbey
9. Heitz Cellars
10. Niebaum-Coppola Vineyards
11. Hanns Kornell Champagne Cellars
12. Charles Krug Winery
13. Markham Vineyards
14. Louis M. Martini Winery
15. Robert Mondavi Winery
16. Joseph Phelps Vineyards
17. Rutherford Hill Winery
18. V. Sattui Winery
19. Spring Mountain Vineyard
20. Sutter Home Winery

William Bowers Bourne, who, quite notably, also built the Filoli Mansion (featured in TV's *Dynasty*) at Woodside, California. It now houses the Culinary Institute of America.

Close by, and also worth visiting, is the historic Charles Krug Winery, claimed to be the oldest operating winery in the valley. It was originally founded in the 1850s by immigrant Charles Krug, who, we are told, was the first in the Napa Valley to make wine using a grape press, rather than by means of the traditional method of crushing grapes by stomping by foot. The winery has public tours, wine tasting and sales. There is also a gift shop on the premises.

North still, are the historic Markham Winery, Freemark Abbey—which has a tasting room in a small complex with two unusual gift shops—and the Kornell Champagne Cellars, which actually lies on a side street, Larkmead Lane, east off the highway. This last, of course, is the most interesting of them all, offering a superb winery tour on which visitors can view, first hand, the champagne-making process. The tour also includes a visit to the winery's ancient aging caves, where you can see the original Victorian cupola, dating from 1901.

Among other interesting wineries in the St. Helena area, north of town, are the Round Hill Cellars—a small, charming 19th-century winery—and the equally historic Spring Mountain Vineyards, famous as the setting for the TV drama, *Falcon Crest*. Tours of Spring Mountain Vineyards are available by appointment, and the winery, besides, offers a line of "Falcon Crest" wines for tasting. Here also you can view the picturesque Falcon Crest mansion featured on the TV series, although it is usually not open to the public for touring.

Just to the south of St. Helena on Highway 29 are other historic and well-known wineries, among them Louis M. Martini, Sutter Home, and Heitz Cellars, a delightful little family-owned-and-operated winery, notable increasingly for its Martha's Vineyard Cabernet Sauvignon. Sutter Home, too, has a distinction; it is the largest of Napa Valley's historic wineries built entirely from wood, besides which it is also one of the best known and largest producers of Zinfandel in California. Sutter Home dates from 1874, and Louis M. Martini from 1922.

Two other St. Helena wineries of special tourist interest, also south of town, are the native-stone V. Sattui Winery—which dates from 1885 and is enormously popular with wine country visitors, featuring a large picnic area, a fully-stocked delicatessen, and wine and gourmet shops—and Franciscan Vineyards, housed in a large redwood building, with an ancient German grape press on display, as well as a good collection of antique corkscrews. Franciscan also offers a public tour, which includes a brief course in the sensory evaluation of wines.

Worth visiting, too, are a handful of wineries on the east side of the valley floor, along the Silverado Trail; among them the small, French-style Duckhorn Vineyards, and the Casa Neustra Winery, situated on a 10-acre vineyard estate. Also on the Silverado Trail are the Napa Creek, Raymond and Joseph Phelps wineries, all of which offer wine tasting and sales, and the large, well-known Rutherford Hill Winery which has, in addition, scheduled public tours of its modern winemaking facility as well as its 30,000 square feet or so of recently-excavated ageing cellars.

If time permits, try to also visit Rutherford and Oakville just south of St. Helena, two small but important wine-growing centers, and also part of the Napa Valley. At Rutherford you can tour the Niebaum-Coppola (formerly Inglenook) and Beaulieu wineries, both historic, and with good visitor facilities. At Oakville, of course, the chief attraction is the Robert Mondavi Winery, housed in a dramatic, Italian-style stucco building, which also features a superb art gallery displaying works of Napa artists. Mondavi has a good winery tour, and during the summer months it also schedules open-air music concerts.

HOW TO GET THERE

St. Helena is situated in the heart of the famous Napa Valley, roughly 55 miles northeast of San Francisco. It can be reached by taking *Highway 101* directly north from San Francisco to Novato (26 miles), then *Highways 37* and *121* northeast to the city of Napa, another 25 miles. From Napa, follow *Highway 29* directly to St. Helena, 18 miles northwest.

An alternative route is by way of *Interstate 80* east from San Francisco to Vallejo (31 miles), then *Highway 29* directly north to Napa, another 14 miles. From Napa, again, you can continue on *Highway 29* to St. Helena.

TOURIST INFORMATION

St. Helena Chamber of Commerce. 1020 Main St., St. Helena; (707) 963-4456. Tourist brochures, including restaurant and bed & breakfast listings; winery maps, and information on local events.

Napa Chamber of Commerce. 1556 First St., Napa; (707) 226-7459. Tourist literature for the Napa Valley wine country, including lodgings, restaurants, wineries, seasonal events and recreational facilities. There is also a *Wine Country Bed & Breakfast Reservations* service in the Napa Valley area; for referrals and reservations, call (707) 963-9114, or write Wine Country Bed & Breakfast Reservations, P.O. Box 5059, Napa, CA 94581.

ACCOMMODATIONS

Bed & Breakfast Inns

Ambrose Bierce House. *$115-$195.* 1515 Main St.; (707) 963-3003. Luxury inn, formerly home of author Ambrose Bierce, built in 1872. 4 antique-furnished suites with brass beds and armoires; private baths, with claw foot tubs. Suites are named after notable 19th-century personages—Lily Langtree, Lillie Coit, Eadweard Muybridge, and Bierce. Country breakfast, comprising homemade pastries and fresh fruit. Bicycles available for guests' use.

Bartel's Ranch. *$185-$425.* 1200 Conn Valley Rd.; (707) 963-4001. Romantic country home on secluded 100-acre estate. 3 delightful guest rooms, with private baths. Jacuzzi, swimming pool and games room; complimentary wine and sherry, full breakfast, and in-room dinner service. Also, bicycles available for guests' use, and private vineyard and cave tours.

Bylund House. *$95-$175.* 2000 Howell Mountain Rd.; (707) 963-9073. Secluded country estate, with two well-appointed guest rooms with private baths and balconies. Complimentary wine and hors d'oeuvres; hearty country breakfast.

Chestelson House. *$120-$170.* 1417 Kearney St.; (707) 963-2238. Centrally located, turn-of-the-century Victorian home; wide veranda, superb mountain views; 3 rooms. Delicious gourmet breakfast; complimentary wine.

The Cinnamon Bear. *$115-$190.* 1407 Kearney St.; (707) 963-4653. 3 guest rooms in small, comfortable home, dating from the early 1900s; antique quilts and toys, polished brass, private, old-fashioned baths. Full breakfast, served on the porch or in the dining room. Downtown location.

Deer Run Inn. *$140-$195.* 3995 Spring Mountain Rd.; (707) 963-3794. Secluded mountain retreat, tucked away in the forest on Spring Mountain. 2 guest rooms with private baths, 1 with a fireplace. Pool on premises.

Erika's Hillside. *$95-$250.* 285 Fawn Park Rd.; (707) 944-8101. Century-old hillside chalet, situated on wooded 3-acre estate. 3 spacious rooms, with private entrances, hot tubs and fireplaces. Patio and garden room; continental breakfast, featuring German specialties.

Hotel St. Helena. *$155-$325.* 1309 Main St.; (707) 963-4388. Restored Victorian hotel in downtown St. Helena. 18 rooms, most with private baths. Sun deck; wine bar, continental breakfast. Close to shops and restaurants.

Ink House. *$99-$195.* 1575 St. Helena Hwy.; (707) 963-3890. 1884 Italianate Victorian home with 3 charming rooms, each decorated with period furnishings. Superb vineyard views. Continental breakfast served in the dining room. Antique pump organ in front parlor.

La Fleur. *$150.* 1475 Inglewood Ave.; (707) 963-0233. Beautifully restored 100-year-old Victorian inn with solarium and 3 guest rooms featuring French decor. Breakfast comprises homemade pies and pastries.

Judy's Bed & Breakfast. *$95-$105.* 2036 Madrona Ave.; (707) 963-3081. Charming country cottage set among vineyards in St. Helena. Large bedroom-cum-sitting room, with private bath, private entrance, fireplace, and TV; also pool on premises. Freshly baked pastries for breakfast; complimentary wine.

Oliver House. *$85-$305.* 2970 Silverado Trail; (707) 963-4089. Swiss chalet on private 4-acre estate in the hills above Napa Valley. 4 charming guest rooms, furnished with antiques and brass beds; large stone fireplace in parlor. Continental-style breakfast, comprising muffins, pastries and fresh fruit.

Prager Winery Bed & Breakfast. *$185.* 1281 Lewelling St.; (707) 963-3720. 2 spacious suites, situated above the barrel aging cellar of Prager Winery.

Fireplaces and private baths; veranda with mountain and vineyard views. Breakfast served in suite.

Shady Oaks Country Inn. *$159-$195.* 399 Zinfandel Lane; (707) 963-1190. Delightful country inn, housed in 1920s home, and set among scenic vineyards on 2-acre estate. 4 antique-decorated rooms with private baths; complimentary wine. Homemade breakfast, served on the veranda or by the fireplace.

Wine Country Inn. *$146-$268.* 1152 Lodi Lane; (707) 963-7077. 25 rooms, individually decorated with antiques and handmade quilts; some fireplaces and balconies; also pool, and spa. The inn is situated atop a knoll overlooking vineyards.

Hotels and Motels

El Bonita Motel. *$79-$135.* 195 Main St.; (707) 963-3216. 41 units, with phones and TV; some units with whirlpool spas. Pool.

Harvest Inn. *$199-$529.* 1 Main St.; (707) 963-9463. 32 individually-decorated rooms in Tudor-style inn. TV, phones, wet bars, fireplaces. Pool, spa. Vineyard views.

Meadowood Resort. *$345-$660.* 900 Meadowood Lane; (707) 963-3646/(800) 458-8080. Luxury resort complex, set on 250 acres. 70 rooms and suites, restaurant, golf course, tennis courts, croquet, pool.

SEASONAL EVENTS

June. *Robert Mondavi Summer Festival.* At the Robert Mondavi Winery in Oakville, just south of St. Helena. Series of six jazz concerts, held on Sunday evenings, in June and July. Also wine and cheese tasting, featuring Rouge et Noir cheeses; informal picnics. Advance reservations required; for schedule and tickets, call the winery at (707) 963-9611. *Napa Valley Wine Auction.* At the Meadowood Resort; last week of the month. Auction sponsored by Napa Valley Vintners Association to benefit local medical facilities. Candlelight banquet and dancing; barrel tastings, wine futures. For details, call (707) 942-9775.

October. *Hometown Harvest Festival.* Oak and Adams Sts., St. Helena. Lively celebration, with wine and food booths, arts and crafts show, 5-kilometer and 10-kilometer races, a carnival, and live music. For a complete schedule, call (707) 963-5706. *Old Mill Days.* At Bale Grist Mill State Historic Park, Hwy. 29, St. Helena. Living history recreation of life in the 1860s. Harvest activities, food, and live entertainment. Also offers opportunities to see the mill in operation. Call (707) 963-2236 for additional information.

PLACES OF INTEREST

Bale Grist Mill. 3 miles north of St. Helena on Hwy. 29; (707) 963-2236. Historic, water-powered mill, built in 1846 by pioneer settler Dr. Edward Turner Bale, to grind corn. The mill is now owned and maintained by the State Parks Department, and is presently being restored. Mill building houses a small museum, with displays of old photographs and local-interest artifacts. Some walking possibilities in park. Open daily 10-5, with live demonstrations on weekends; admission for museum: $1.00.

Silverado Museum. 1490 Library Lane; (707) 963-3757. Small museum, devoted to the collecting, preserving and exhibiting of artifacts pertaining to the life and works of Robert Louis Stevenson (author of *Kidnapped, Treasure Island* and *Doctor Jekyll and Mr. Hyde,* among others). Contains over 7,800 items of Stevenson memorabilia, believed to be the largest collection of Stevensoniana in the world. Exhibits include many first editions, letters, photographs, original manuscripts, personal and work-related items, and paintings and sculptures of the author. Free admission; open Tues.-Sun. 12-4.

Napa Valley Wine Library. Housed in the St. Helena Public Library Building, at 1492 Library Lane; (707) 963-5244. Contains approximately 3,000 volumes on wine and wine-related subjects—including books, magazines, journals and special publications—claimed to be one of the largest such collections of wine literature on the West Coast. The library also schedules wine appreciation seminars and wine tastings during summer.

Bothe-Napa Valley State Park. 3801 N. St, Helena Hwy., (707) 942-4575. Delightful 1,800-acre park, with forests of redwood, fir, oak and madrone, and wildflowers in spring. Park facilities include camping, picnicking, hiking and swimming. Day use fee: $5.00 per car, additional fee for use of pool; camping fee: $15.00-$16.00 per site. Park open daily; pool open summer only.

WINERIES

Beringer Vineyards. 2000 Main St.; (707) 963-7115. Historic winery, founded in 1876 by brothers Jacob and Frederich Beringer, and now one of Napa Valley's great attractions. The estate-owned Rhine House, a majestic 19th-century mansion which was once the home of Frederich, is now a visitor center and one of the most photographed structures in the wine country. Also view Beringer's 1,000 feet of ancient tunnels and caves, dug into the hillside by hand in the 1880s. Victorian tasting room, and wine and gift shop on premises. Scheduled tours daily. Winery open 10-5.

Beaulieu Vineyard. 1960 St. Helena Hwy.; (707) 963-2411. One of Napa Valley's best-known large wineries, housed in an imposing, ivy-covered brick and concrete building, dating from 1885. Beaulieu is notable mainly for its red table wines, and its open-tank-fermentation winemaking method. Guided tours daily, with audio visual presentation; also tasting and sales. Winery open 10-4.

Duckhorn Vineyards. 1000 Lodi Lane; (707) 963-7108. Visitors by appointment only, Mon.-Fri. 9-4.30. No tours or tasting; retail sales.

Franciscan Vineyards. 1178 Galleron Rd.; (707) 963-7111. Housed in large, redwood building on the highway, with an outdoor display of an antique German grape-press. Self-guided tours. Wine tasting and sales 10-5 daily.

Freemark Abbey Winery. 3022 St. Helena Hwy.; (707) 963-9694. Housed in 19th-century stone cellar. Features estate-bottled varietals and one or two proprietary wines. Tasting and sales 10-4.30 daily; tours at 2 p.m.

Heitz Wine Cellars. 500 Taplin Road; (707) 963-3542. Family owned and operated winery, founded in 1961 by Joseph and Alice Heitz. Famous primarily for its Martha's Vineyard Cabernet Sauvignon, Heitz also offers one or two other varietals, as well as some generic and dessert wines. Open 11-4.30; tours by appointment.

Kornell Champagne Cellars. 1091 Larkmead Lane; (707) 942-0859. Maker of *méthode champenoise* sparkling wines. Superb winery tour, highlighting the champagne-making process and including a visit to the winery's historic ageing cellars, originally built in 1906. Kornell bottles seven different types of champagne. Tasting and retail sales 10-4.30 daily.

Charles Krug Winery. 2800 St. Helena Hwy.; (707) 967-2201. Napa's oldest operating winery, founded in 1861 by immigrant Charles Krug. Offers a full line of varietal, generic and jug wines. Gift shop and tasting room on premises; guided tours. Open daily 10-5.

Markham Vineyards. 2812 St. Helena Hwy.; (707) 963-5292. Historic, 18th-century Napa Winery, restored and re-opened in 1978. Bottles primarily estate varietal wines. "Sensory evaluation" wine seminar on weekdays. Wine tasting and sales; tours by appointment. Winery open daily 10-5.

Louis M. Martini Winery. 254 St. Helena Hwy.; (707) 963-2736. Large, well-known producer of dry table wines, established in 1922. Scheduled winery tours; tasting and sales. Open daily 10-4.30.

Robert Mondavi Winery. 7801 St. Helena Hwy.; (707) 226-1335. Impressive, Italian-style stucco winery, founded in 1966 by Robert Mondavi of Napa Valley's respected Mondavi family. Winery tours daily; jazz concerts scheduled during summer. Reservations advised for tours and other events. Art gallery and wine and gift shop on premises. Winery open daily, 9-5 in summer, 10-4.30 in winter.

Niebaum-Coppola Estate. 1991 St. Helena Hwy.; (707) 963-9099. Grand old Napa winery (formerly Inglenook), established in the 1880s by Finnish sea-captain Gustave Niebaum, and housed in an ivy-covered, Gothic stone chateau set amid estate vineyards. View wine museum and library. Daily tours, and wine appreciation; also wine tasting and retail sales. Winery hours: 10-5.

Joseph Phelps Vineyards. 200 Taplin Rd.; (707) 963-2745. Winery housed in wood-frame building consisting of two separate pavilions, joined together by an enclosed bridge, built in 1973. Offers a full line of premium varietal wines. Tasting and sales 8-5 daily; tours by prior arrangement.

Raymond Vineyards and Cellar. 849 Zinfandel Lane; (707) 963-3141. 100% varietal wines. Tasting and sales 10-4 daily; tours by appointment.

Round Hill Cellars. 1680 Silverado Trail; (707) 963-9503. Modest-sized winery, offering a full line of varietal and generic wines. Open for wine sales daily, 10-4.30; tours by appointment.

Rutherford Hill Winery. 200 Rutherford Hill Rd.; (707) 963-7194. Large winemaking facility at the foot of the eastern hills of Napa Valley. Scheduled tours, highlighting the winery's state-of-the-art winemaking equipment and technology, and its 30,000 square feet of recently-excavated hillside caves. Winery and tasting room open 10-5 daily. Shaded picnic area on premises.

V. Sattui Winery. 1111 White Lane; (707) 963-7774. Tourist-alluring, historic Napa winery, originally established in 1885 by pioneer vintner Vittorio Sattui. Features fully-stocked deli, gift shop and picnic area. Wine sales limited to winery. Open daily 9-5; tours by appointment.

Spring Mountain Vineyards. 2805 Spring Mountain Rd.; (707) 967-4188. Historic winery, housed in splendid, 1880s Victorian mansion with stained-glass windows and hand-hewn tunnel for ageing wines. The winery is also famous as the setting for TV's *Falcon Crest*. Tasting room open daily 10-5; tours by appointment only.

Sutter Home Winery. 277 St. Helena Hwy.; (707) 963-3104. Oldest wooden winery in the Napa Valley, built in 1874. Notable as one of the largest producers of Zinfandel in the country. No formal tours; wine tasting and retail sales 10-4.30 daily.

RECREATION

Ballooning. *Adventures Aloft,* at Vintage 1870, Yountville; (707) 255-8688/(800) 944-4408. Offers champagne flights over the Napa Valley; $185.00 per person. *Napa Valley Balloons, Inc.,* Yountville; (707) 253-2224. One-hour flights; champagne reception, picnic lunch. $185.00 per person. *Above the West Ballooning,* P.O. Box 2290, 6744 Washington St., Yountville; (707) 944-8638. Balloon flights above the valley; champagne reception. $185.00. *Balloon Aviation of Napa Valley*, Vintage 1870, Yountville; (707) 944-4400/(800) 367-6272.

Bicycling. The St. Helena area offers good bicycling opportunities, with several back-country roads crisscrossing between vineyards. Bicycle rentals are available locally from *St. Helena Cyclery,* 1156 Main St.; (707) 963-7736.

Golf. *Meadowood Resort,* 900 Meadowood Lane; (707) 963-3646. 9-hole course, 4170 yards, par 62; green fees: $35.00. Pro shop, hand-cart rentals, dining room and snack bar.

Tennis. *Crane Park,* Grayson Ave. 6 lighted tennis courts, and 4 lighted bocce courts. *Robert Louis Stevenson School,* 1316 Hillview Place. 2 courts; no lights. *St. Helena High School,* 1401 Grayson Ave. 2 courts with lights.

Swimming. *Bothe-Napa Valley State Park,* 3601 St. Helena Hwy. North; (707) 942-4575. Admission $5.00 per car, additional fee for pool use. *St. Helena Community Pool*; (707) 963-7946.

RESTAURANTS

(Restaurant prices—based on full course dinner, excluding drinks, tax and tips—are categorized as follows: *Deluxe,* over $30; *Expensive,* $20-$30; *Moderate,* $10-$20; *Inexpensive,* under $10.)

Auberge du Soliel. *Deluxe.* 180 Rutherford Hill Rd., Rutherford; (707) 963-1211. Elegant French restaurant, located high above the valley floor, with spectacular vineyard views. Prix fixe meals; menu changes daily. Extensive wine list. Open for lunch and dinner Thurs.-Tues. Reservations required.

Brava Terrace. *Moderate-Expensive.* 3010 N. St. Helena Hwy.; (707) 963-9300. American-French bistro-style cuisine, featuring fresh local ingredients. Outdoor dining on garden terrace, or indoor, hearthside dining. Open for lunch and dinner daily.

Gail's Oldies and Goodies. *Inexpensive-Moderate.* 1347 Main St.; (707) 963-3332. Old-fashioned ice cream parlor and cafe, serving soups, salads and sandwiches. Open for breakfast and lunch daily; dinner on weekends.

Gillwoods Bakery Cafe. *Inexpensive-Moderate.* 1313 Main St.; (707) 963-1788. Homestyle cooking, with fresh, home-baked breads, pies, cakes, muffins, scones and pastries. Open for breakfast and lunch daily.

Meadowood Resort Restaurant. *Expensive.* Meadowood Resort, 900 Meadowood Lane; (707) 963-3646. Elegant Napa Valley restaurant, overlooking golf course. Menu features California country cuisine, with emphasis on duck, venison and seafood preparations. Prix fixe dinners, from 6 p.m. daily; also Sunday brunch.

Terra Restaurant. *Expensive-Deluxe.* 1345 Railroad Ave.; (707) 963-8931. Well-regarded St. Helena restaurant, housed in handsome 1884 building. Features Continental and California cuisine, with an Oriental flavor, with emphasis on seafood, poultry and pork. Open for dinner, Wed.-Mon. Reservations suggested.

The Spot. *Inexpensive.* 587 St. Helena Hwy.; (707) 963-2844. Fifty's-style hamburger joint, authentic down to the jukebox and black and white checkered floor. Hamburgers, sandwiches, salad bar and pizza. Hours: 11.30 a.m.-9 p.m.

Spring Street. *Moderate.* 1245 Spring St. (cnr. of Oak); (707) 963-5578. Housed in delightful, early 1900s bungalow, with vine-covered patio. Homestyle dinners, featuring steaks, pasta, fish and barbecued specialties; also homemade desserts, and light luncheons. Open daily, 11 a.m.-2.30 p.m. and 5 p.m.-8.30. p.m.; brunch on weekends.

Showley's at Miramonte. *Moderate-Expensive.* 1327 Railroad Ave.; (707) 963-3970/963-1200. Continental cuisine, featuring seafood, lamb, poultry, and New York Steak; menu changes daily. Open for lunch and dinner daily (except Mon.). Reservations suggested.

Tomatina. *Inexpensive-Moderate.* 1016 Main St.; (707) 967-9999. Casual, family-style Italian restaurant, serving pizza and pasta. Open for lunch and dinner daily.

Trilogy. *Moderate-Expensive.* 1234 Main St.; (707) 963-5507. Small, intimate restaurant, offering French and California cuisine, with emphasis on fresh fish, poultry and local produce. Extensive wine list. Open for lunch and dinner Thurs.-Tues. Reservations recommended.

SAN LUIS OBISPO

The Middle Kingdom

San Luis Obispo lies happily amid the gentle hills of the Santa Lucia Range, approximately midway between Los Angeles and San Francisco—some 200 miles or so from either city—claiming for itself the title, "The Middle Kingdom." It is a largely pastoral—and to some degree, historic—town in a modern-day setting, at the center of an agriculturally rich county. Its chief interest lies in its weekly farmers' markets and varied domestic architecture, besides which it also has a university of some interest, and several places of supreme tourist interest quite close at hand, including the fabled Hearst Castle, Cambria, Morro Bay, Pismo Beach and Avila Beach.

The best and most direct way to reach San Luis Obispo is on Highway 101, both from Los Angeles and San Francisco. Highway 1 is a handy, but slower, alternative, journeying along the coast for the most part, with a small detour inland to arrive at San Luis Obispo.

SAN LUIS OBISPO

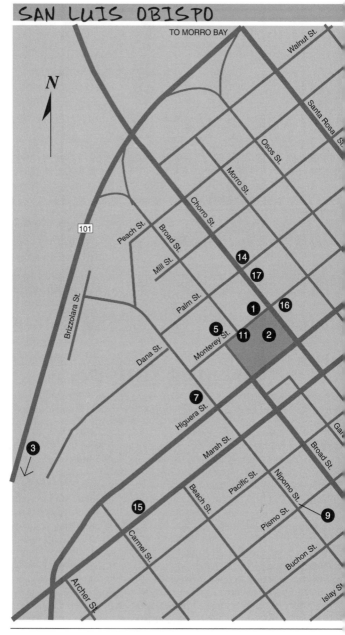

1. Mission San Luis
   Obispo de Tolosa
2. Mission Plaza
3. Madonna Inn
4. California Polytechnic
   State University
5. San Luis Obispo
   County Historical
   Museum
6. Fremont Theater
7. The Creamery
8. Presbyterian
   Church

SAN LUIS OBISPO

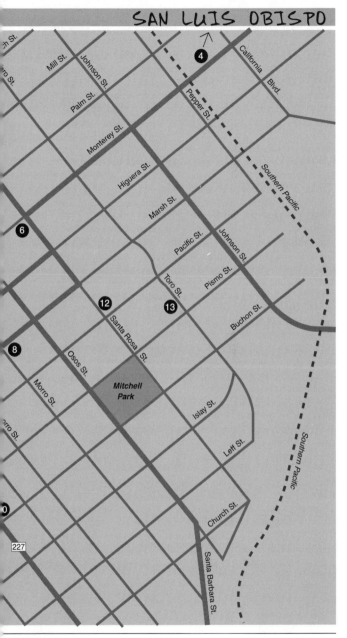

9. St. Stephen's
   Episcopal Church
10. Myron Angel Home
11. Judge Walter Murray
    Adobe
12. Kundert Medical
    Building
13. Dallidet Adobe
14. Ah Louis Store
15. Jack House
16. Sinsheimer
    Brothers' Store
17. Sauer Adobes

DISCOVERING SAN LUIS OBISPO

San Luis Obispo, first and foremost, is a market town, with lively, colorful farmers' markets, quite interesting to residents and visitors alike. There are two well-known markets here, on Higuera Street, between Osos and Broad streets, and at the Central Coast Mall, Hwy. 1 and Madonna Rd., held on Thursday evenings and Saturday mornings, respectively. The downtown market is especially to be recommended to first time visitors to the area. It is a festive event, featuring market stalls laden with farm produce—backed, quite in contrast, by modern shops and boutiques—as well as street barbecues and musicians at street corners playing banjos, guitars and bagpipes. The market remains open until 9 p.m.

Architecturally, too, the town has something of interest, but nothing greater than its ancient and lovely Mission San Luis Obispo de Tolosa, located in the heart of town, on Monterey and Chorro streets, and dating from 1772. The adobe mission is the work of native Chumash Indians, and, more importantly, it is the fifth of the twenty-one California missions founded by Franciscan monk, Father Junipero Serra. The mission is open to public tours, and its chapel, beautifully restored, still serves as the parish church. There are some well-kept gardens here, overflowing with geraniums and begonias, and several eucalyptus and other splendid shade trees. The delightful, brick-paved plaza at the front of the mission, recreated in 1971, is quite popular with walkers and picnickers, a good place to linger in, and frequently the scene of community and cultural events, including the well-liked Mozart Festival, held here in August every year, featuring classical music concerts and recitals.

The mission is also a good starting point for the prescribed 2-mile tour of the town's old adobes, Victorians and other historic and architecturally interesting buildings—with good maps for this available from the local Chamber of Commerce on Chorro Street, quite close by. Highlights of the tour include the ancient Judge Walter Murray Adobe (1846), the Dallidet Adobe (1853), the Sauer adobes (circa 1860), and the Victorian home of Myron Angel, founder of the California Polytechnic, dating from 1883. Also on the tour are the Chinese Ah Louis Store (1874); the Sinsheimer Brothers Store (1874), with its cast-iron facade; the wood-frame St. Stephen's Episcopal Church (1867), believed to be the oldest Episcopal church in California; and the splendid Presbyterian Church (1905), built entirely from granite rock taken from nearby Bishop's Peak, the second of the seven volcanic peaks lying between San Luis Obispo and Morro Bay farther to the northwest.

Among other architectural treasures here are the Art Deco-style Fremont Theater on Santa Rosa Street, dating from 1941, and the Kundert Medical Center at the corner of Santa Rosa and Pacific streets, notably the work of Frank Lloyd Wright. Also try to see the Old Creamery on Nipomo Street, originally built in 1906 and now converted from its original use to a pleasant little mall; and the San Luis Obispo County Historical Museum at the corner of Monterey and Chorro

Sonoma's City Hall, situated along the south of the Sonoma Plaza

Danish architecture in Solvang

Mt. San Jacinto provides the backdrop for a Palm Springs golf course

La Jolla Cove, one of La Jolla's foremost attractions

Beringer Vineyards' stately Rhine House, situated just outside St. Helena, is open to public tours

Santa Barbara's El Paseo Plaza, dating from 1826, preserves the flavor of Old Spain

South Lake Tahoe enjoys a lovely alpine setting at the southern
edge of Lake Tahoe

Mendocino sits on a bluff overlooking the Mendocino Bay

streets, directly across from the mission, housed in the old Carnegie Library Building, dating from 1905 and quite attractive in its stone and red-brick construction. The museum has displays of items of local historical interest, depicting all eras of the county history.

Just to the north of town, worth visiting too, is the California Polytechnic State University, one of the most popular colleges in the state system, with good programs for agriculture, engineering and computer sciences. It is nestled on some 5,500 hillside acres, with lovely, tree-shaded grounds and one or two Spanish adobes to be found among the more modern campus buildings as well. Another, the Cuesta College, much smaller than the polytechnic but still with something in it of interest to the campus visitor, lies west of town, just off Highway 1. The place to visit here is the old Hollister Adobe, dating from the 1800s and now containing a museum with displays of Chumash Indian artifacts. Visitor passes are available at both colleges.

San Luis Obispo has yet something to surprise the visitor. Just north of town, on Madonna Road which goes off Highway 101, is the famous Madonna Inn, featured on TV's *Evening Magazine*, and referred to by the *New York Times* as an architectural fantasyland. The inn has 104 guest rooms, individually decorated in unusual and sometimes garish themes—such as a Cave Room, Cinderella Room, Barrel Room and Mine Room. There is also a unique, richly furnished dining room here, and a handful of shops retailing equally unusual, one-of-a-kind gifts. Another place of interest at the inn is the men's urinal—which is an actual waterfall!

North, too, on Monterey Street is the ancient Motel Inn, claimed to be the oldest motel in the world—dating from 1925! It is, of course, open to the public for overnight lodging.

DETOURS

San Luis Obispo also makes for an excellent base from which to explore the Central Coast wine country. To its north, for instance, some 30 miles or so, is Paso Robles, a well-known viticultural area with at least twenty established wineries, among them York Mountain, Arciero Winery, Harmony Cellars, Creston vineyards, Meridian Vineyards, Twin Hills Ranch Winery and Martin Brothers. To the south, just 5 miles, is the Edna Valley, another recognized winegrowing region, which has in it seven reputable wineries—including Edna Valley, Cottonwood Canyon, Nichols Winery & Cellars, Laetitia Vineyards and Corbett Canyon, the largest. This last is especially worth visiting, for it has some of the best visitor facilities, including public tours, and tasting of its premium wines.

Also south of San Luis Obispo, 10 to 15 miles distant, are two small but attractive coastal resorts, Pismo Beach and Avila Beach, both with a measure of tourist interest. Pismo Beach is of course famous for clams, dunes and surf, and at Avila Beach there is a nuclear power plant (Diablo Canyon) which can be toured by appointment. Avila also has natural spring baths, beach sports, golfing possibilities, and fishing boat rentals. There are, besides, good motel accommodations at both Pismo and Avila beaches, and some worthwhile restaurants.

North of San Luis Obispo, too, there is something of tourist value. Morro Bay, 12 miles up the coast, is a picturesque little fishing village, named for the historic, 576-foot-high Morro Rock just offshore, claimed to be the second largest such monolith in the world. For tourists, Morro Bay has good fishing, a fine selection of seafood restaurants, a superb natural history museum, and its colorful and lively Embarcadero, where hundreds of artists display and sell their works, and where there is a most interesting jumble of waterfront shops, bursting with souvenirs, gifts, beachwear, seashells, and the like. Fishing charters are also available here, for sportfishing excursions out to sea, as well as trips to the small sand dunes lying just off the coast.

From Morro Bay it is another 27 miles or so northward on the scenic coastal route, Highway 1, to the tiny, seaside community of Cambria, a mecca for artists and vacationers, and notable, too, as the place where "the pines meet the sea." There are some good gift shops and beach areas at Cambria, and abundant opportunities for ocean viewing.

Farther along the coast, 6 miles, is San Simeon, the star attraction of the Central Coast, which not only has good beaches but also one of California's great treasures—the Hearst Castle. The "castle" is indeed a place not to be missed, visited by more than a million tourists each year. It was originally the home of newspaper legend William Randolph Hearst, and was built over a period of some twenty years, 1922-1941, by noted San Francisco architect Julia Morgan. It comprises a magnificent, Spanish cathedral-style main building and a handful of adjoining, and equally lovely, mansions, all perched on a hill—in the Santa Lucia Range—overlooking the ocean. Within the castle one can view the astonishing Hearst art collection, and countless rare and priceless treasures—among them, rugs, tapestries, exquisite antique furniture, and ornate, one-of-a-kind ceilings. On the grounds, too, are beautiful gardens, with exotic trees and plants, and lavish pools, both outdoor and indoor. The estate itself encompasses some 250,000 acres, mostly wild, rolling country, where zebra, elk, goats and other wild animals once roamed free, in what was then considered to be the largest private zoo in the world. The estate was deeded to the state by the Hearst Corporation in 1958, and is now maintained by the State Parks Department, who conduct guided tours of the castle daily. There are four tours offered, by which to see the castle, each covering a different section of it; reservations are advised, especially for tours on weekends and holidays.

HOW TO GET THERE

San Luis Obispo lies approximately midway between San Francisco and Los Angeles, easily accessible on *Highway 101* from either city. From San Francisco it is 225 miles south; and from Los Angeles, 196 miles northwest.

An alternative, but slower, route from San Francisco to San Luis Obispo is by way of *Highway 1*, directly south to Monterey, then along the spectacular Big Sur coastline to the little fishing village of Morro Bay, covering a distance of around 246 miles. From Morro Bay, *Highway 1* journeys inland some 14 miles directly to San Luis Obispo.

TOURIST INFORMATION

San Luis Obispo County Visitors & Convention Bureau. 1037 Mill St., San Luis Obispo; (805) 541-8000/(800) 634-1414. Accommodation and restaurant listings, information on Hearst Castle, Morro Bay, Pismo and Avila beaches. The bureau also publishes a *Visitors Guide*, with a map pinpointing places of local historical interest.

San Luis Obispo Chamber of Commerce. 1031 Chorro St., San Luis Obispo; (805) 781-2777. Local maps, information on accommodations and restaurants.

Morro Bay Chamber of Commerce. 880 Main St., Morro Bay; (805) 772-4467/(800 231-0592. Wide variety of tourist literature, including information on accommodations, restaurants, local activities and attractions; also maps.

Reservations for tours of the *Hearst Castle* can be made directly by calling the park service at (800) 444-4445.

ACCOMMODATIONS

Bed & Breakfast Inn

Heritage Inn. *$85-$120.* 978 Olive St.; (805) 544-7440. Beautifully restored Victorian bed and breakfast inn, with 9 antique-filled guest rooms, some with fireplaces. Creekside setting.

Hotels and Motels

Apple Farm Inn & Trellis Court. *$60-$150.* 12015 Monterey St.; (805) 544-2040/(800) 255-2040. 103 individually-decorated rooms, all with fireplaces. Hot tub and pool. Full breakfast included. Also restaurant, gift shop and bakery on premises.

Campus Motel. *$44-$68.* 404 Santa Rosa Rd.; (805) 544-0881/(800) 447-8080. 35 modern motel units, some with whirlpool or steam bath; TV, phones, pool. Close to downtown.

Coachman Inn Motel. *$40-$55.* 1001 Olive St.; (805) 544-0400. 27 rooms; TV, phones, pool; in-room coffee, restaurant nearby.

Holiday Inn Express. *$60-$120.* 1800 Monterey St.; (805) 544-8600/ (800) HOLIDAY. 99 units; TV, phones, pool and jacuzzi; also restaurant adjacent.

Homestead Motel. *$35-$50.* 920 Olive St.; (805) 543-7700. 25 units, including family and kitchen units; phones, TV, pool.

Howard Johnson Express. *$60-$90.* Hwy. 101 and Los Osos Valley Rd.; (805) 544-5300. 64 well-appointed units; TV, phones, pool; restaurant on premises. Complimentary continental breakfast.

La Cuesta Motor Inn. *$57-$90.* 2074 Monterey St.; (805) 543-2777/ (800) 543-2777. 72 units, with TV and phones; also pool and jacuzzi for guest use. Complimentary coffee and danish in the morning.

Madonna Inn. *$89-$225.* 100 Madonna Rd.; (805) 543-3000/(800) 543-9666. Unique inn, with 104 units, each decorated in an individual, often unusual, theme, such as Cave Room, Cinderella Room and Mine Room. Restaurant and gift shop on premises. Reservations required.

Olive Tree Motor Inn Best Western. *$59-$80.* 1000 Olive St.; (805) 544-2800/(800) 528-1234. 38 rooms, some family suites; TV, phones, pool, sauna, restaurant and laundromat.

Embassy Suite Hotel. *$95-$140.* 333 Madonna Rd.; (805) 549-0800/ (800) 362-2779. 196 luxury suites. Hotel facilities include an indoor pool, fitness room, 3 spas, restaurants and cocktail lounge; also complimentary breakfast, and bicycle rentals for guests.

Peach Tree Inn. *$50-$80.* 2001 Monterey St.; (805) 543-3170/(800) 227-6396. 51 rooms; phones, TV. Complimentary continental breakfast.

Best Western Royal Oak. *$53-$120.* 214 Madonna Rd.; (805) 544-4410/ (800) 528-1234. 99 rooms; phones, TV, coffee; also pool, and restaurant and cocktail lounge.

Sands Motel. *$59-$99.* 1930 Monterey St.; (805) 544-0500/(800) 441-4657. 70 units, including some suites. TV, phones, pool.

Somerset Manor-Best Western. *$59-$89.* 1895 Monterey St.; (805) 544-0973/(800) 528-1234. 40 units; TV, phones, pool, spa, coffee shop and restaurant.

San Luis Obispo Travelodge. *$46-$80.* 1825 Monterey St.; (805) 543-5110. 38 units, some family rooms; TV, phones, pool.

The Lamplighter Inn. *$49-$79.* 1604 Monterey St.; (805) 547-7777/ (800) 547-7787. 40 rooms and suites; phones, TV, in-room coffee. Heated pool and spa. Complimentary breakfast.

Vagabond Motor Inn. *$59-$99.* 210 Madonna Rd.; (805) 544-4710/(800) 522-1555. 61 units; TV and phones; pool. Complimentary continental breakfast. Restaurant nearby.

Villa San Luis Motel. *$49-$89.* 1670 Monterey St.; (805) 543-8071. 14 rooms with phones and TV. Pool. Complimentary continental breakfast.

SEASONAL EVENTS

April. *Italian Street Painting Festival.* At the Mission Plaza. Professional and amateur artists create chalk murals on the pavement. (805) 544-9251.

May. *La Fiesta.* Held at the Mission Plaza, in the heart of the city. Celebration of the town's Spanish heritage; features music and dance. Call for more information; (805) 543-1710.

July. *Renaissance Fair.* Two-day fair, featuring period costumes and a variety of festivities. Popular annual event. (805) 474-9571.

August. *Mozart Festival.* Annual, week-long festival, held during the first and second weeks of the month. Classical music concerts, featured at the historic Mission Plaza and other locations around town. For program information and reservations, call (805) 781-3008. *Heritage Day at the Dallidet Adobe.* Festivities include craft demonstrations and live entertainment. Call (805) 781-2777 for more information.

September. *Central Coast Wine Festival.* Held at the Mission Plaza, downtown San Luis Obispo. Many of the county's fine wineries participate in this celebration of the year's harvest. (805) 541-1721.

October. *Harbor Festival.* At Morro Bay; first weekend of the month. Features a sand sculpture competition, kite festival and children's treasure hunt, golf tournament, life-size chess and monopoly tournaments, and sprint triathlon. Also, live music and dancing. For a schedule of events, call (805) 772-1155. *Clam Festival.* At Pismo Beach, second weekend. Celebration of area's rich clam harvest. Arts and crafts show, food concessions featuring clams, and parades and festivities. For more information, call (805) 773-4382.

November. *International Film Festival.* Screenings of selected films from around the world are held at various locations around San Luis Obispo. Call (805) 546-FILM for a schedule.

Ongoing. *Downtown Farmers' Market,* on Higuera St., between Osos and Broad streets; every Thursday night, 6.30 p.m.-9 p.m. Market stalls, street barbecues, entertainers and musicians. (805) 543-1323. *Central Coast Plaza Farmers' Market,* at Hwy. 101 and Madonna Rd. Year-round market, held on Saturdays, 8 a.m.-10.30 a.m. (805) 544-9570.

PLACES OF INTEREST

Mission San Luis Obispo de Tolosa. Cnr. Chorro and Monterey Sts. (at the Mission Plaza). Fifth of California's 21 missions, founded in 1772 by Franciscan Father, Junipero Serra. The mission museum and the old, restored chapel—which still serves as the parish church—are open to the public daily. A delightful, brick-paved plaza at the front of the mission, recreated in 1971, offers picnicking and strolling possibilities. Gift shop on premises. Open 9-4 daily; mission phone, (805) 543-6850.

San Luis Obispo Path of History. Self-guided walking/driving tour of more than a dozen historical buildings in downtown San Luis Obispo (detailed map available from local Chamber of Commerce or Visitors Bureau on Chorro St.). Highlights of the tour include the *Myron Angel Home,* a red Victorian built in 1883, formerly the home of Myron Angel, founder of the California Polytechnic; the *Judge Walter Murray Adobe* (1846), where the first copies of the local newspaper, "The Tribune," were printed; and the *Dallidet Adobe* (1853) and *Sauer Adobes* (c.1860). Other points of interest here include *The Creamery,* built in 1906 and now housing a mini-arcade; the Art Deco-style *Fremont Theatre,* dating from 1941; the *Kundert Medical Building,* dating from 1956 and notable as the work of Frank Lloyd Wright; and the *Ah Louis (Chinese) Store,* built in 1874. Also on the tour are the local *Presbyterian Church,* built entirely from locally-quarried granite rock, in 1905; and the lovely, wood-frame *St. Stephen's Episcopal Church,* dating from 1867 and claimed to be one of the first Episcopal churches in California.

San Luis Obispo County Historical Museum. 696 Monterey St. (cnr. Broad St.); (805) 543-0638. Housed in the old brick and stone Carnegie Library Building, dating from 1905. The museum features displays of artifacts of local historical interest, representing every era of San Luis Obispo County's history, from Chumash Indian days to the present time. There is also a priceless collection of antique dolls and toys, furniture, clothing, textiles and arts, together with over 17,000 photographs. Open 10-4 Wed.-Sun.

San Luis Obispo Children's Museum. 1010 Nipomo St., San Luis Obispo; (805) 544-5437. Features interactive exhibits to encourage learning through exploration. Open Mon. and Sat. 10-5, Tues., Thurs., Fri., and Sun. 1-5, closed Wednesday. Admission: $4.00 per person (children under 2 free).

California Polytechnic State University. Located just to the north of the San Luis Obispo township, reached on California Blvd. This is one of the most popular colleges in the state system, noted for its agriculture, engineering and computer sciences programs. Campus comprises roughly 5,500 hillside acres, with one or two Spanish-style adobes situated amid the modern campus buildings as well. Two places of special interest here are the *Shakespeare Museum* which has displays of vintage printing equipment, and *The McPhee University Union Gallerie*, (805) 756-1182, which presents educational, historical, modern, and student art exhibits. Also, the university's *School of Agriculture* has tours of on-campus farm units, including the dairy cattle grounds, horse-breeding stables, vegetable gardens and food-processing plant. Visitor passes are available at the university entrance on Grand Avenue. For further information, call (805) 756-1182.

The Jack House. Located at 536 Marsh St., 2 blocks off Hwy. 101. Splendid two-story Victorian house, dating from 1880, set amid delightful gardens and lawns. The house is fully restored, with antique furnishings, 19th-century artifacts, and old photographs. Open Wed. and Fri., 1-4, May-Oct., and the first Sunday of each month during the rest of the year. (805) 781-7222.

Madonna Inn. On Madonna Ave., just off Hwy. 101; (805) 543-3000. A most unique inn, referred to by the *New York Times* as an architectural fantasyland. Comprises 104 guest rooms, each individually decorated—often in garish themes—such as Cave Room, Mine Room and Cinderella Room. Gift shops and one-of-a-kind dining room on premises; also, the men's urinal is an actual waterfall! Must-see attraction for first-time visitors to the area.

Avila Beach. 10 miles southwest of San Luis Obispo, off Hwy. 101. Good swimming beach with picnic and barbecue facilities and hot mineral baths. 3 miles of beach; pier and restaurants.

Pismo Beach. 12 miles south of San Luis Obispo, off Hwy. 101. Seaside resort with large, sandy beach, famous for its surf, sand dunes and clams. It is also the site of the annual Pismo Clam Festival, usually held in mid-October. Some good restaurants in area.

Morro Bay. 12 miles northwest of San Luis Obispo on Hwy. 1. Colorful little fishing village, named for the 576-foot Morro Rock just offshore, believed to be the second largest such monolith in the world. Excellent seafood restaurants and shops and galleries along waterfront, and sportfishing charters available year-round. Also worthwhile is the *Morro Bay Museum of Natural History*, located on State Park Rd. (off South Bay Blvd.), which has environmental exhibits, as well as displays of native marine life and wildlife. There is also a hands-on "discovery center" at the museum. The museum is open 10-5 daily; phone, (805) 772-2694. Also at Morro Bay State Park is a *Heron Rookery* which is easily viewed from a nearby observation point. Courtship season for the great blue herons begins in January.

Cambria. Located on Hwy. 1, 33 miles northwest of San Luis Obispo. This peaceful village was once known for its dairy farming, but is now home to many artists. There are numerous art galleries, quaint shops, fine restaurants and oceanside inns in and around Cambria. For tourist information, contact the *Cambria Chamber of Commerce,* 767 Main St., Cambria; (805) 927-3624.

Hearst Castle. 45 miles northwest of San Luis Obispo on Hwy. 1, at San

Simeon. Spectacular, multilevel Spanish- cathedral-style "castle," perched on a hill overlooking the ocean; formerly home of newspaper legend William Randolph Hearst. Now owned and operated by the State Parks Department, the castle houses the fabulous Hearst art collection, featuring priceless paintings, sculptures, antiques, period furniture, rare tapestries and rugs, and several hand-crafted, one-of-a-kind ceilings. Also featured here are superb, landscaped grounds, with exotic trees and plants, and lavish indoor and outdoor pools. The estate itself comprises approximately 250,000 acres of rolling coastal land, in the Central Coast's Santa Lucia Range, where once buffalo, zebra, elk, exotic deer and other animals roamed free, in what was described as the largest private zoo in the world. Castle originally built between 1922 and 1941, designed by architect Julia Morgan. There are four different tours of the castle and grounds, conducted by park personnel, each covering a different section of the estate. For tour information and reservations, call (800) 444-4445.

RECREATION

Golf. *Avila Beach Golf Resort.* Avila Beach Rd. (off Hwy. 101), Avila Beach; (805) 595-2307. 18-hole championship course, par 71, 6,443 yards. Driving range, lessons; restaurant. Open to the public daily. *Dairy Creek Golf Course.* 2950 Dairy Creek Road, San Luis Obispo; (805) 728-8060. 18-hole, par 72, 6,548 yard, public course. *Laguna Lake Golf Course.* 11175 Los Osos Valley Rd., San Luis Obispo; (805) 781-7309. 9-hole executive course, 1,306 yards. Driving range, lessons; snack bar. *Morro Bay Golf Club.* Situated in the Morro Bay State Park, 201 State Park Rd., Morro Bay; (805) 782-8060. 18-hole public course, overlooking Morro Bay, par 71, 6,360 yards. *Sea Pines Golf Club.* 1945 Solano Ave., Los Osos (northwest of San Luis Obispo); (805) 528-5252. 9-hole, par 28, executive course, overlooking the ocean. Driving range, pro shop, restaurant.

Hot Springs. *Avila Hot Springs Spa,* 250 Avila Beach Dr., Avila Beach; (805) 595-2359. Hot mineral pools, swimming pool, massage facilities; also RV park on premises. Open daily, year-round. *Sycamore Mineral Springs Resort,* 1215 Avila Beach Dr., Avila Beach; (805) 595-7302. Hot mineral pools, individual hot tubs, swimming pool. Open to the public daily.

Sport Fishing. The seaside village of Morro Bay, 12 miles northwest of San Luis Obispo, is a popular place for sport fishing and boating. For charters and fishing trips, contact *Virg's Deep Sea Fishing,* 1215 Embarcadero, (805) 772-1222, or *Bob's Sport Fishing of Morro Bay,* 845 Embarcadero, (805) 772-3340.

Dune Buggies. Pismo Beach, south of San Luis Obispo, is famous for its sand dunes, with dune buggy and ATV recreation facilities available at the Pismo Dunes Vehicle Recreational Area, just off Hwy. 101. For dune buggy and ATV rentals, contact any of the following: *The Sand Center,* 306 Pier Ave., Oceano, (805) 489-0395; *Joe's Buggy Haus,* 239 3rd St., Grover City, (805) 489-0658; or *BJ's ATV Rentals,* 197 Grand Ave., Grover City, (805) 481-5411.

RESTAURANTS

(Restaurant prices—based on full course dinner, excluding drinks, tax and tips—are categorized as follows: *Deluxe*, over $30; *Expensive*, $20-$30; *Moderate*, $10-$20; *Inexpensive*, under $10.)

Angelo's Italian Restaurant. *Moderate.* 969 Monterey St.; (805) 544-5888. Authentic Italian food, including pizza. Open for lunch and dinner.

Apple Farm Restaurant. *Inexpensive-Moderate.* 2015 Monterey St.; (805) 544-6100. Old-fashioned dinners, featuring homemade soups and pies, and freshly baked cornbread with honey butter. Also serving breakfast and lunch. Hours: 7 a.m.-9 p.m., daily.

Big Sky Cafe. *Inexpensive-Moderate.* 1121 Broad St.; (805) 545-5401. Popular, casual restaurant, serving New American cuisine. Open for lunch and dinner daily.

Buena Tavola. *Moderate-Expensive.* 1037 Monterey St.; (805) 545-8000. Northern Italian cuisine, featuring fresh antipasti, homemade pasta and seafood. Open for lunch and dinner daily. Patio for outdoor dining.

Cafe Roma. *Moderate.* 1020 Railroad Ave.; (805) 541-6800. Northern Italian fare, comprising delicious homemade pastas and unusual desserts. Lunch and dinner, Tues.-Sat.

Caffe Brio. *Inexpensive-Moderate.* 1203 Marsh St.; (805) 541-5282. Specializing in fresh and natural vegetarian and vegan meals. Also homemade focaccias, pastas and pastries. Take-out deli on premises. Open for lunch and dinner daily; also weekend brunches.

China Bowl & Kyoto Restaurant. *Moderate.* 685 Higuera St.; (805) 546-9700. Unique blend of Chinese and Japanese cuisine; Szechuan, Hunan and Mandarin dishes, as well as large Sushi Bar. Lunch and dinner daily.

DaVinci's. *Moderate.* 1761 Monterey St.; (805) 543-0777. Homemade pasta and other Italian food; sunny patio for outdoor dining. Open for lunch and dinner.

Golden China Restaurant. *Moderate.* 1085 Higuera St.; (805) 543-7354. Mandarin and Szechuan cuisine. Lunch and dinner daily.

1865. *Moderate-Expensive.* 1865 Monterey St.; (805) 544-1865. Loft dining; hanging gardens. House specialty is prime rib; also seafood and pasta dishes. Live entertainment. Open for lunch and dinner.

Imperial China Restaurant. *Moderate.* 667 C Marsh St.; (805) 544-1668. Cantonese, Mandarin and Szechuan dishes. Daily lunch specials; family dinners. Open 11.30 a.m.-10 p.m.

Izzy Ortega's. *Inexpensive-Moderate.* 1850 Monterey St.; (805) 543-3333. Authentic Mexican food; multi-flavored margaritas and Mexican beer. Patio for outdoor dining. Lunch and dinner daily.

F. McLintock's Saloon. *Moderate-Expensive.* 686 Higuera St.; (805) 541-0686. Steak, prime rib and seafood. Open for breakfast, lunch and dinner. Patio for outdoor dining.

This Old House. *Moderate-Expensive.* 740 W. Foothill Blvd. (near Los Osos Valley Rd.); (805) 543-2690. Delightful little restaurant, housed in an old farmhouse. Menu features ribs, seafood, and other items from the oakwood barbecue. Dinners from 5.30 p.m. daily.

Tsurgi. *Moderate.* 570 Higuera St. (in the old Creamery); (805) 543-8942. Sushi and tempura specialties. Open for lunch and dinner daily.

SANTA BARBARA

Old Spain and Palm-Fringed Beaches

Santa Barbara, situated on the beautiful Southern California coast, just 90 miles or so north of Los Angeles, has more in it that is reminiscent of Old Spain than perhaps any other city in California. It is, typically, filled with Spanish-colonial architecture, Spanish gardens and terrazzo walks, Spanish-style courtyard restaurants and sidewalk cafes, Spanish names, and a rich, colorful Spanish past—all of which go to give the city a distinctly Spanish flavor. Here also, we might add, are some of the West's loveliest white sand beaches, lined with picturesque palms and backed by the ancient Santa Ynez Mountains, and one or two of America's most exclusive residential communities, where the rich and the famous and Hollywood celebrities make their homes. The city, besides, is a well-liked vacation retreat, with good accommodations, restaurants and shops, and with art and history museums, botanic gardens, a zoo and bird refuge, and festivities year-round.

The city can quite easily be reached on Highway 101, from either Los Angeles or San Francisco (331 miles).

DISCOVERING SANTA BARBARA

Santa Barbara has two tours by which to see the city—the Red Tile Tour and the Scenic Drive, with good maps and brochures available for both from the local Chamber of Commerce on State Street. The first of these is primarily a walking tour of the downtown area—taking in roughly twelve city blocks—along State, Anapamu, Anacapa, Canon Perdido, De La Guerra and Santa Barbara streets. It has on it more than twenty points of interest, most notable being the Santa Barbara County Courthouse on Anacapa Street, a truly magnificent example of Spanish-Moorish architecture and, indeed, claimed to be the most beautiful Spanish-style building in North America. It dates from 1929, and is still partially in use as a courthouse, with a judge's chamber, a district attorney's office and a holding cell. It also has a superb Spanish-style courtroom on its second floor, with antique furnishings and wrought-iron chandeliers, and a splendid hand-painted ceiling and wall murals depicting the story of Santa Barbara. The courthouse tower, 70 feet high (approximately four stories), has expansive, all-round views of the city and its vast sea of red-tiled roofs, sweeping across, all the way, to the ocean. It is, of course, open to the public. Also of tourist interest, lying between its two glorious wings, are the delightful, tropical sunken gardens of the courthouse—notable as the site of the first courthouse, built here in 1786, and more recently, in 1983, the site of the reception for Queen Elizabeth II during her visit to the city. The gardens are also the scene of open-air concerts during the annual Spanish Days celebration, usually held in July-August.

Near at hand on State Street is the Santa Barbara Museum of Art—a place not to be missed—acknowledged as one of the finest small museums in America. It has a remarkable collection of contemporary art, and some famous works of Monet, Matisse, Chagall, Peele, Moore and Kadinsky, among others. In a center gallery, which has natural skylight lighting, are displayed sculptures from Egypt, Rome and Greece, with an adjoining room containing treasures from the Orient, as well as some rare African art. There is also a floor devoted entirely to photographic exhibits, and on its lower floor the museum features notable visiting exhibitions. A gift shop on the premises carries a line of greeting cards featuring reproductions of some of the museum's most prized art properties.

There are also several splendid, Spanish-style malls and plazas here, most of them of adobe construction, and all of them colorfully decorated with banners, flags and flowers. The loveliest and oldest of these is of course the El Paseo (or Casa De La Guerra) on Anacapa and De La Guerra streets, where the atmosphere of Old Spain has been wonderfully preserved. It dates from 1826 and is the former home of the Spanish-born De La Guerra family, frequently at the center of Santa Barbara's social life. The "casa," notably, was also the setting for Richard Henry Dana's 19th-century classic, *Two Years Before The Mast*. It now contains a delightful courtyard restaurant, a bar and sidewalk cafe, and a dozen or so charming little shops and galleries.

For history buffs, the best of all places to visit is the Santa Barbara

Historical Society Museum on De La Guerra Street, which has in it a wealth of mementos and artifacts from all four eras of the city's history —Indian, Spanish, Mexican and American. There are some worthwhile outdoor displays as well, and two adjoining adobes, Casa de Covarrubias (1817) and the Historic Adobe (1836), although usually not open to the public, add to the interest. Also try to visit the site of the old Presidio on nearby Canon Perdido Street, where the ancient Caneda Adobe (part of the original Presidio quadrangle) can still be seen, dating from 1782 and recently restored to its former glory; and where the reconstructed Presidio Chapel, quite lovely with its hand-painted tiles, is also open to public viewing. Across from the Presidio site is El Cuartel ("The Guard House"), another small but enchanting adobe, dating from 1788. It now houses a gift shop, with Santa Barbara souvenirs, mainly.

Among other notable structures are the Orena Adobes (1848-1858) on East De La Guerra Street, formerly the home of a California Don; the Hill-Carrillo Adobe (1826) on East Carrillo Street, which has in it the city's first wooden floor; and the Rochin Adobe (1855) on Santa Barbara Street, now a private residence, but nevertheless worth seeing. Two other superb, historic buildings, a little way from the center of town on Montecito Street, are the Fernald House—a 14-room, gabled Victorian mansion—and the Trussell-Winchester Adobe, dating from 1854 and built, quite interestingly, from adobe bricks and timbers taken from the *Winfield Scott*, a ship wrecked just off the Santa Barbara coast. Both the Fernald House and the Trussell-Winchester Adobe are owned and maintained by the historical society, and are open to the public on weekends.

State Street, in the center of town, is also much to be recommended to visitors. It is of course the city's main street, and the only one in the downtown area with a non-Spanish name. It has on it scores of fine shops, galleries, restaurants and sidewalk cafes, and its lovely mall-style setting is ideally suited to strolling and browsing. The street is also the scene of the colorful Summer Solstice parade, usually held in late June each year.

Leaving the center of town, the Scenic Drive, the second and lengthier of the city's two tours, follows a circuitous route around the city, enchantingly weaving through the foothills of the picturesque Santa Ynez Mountains that surround the city on two sides. The tour takes in some fifteen points of supreme tourist interest, including one or two of America's most opulent residential communities, and the increasingly popular waterfront, with its sandy, palm-fringed beaches.

The Scenic Drive, much like the Red Tile Tour, can be joined at virtually any point enroute, although it is a good idea, we might suggest, to begin at the north end—an especially logical choice if you are already in the city. In any case, first off is the glorious Mission Santa Barbara, situated on a hill on Laguna Street, overlooking the city. This is said to be one of the most beautiful of California's missions —the "Queen of the Missions"—and the only one with two identical towers. This is also, most notably, the tenth of California's twenty-one missions founded by Franciscan fathers, originally built in 1786. It has in it a delightful mission museum, with old photographs detailing

SANTA BARBARA

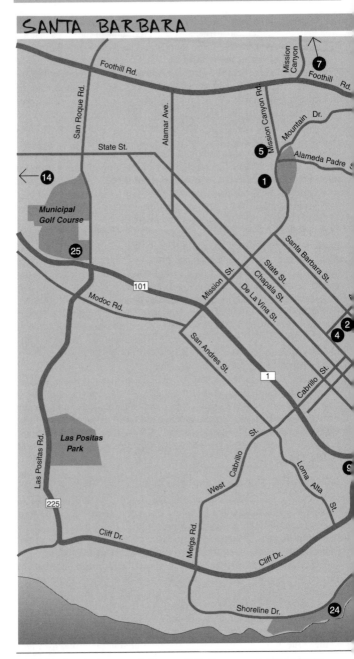

1. Mission Santa Barbara
2. Santa Barbara County Courthouse
3. El Paseo
4. Museum of Modern Art
5. Museum of Natural History
6. Santa Barbara Historical Society Museum
7. Santa Barbara Botanic Garden
8. Moreton Bay Fig
9. Fernald House and Trussell-Winchester House
10. El Presidio de Santa Barbara

SANTA BARBARA

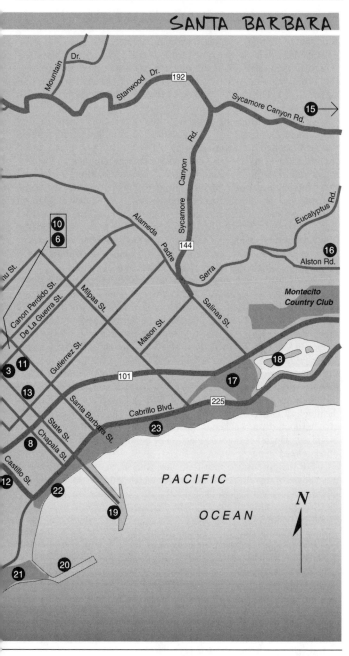

11. El Cuartel
12. Carriage House Museum
13. Santa Barbara Visitors Bureau
14. U.C. Santa Barbara
15. Montecito Village
16. Brooks Institute of Photography
17. Santa Barbara Zoo
18. Andree Clark Bird Refuge
19. Stearns Wharf
20. Breakwater
21. Leadbetter Beach
22. West Beach
23. East Beach
24. Shoreline Park
25. Earl Warren Showgrounds

the building of the mission, as well as historic mission artifacts and a typical Franciscan monk's room, with its original, 18th-century furnishings. There is also a gift shop on the premises, and some well-kept gardens, both in the courtyard and at the rear of the mission—where, further, there is a small selection of trees from various parts of the world, including China and Australia, and a chapel cemetery of some interest. The mission chapel, by the way, still serves as the parish church.

A little way from the mission (traveling in a clockwise direction) is the Santa Barbara Museum of Natural History, home to countless fine exhibits and dioramas featuring native fauna, flora, geology, and the life and ways of the native Shoshone Indians. Among the displays are an exhibit of a "volcanic bomb," a diorama featuring prehistoric elephants, and another detailing the ocean shelf between the Santa Barbara coast and the Channel Islands—which lie some 30 to 40 miles distant, and comprise four islands, Anacapa, Santa Cruz, Santa Rosa and San Miguel. There is also an outdoor display here, of the skeleton of a 72-foot blue whale that washed up on the Santa Barbara shores in the early 1960s. The museum, besides, has a gift shop and a planetarium which schedules programs on Sundays.

North still, on a small detour off the Scenic Drive, is Santa Barbara's lovely Botanic Garden, with sixty-five acres of native California trees, shrubs, flowers and cacti. Most of the plants and trees are in a natural setting, and there are, besides, several individual theme settings here, such as a Redwood Section with its splendid groves of California redwoods, a Meadow Section, a Desert Section, an Island Section, and—best of all—a Canyon Section which has in it the historic Mission Dam, built in 1806 by the native Shoshone Indians, under the supervision of the Franciscan padres, to supply water for the mission. There are at least five miles of enchanting little trails dashing off all over the garden, by which to explore, and guided tours are conducted on weekends. There is also a garden shop on the premises, which has a good selection of botany and nature books and other related items.

For the purposes of our tour, however, let us now return to our main route of travel, the Scenic Drive, which journeys east along the glorious Santa Ynez foothills, several miles, to Montecito, passing by the Brooks Institute of Photography, renowned the world over for its excellent instruction in the art of photography, and which also has a gallery featuring students' works. Montecito itself has a distinction too. It is one of America's most luxurious residential communities, home to scores of lavish mansions—residences of the rich and famous—tucked away among age-old shade trees and towering palms, overlooking the city and the vast, blue ocean. The Montecito village also has a charming little shopping district, filled with specialty and import shops, antique stores, art galleries, and a handful of outdoor, patio-style restaurants and cafes. Just to the south of the village, of course, lies the Montecito Country Club, with its manicured greens and picturesque white clubhouse.

Immediately below Montecito and its country club—with the Scenic Drive now westbound, having looped around Montecito—are the Andree Clark Bird Refuge, where you can observe a variety of freshwater fowl; and the Santa Barbara Zoological Gardens, which feature all sorts of exotic birds and animals, including elephants, lions and monkeys. The zoo has miniature train rides as well, quite enjoyable to children.

Westward, journeying toward the center of town, the Scenic Drive swoops down to the Santa Barbara coast and passes by the sandy East Beach, where arts and crafts shows are held on weekends and holidays all year, featuring works of over 300 local artists. East Beach is adjoined, quite naturally, by West Beach, another delightful sandy beach which, most interestingly, is bisected by the ancient Stearns Wharf, said to be the oldest operating wharf on the West Coast. The wharf is actually a three-block-long extension of the city's main street, State Street, and boasts a collection of colorful little gift and souvenir shops and kiosks, fish markets, three or four well-liked seafood restaurants, and a Sea Center which has some outstanding displays of Santa Barbara's marine life. The wharf has good pier fishing and fishing boats can also be chartered here, for sportfishing trips out to sea. Nearby, at the corner of Chapala Street and Highway 101, and well worth seeing, is the amazing Moreton Bay Fig Tree, with a branch spread of nearly 165 feet, and which, it is claimed, can shade more than 10,000 people at noon! The Moreton Bay Fig is native to Australia, and was planted here by a pioneer family in 1877.

Also near to Stearns Wharf is the Santa Barbara Yacht Harbor—home to over 1,000 working and pleasure craft—and the half-mile-long Breakwater, a man-made marvel, on which you can stroll, and which has great views—looking back from it—of the city and the Santa Ynez Mountains.

Next up, adjacent to the Breakwater, is Leadbetter Beach, another of Santa Barbara's beautiful, white sand beaches, quite popular with swimmers, surfers and sunbathers, and directly above which one can visit the Shoreline Park, which offers commanding views of the Leadbetter Beach, Breakwater, Stearns Wharf, and the city and mountains farther inland.

In order to complete our tour along the Scenic Drive, however, we must continue inland from Shoreline Park a little way, to the much-talked-about Hope Ranch, sprawled among the scenic, coastal hills, and claimed to be one of Santa Barbara's most exclusive neighborhoods. From Hope Ranch the Scenic Drive heads north to the Earl Warren Showgrounds, site of the city's horse, dog and flower shows, among others; then on to the Santa Barbara Mission, our starting point.

West and east of Santa Barbara are two other places of interest —Goleta Beach and Carpenteria Beach, respectively. Both have good, sandy beaches, and Goleta also has a notable museum, devoted to early day railroad signaling and other communications equipment, with several working exhibits. A short distance past Goleta is the University of California, Santa Barbara, which has its very own lagoon, with spectacular ocean vistas, and some splendid campus buildings and tree-shaded grounds. Campus maps are available at the university gates.

Another worthwhile detour from Santa Barbara is Ojai, some 34 miles to the southwest, by way of Highway 101, Casitas Pass Road and Highway 150. Ojai—pronounced, "O-High"—enjoys a lovely valley setting, notable, too, as the setting for the "Valley of Shangri-La" in the movie *Lost Horizon.* There is a good museum here, with displays of Indian artifacts, as well as Biblical Gardens which feature most of the plants mentioned in the Bible. Ojai is also home to the largest Theosophical Library on the West Coast.

If time permits, a visit to the Channel Islands—which comprise four islands, Santa Cruz, Santa Rosa, San Miguel and Anacapa, lying some 20-40 miles off the coast of Santa Barbara—is also much to be recommended. The islands are now part of the National Parks System, and are open to the public for day trips only. Their chief interest lies in fishing, hiking, and observing native sea life and some unique trees and wildflowers, indigenous to the islands. Boat excursions to one or two of the nearer islands depart from the park headquarters at Ventura, 20 miles south of Santa Barbara; call (805) 644-8262 for reservations.

HOW TO GET THERE

Santa Barbara lies on the beautiful Southern California coast, approximately 90 miles northwest of Los Angeles, by way of either *Highway 1* or *Highway 101.*

From San Francisco it is 331 miles, southeastward, to Santa Barbara, also by way of *Highway 101.* An alternative route from San Francisco is on coastal *Highway 1,* slower but infinitely more scenic.

Santa Barbara also has a commercial airport, situated just to the northwest of town, in Goleta. Airlines servicing the Santa Barbara airport include *American Airlines* (800) 433-7300, *United Airlines* (800) 241-6522, and *Sky West* (800) 453-9417. There are also several companies providing shuttle service from Los Angeles International Airport, including *Super Ride* (805) 683-3526, *Santa Barbara Airbus* (805) 964-7759, and *Santa Barbara Shuttle Service* (805) 962-0507.

TOURIST INFORMATION

Santa Barbara Conference & Visitors Bureau. 504 State St., Santa Barbara; (805) 966-9222. Wealth of tourist literature, including visitor magazines and brochures on accommodations, restaurants, tours and fishing charters, annual events, and camping and recreational facilities. The Chamber also publishes brochures on Santa Barbara's "Red Tile Tour" and "Scenic Drive," with good maps to go by. For accommodation information and reservations, call *Accommodations in Santa Barbara,* (805) 687-9191.

ACCOMMODATIONS

Bed & Breakfast Inns

Bath Street Inn. *$100-$190.* 1720 Bath St.; (805) 682-9680. Restored Queen Anne Victorian with delightful gardens. 7 rooms; private baths. Complimentary wine and cheese. Continental breakfast. Bicycles for guests' use.

Blue Dolphin Inn. *$69-$195 .* 420 W. Montecito St.; (805) 962-4907. Victorian inn located two blocks from the beach. 9 rooms with private baths, including 3 rooms with jacuzzi tubs and 5 rooms with fireplaces. Jacuzzi. Full breakfast; afternoon wine and cheese.

Cheshire Cat. *$140-$300.* 36 W. Valerio St.; (805) 569-1610. Side-by-side Victorians, beautifully restored and decorated with antiques and period furnishings. 14 rooms, each with private bath and phone; some fireplaces, private spas, and balconies. Lovely garden, with gazebo spa and private patio. Continental breakfast.

Glenborough Inn & Cottage. *$100-$360.* 1327 Bath St.; (805) 966-0589. Quiet Victorian Inn with 9 guest rooms; hot tub in garden setting, bicycles available for guest use. Breakfast served in room.

Olive House. *$110-$180.* 1604 Olive St.; (805) 962-4902. Beautifully restored home within easy walking distance of the Mission. 7 rooms with private baths. Country breakfast. Children welcome.

Secret Garden Inn. *$110-$195.* 1908 Bath St.; (805) 687-2300. 2 guest rooms in main house, and 7 cottages, with private entrances; private baths, some fireplaces. Wine and cheese in the evening; full breakfast.

Simpson House Inn. *$160-$365.* 121 E. Arrellaga St.; (805) 963-7067. 1874 inn, set on an acre of lush gardens. 4 guest rooms, furnished with antiques, lace and oriental rugs. Afternoon tea and hors d'oeuvres; continental breakfast.

Hotels and Motels

BestWestern Beachside Inn. *$119-$169.* 336 W. Cabrillo Blvd.; (805) 965-6556/(800) 528-1234. 60 motel units; TV, phones and refrigerators; harbor views; heated outdoor pool, tennis court; restaurant on premises. Handicapped facilities.

BestWestern PepperTree. *$128-$158.* 3850 State St.; (805) 687-5511/ (800) 528-1234. Located near Santa Barbara Mission and Showgrounds. 150 rooms with private patios overlooking gardens. Pool, spa, sauna, gym, restaurant, cocktail lounge, and gift shop. Golf and tennis facilities nearby. Handicapped facilities.

Casa del Mar. *$69-$229.* 3714 State St.; (805) 687-2468/(800) 433-3097. 114 units; some suites and kitchen units. Heated pool, spa, sauna, weight room. Complimentary continental breakfast, evening wine and cheese.

Coast Village Inn. *$85-$155.* 1188 Coast Village Rd., Montecito; (805) 969-3266. 25 rooms and suites, most with ocean views. TV, phones; some kitchenettes. Heated pool. All rooms in the hotel are non-smoking.

Days Inn. *$55-$90 .* 116 Castillo St.; (805) 963-9772. 45 rooms with TV and phones; jacuzzi. Located one block from beach, wharf and harbor. Handicapped facilities.

Eagle Inn. *$65-$95.* 232 Natoma Ave.; (805) 965-3586. Spanish-style inn, close to beach and marina. 18 units, with TV and phones; some kitchen units.

El Encanto Hotel & Garden Villas. *$229-$469.* 1900 Lasuen Rd.; (805) 687-5000. 100 cottages, set amid 10 acres of tropical gardens. Many of the cottages have fireplaces, kitchens and patios. City and ocean views; restaurant, cocktail lounge, tennis court, heated pool, room service. Handicapped facilities

El Prado Motor Inn. *$55-$90.* 1601 State St.; (805) 966-0807. 66 rooms with TV and phones. Heated pool. Complimentary continental breakfast. Handicapped facilities.

Encina Lodge-Best Western. *$124-$164.* 2220 Bath St.; (805) 682-7277/(800) 528-1234. 121 guest rooms, suites, kitchen units and apartments; some private patios. Restaurant, pool, spa and sauna. Handicapped facilities.

Fess Parker's Doubletree Resort Hotel. *$179-$259.* 630 E. Cabrillo Blvd.; (805) 564-4333/(800) 222-8733. Oceanside setting; 360 luxury units, including 32 suites. Facilities include a pool, spa, sauna, exercise room, tennis courts, two restaurants and cocktail lounge. Handicapped facilities.

Franciscan Inn. *$75-$145.* 109 Bath St.; (805) 963-8845. 53 units, including 24 kitchen units and some 2-bedroom apartments. TV and phones; pool, spa, continental breakfast. Located one block from the beach.

Harbor View Inn. *$120-$325.* 28 W. Cabrillo Blvd.; (805) 963-0780. 64 units; views of ocean and Stearns Wharf. TV, phones; heated pool, spa and sun deck. Complimentary continental breakfast.

Kings Inn. *$75-$120.* 128 Castillo St.; (805) 963-4471. 45 units, 4 suites; TV and phones, some balconies. Also heated pool, spa and sauna.

Lemon Tree Inn. *$75-$150 .* 2819 State St.; (805) 687-6444/(800) 536-6764. Full service hotel. TV and phones. Tropical garden courtyard with heated swimming pool and spas. Restaurant. Handicapped facilities.

Marina Beach Motel. *$55-$85.* 21 Bath St.; (805) 963-9311. 32 rooms and suites with TV and phones; some with fireplaces, kitchens and spas. Close to beach and wharf.

Mason Beach Inn. *$68-98.* 324 W. Mason St.; (805) 962-3203/(800) 446-0444 in CA. 47 rooms and suites with TV and phones; some kitchenettes. Heated pool, jacuzzi. Continental breakfast.

The Montecito Inn. *$185-$350.* 1295 Coast Village Rd., Montecito; (805) 969-7854. Elegant, Mediterranean-style full-service hotel; 60 units. Health spa, saunas, massage rooms, pool and spa; also restaurant.

Ocean Palms Resort Hotel. *$70-$125.* 232 W. Cabrillo Blvd.; (805) 966-9133. 33 rooms with ocean views; TV, phones, heated pool and spa. Cottages and kitchen units available.

Polynesian Motel. *$60-$120.* 433 W. Montecito St.; (805) 963-7851. 41 units, 22 with kitchens; TV and phones, heated pool and spa; tennis courts next door. Close to beach.

Radisson Santa Barbara Hotel & Spa. *$179-$229.* 1111 E. Cabrillo Blvd.; (805) 963-0744/(800) 333-3333. 174-unit beachfront hotel with panoramic ocean views. Pool, health spa, restaurant.

Sandpiper Lodge. *$49-$79.* 3525 State St.; (805) 687-5326. 92 units, including some family suites and kitchen units; TV, phones, heated pool. Close to showgrounds and golf course.

Santa Barbara Biltmore. *$395-$565.* 1260 Channel Dr., Montecito; (805) 969-2261. Superb oceanside hotel with 229 luxurious guest rooms. Spectacular views, and complete range of recreational facilities.

Santa Barbara Inn. *$139-$249.* Cnr. E. Cabrillo Blvd. and Milpas St.; (805) 966-2285. Charming resort hotel on the beach; 71 rooms, each with private lanai. Pool, spa, restaurant. Spectacular views of ocean and harbor.

San Ysidro Ranch. *$399-$3,000.* 900 San Ysidro Lane, Montecito; (805) 969-5046. 39 cottage units in rustic hideaway, set on over 500 acres of private grounds, with ocean and mountain views. Pool and tennis courts; excellent restaurant; also hiking and horseback riding. Member of Relais de Chateaux.

Schooner Inn. *$50-$70.* 533 State St. (cnr. Cota St.); (805) 965-4572. 96 rooms, with TV and phones.

Upham-Victorian Hotel & Garden Cottages. *$170-$225.* 1404 De la Vina St.; (805) 962-0058/(800) 727-0876. Oldest hotel in continuous operation in Southern California; offers 38 beautifully-renovated rooms and cottages in a garden setting. Continental breakfast; restaurant on premises. Centrally located.

Villa Rosa. *$100-$230.* 15 Chapala St.; (805) 966-0851. Restored, 1930s Spanish-style inn. 18 units, with ocean, harbor, or mountain views; some fireplaces, and sunken tubs. Also kitchen units and suites available. Pool and spa in garden courtyard; continental breakfast, afternoon wine and cheese. Located near beach.

West Beach Inn. *$101-$133.* 306 W. Cabrillo Blvd.; (805) 963-4277. Located at the beach; 44 rooms with ocean or garden views. Heated pool and spa; complimentary continental breakfast.

SEASONAL EVENTS

March. *Santa Barbara International Film Festival.* 1st week of the month. Premieres of American and international motion pictures and documentaries; also workshops and seminars, conducted by film professionals, including stars, movie makers, critics and writers. For festival details and tickets, call (805) 963-0023.

April. *Santa Barbara Arts Festival.* Two-week-long celebration of Santa Barbara's performing and visual arts, featuring art exhibitions, orchestras, dance, theater, jazz, mime and puppets; also tours of artists' studios. For more information, call the Santa Barbara Arts Council, (805) 966-9222.

May. *Children's Festival.* Held at Alameda Park. Includes sporting activities, arts and crafts, live entertainment, and a barbecue. For more information, call (805) 965-1001. *Chinese Festival.* At Oak Park. Celebration of Chinese culture, with Chinese food, music, dance, arts and crafts, and a dragon parade. (805) 683-3571.

June. *Scandinavian Midsummer Festival.* Held at Oak Park (cnr. Alamar and Junipero Sts.); 2nd Saturday of the month. Features music and dancing around the Maypole, folk dance exhibitions, and polka contest; also handicrafts, homemade pastries and Scandinavian buffet-style lunch. Free admission. (805) 969-6756. *Summer Solstice.* 3rd week. Celebration of the year's longest day; spectacular, colorful parade down State Street, music festival, dance, and more. Multi-arts extravaganza. For schedule and information, call (805) 965-3396. *Semana Nautica.* Last week of the month. Famous week- long summer sports festival, with over 50 ocean, beach and land events. Open to amateurs. Hosted by the Semana Nautica Association, (805) 564-2052, or call (805) 966-9222.

July. *Fourth of July.* Parade and fireworks, on State St. and Stearns Wharf; also arts and crafts show at the Old Mission, and other festivities. *Bastille Day.* Oak Park. A day of French food and music, followed by a fireworks display. Call (805) 564-7274 for further information. *Santa Barbara National Horse & Flower Show.* Held at the Fairgrounds; 3rd week of the month. One of the best-known horse shows in the country; also spectacular flower show. (805) 687-0766. *Santa Barbara County Fair.* 4th week. Large county fair, with carnival, agricultural exhibits, wine show, live entertainment, and more. Held at the Fairgrounds in Santa Maria. For information, call (805) 925-8824.

August. *Old Spanish Days Fiesta.* 2nd week in August. Celebration of city's Spanish heritage; variety of colorful events, including open-air music concerts at the historic County Courthouse, and parades, mercados and rodeo. Schedule and information on (805) 966-9222. *Pacific Coast Open Polo Tournament.* At the Santa Barbara Polo Club; 2nd and 3rd weeks. Second most prestigious polo tournament in the nation, featuring several well-known international teams. (805) 684-6683/(805) 966-9222.

September. *Santa Barbara Concours d'Elegance.* Superb antique and classic automobile show, featuring a winners' parade, and picnic. Held during the 4th weekend of the month. (805) 966-9222.

October. *Goleta Lemon Days.* 2nd week. Goleta's annual festival; features cross-town parade, arts and crafts show, old time fiddlers' convention, crowning of Goleta Queen, hoedown and dinner, and, of course, lots of lemonade. (805) 967-4618. *Goleta Depot Day.* Held at the old Goleta Depot; 3rd Sunday of the month. Events include steam train rides, special railroad exhibits, and an auction of "unclaimed baggage and freight." (805) 964-3540/(805) 967-4618.

November. *Santa Barbara National Amateur Horse Show.* Last week of the month. Country's largest amateur horse show; junior and adult amateurs compete in Western and English-style riding. (805) 687-0766/687-8711.

Ongoing Event. *Arts & Crafts Show.* Held at the beach, along Cabrillo Blvd., east of Stearns Wharf; fair-weather Sundays and public holidays, year-round. Features works of some 300 local, Santa Barbara artists. Variety ranges from paintings, graphics, sculpture and photography to stained glass, textiles, jewelry, quilts and ceramics. (805) 963-0611, ext. 4530.

PLACES OF INTEREST

Santa Barbara has two main tours by which to see the city's many sights. The *Red Tile Tour* takes in some 12 city blocks in the downtown area, pinpointing more than 20 places of interest, most of them quite historic; and the *Scenic Drive,* which circles the city, highlights at least 15 places of supreme tourist interest. In the following we have listed most of the city's major attractions, although for a detailed and complete listing, with brochures and maps, we suggest you contact the Santa Barbara Visitors Bureau (see *Tourist Information*).

Santa Barbara County Courthouse. 1100 Anacapa St.; (805) 962-6464. Magnificent Spanish-Moorish courthouse, built in 1929. Highlights of a tour of the courthouse include the delightful, sunken tropical gardens; the splendid old courtroom, with wall murals depicting the story of Santa Barbara; and the 85-foot-high clock-tower, believed to be the tallest structure in the downtown area, with sweeping views of the city. The courthouse is still in partial use. Open 9 a.m.-5 p.m. Mon.-Fri., 10 a.m.-5 p.m. Sat.- Sun.; guided tours on Mon.-Sat. 2 p.m., Fri. 10.30 a.m. Free admission.

Santa Barbara Historical Society Museum. 136 E. De la Guerra St.; (805) 966-1601. Exhibits of local historical interest, representing all four eras of Santa Barbara's colorful past—Indian, Spanish, Mexican and early American. Also outdoor displays, and two adjoining historic adobes that are occasionally open to the public. Museum hours: 10 a.m.-5 p.m. Tues.-Sat., 12 p.m.-5 p.m. Sun. Guided tours on Wed., Sat. and Sun. at 1.30 p.m.

Santa Barbara Museum of Art. 1130 State St.; (805) 963-4364. One of the finest small museums in the country, with permanent and changing exhibits. Houses works of Monet, Matisse, Chagall and Kadinsky, among others, as well as contemporary art. Also on display are photographic exhibits, African and

Oriental art, and Greek, Italian and Egyptian sculpture. A newer wing of the museum houses another gallery, a discovery center for children, and cafe and gift shop. Museum hours: 11 a.m.-5 p.m. Tues.-Sat., noon- 5 p.m. Sun, closed Mon. Admission fees: $5.00 adults, $3.00 seniors, $2.00 children (ages 6-17), children under 6 are free.

Mission Santa Barbara. Located at the top end of Laguna Street; (805) 682-4713. This is the 10th of California's 21 Spanish missions, founded in 1786; it is also the only one of the missions with two identical towers, billed as the "Queen of the Missions." Superb mission museum, with an extensive collection of mission artifacts, and old, historic photographs depicting the building of the mission. The mission also has a small garden at the rear, with exotic trees and plants from all over the world. Open daily, 9 a.m. -5 p.m.; admission: $3.00 adults.

Santa Barbara Museum of Natural History. 2559 Puesta de Sol Rd.; (805) 682-4711. Excellent dioramas of the life and ways of native Chumash Indians, as well as the ocean shelf between the Santa Barbara coast and the Channel Islands. Also, outstanding exhibits of Santa Barbara's geology, birds, insects, flora and marine life. The museum complex includes a research library, laboratories, educational facilities, and the Gladwin Planetarium which has regular public programs (call 682-4334 for program information). Museum hours: 9-5 Mon.-Sat., 10-5 Sun. Guided tours available on Sundays at 2 p.m. Admission fees: $5.00 adults, $4.00 seniors, $3.00 children.

El Paseo Plaza. Charming old Spanish-style shopping arcade, housed in the historic De La Guerra Adobe, dating from 1826. Features a courtyard restaurant, sidewalk cafe, import and specialty shops, and art galleries. The arcade runs from Anacapa Street through to State Street. Shops and cafe open daily, usually around 10 a.m.

Stearns Wharf. The wharf is really a three-block-long extension of State Street, built in 1873 and claimed to be the oldest operating wharf on the West Coast. It features gift and souvenir shops, kiosks, fish markets, and seafood restaurants. A *Sea Center* at the wharf has displays of native marine life, a touch tank, undersea dioramas and shipwreck remnants; it is open 11 a.m.-5 p.m. Mon.-Fri., 10 a.m.- 5 p.m. Sat.-Sun. Admission: $3.00 adults, $2.00 seniors, $1.50 children; (805) 962-0885. The wharf also has pier fishing and fishing boat charters. (805) 564-5518.

Andree Clark Bird Refuge. 1400 E. Cabrillo Blvd. (near Hwy. 101). Refuge set amid 42 acres of lush gardens and lagoon; features several varieties of freshwater fowl. Walking and bicycling trails around lagoon. (805) 564-5433.

Moreton Bay Fig Tree. Cnr. Chapala St. and Hwy. 101. Amazing old fig tree, believed to be the largest of its kind in America, with a branch spread of nearly 165 feet. It is claimed that more than 10,000 people can stand in its shade at noon! The tree was originally planted here by a pioneer family in 1877. Moreton Bay Figs are native to Australia.

Fernald House and Trussell-Winchester Adobe. 0414 W. Montecito St. Adjoining historic houses, open to public viewing. The first of these, Fernald House, is a multi-gabled 14-room Victorian mansion, superbly furnished with period antiques; the other, the Trussell-Winchester Adobe, adjacent to the Fernald House, dates from 1854 and is built from adobe bricks and timber taken from the Winfield Scott, a ship wrecked off the shores of Santa Barbara. Both houses are open on the first Sundays of each month, 2-4; admission $1.00. For more information, call (805) 966-1601.

Hope Ranch. Las Palmas Dr. This is Santa Barbara's most exclusive residential area, situated just to the west of town, amid rolling hills and huge, century-old palms. Features a private golf and country club, with a lagoon.

Yacht Harbor and Breakwater. West Cabrillo Blvd. Half-mile-long breakwater, built around a 1,200-berth harbor for working and pleasure craft.

Boat rentals, marine supply stores, restaurants and shops. A paved walkway along the breakwater offers good city and harbor views.

Santa Barbara Carriage House and Western Arts Museum. Pershing Park, 129 Castillo St.; (805) 962-2353. View vintage horse-drawn carriages from Santa Barbara's pioneer days. Also on display is one of the largest collections of saddles and carriages in the United States. Open daily 9 a.m.- 4 p.m.

Santa Barbara Zoological Gardens. 500 Ninos Dr. (just off E. Cabrillo Blvd.). Excellent small zoo, situated on a hill overlooking the ocean and adjacent Andree Clark Bird Refuge. Beautiful gardens; also picnic area and snack bar, children's playground, petting farm, botanical garden, sealarium, and miniature train. Admission: $6.00 adults, $4.00 children and seniors. Open daily 10-5. For information, call (805) 962-5339.

El Presidio de Santa Barbara. 122 E. Canon Perdido St. Site of the last of California's four Spanish presidios, established in 1782. The old *adobe barracks*—part of the original presidio—are still intact, open to public viewing. Also visit reconstructed *Presidio Chapel*. Across the street from the presidio site is *El Cuartel* (the guard's house), another small but lovely adobe, built in the 1780s and now housing a gift shop featuring Santa Barbara souvenirs. Open 10.30-4.30 daily. Free admission. For more information, call (805) 966-9719.

Santa Barbara Botanic Garden. 1212 Mission Canyon Rd.; (805) 682-4726. Splendid 65-acre botanic gardens, featuring California trees, shrubs, flowers and cacti in natural settings. The gardens are divided into 12 sections depicting the different natural habitats of California, such as the Redwoods Section, Woodlands Section, Meadow Section, Desert Section, Island Section, and a Canyon Section which has in it an historic aqueduct and dam, built by native Indians in 1806 to supply water to the Mission. Five miles of foot trails; garden shop on premises. Open weekdays 9 a.m. - 5 p.m., weekends 9 a.m. - 6 p.m.; guided tours on Thurs., Sat. and Sun. at 10.30 a.m. and 2 p.m. Free admission.

University of California, Santa Barbara. Situated at the end of Ward Memorial Highway, Isla Vista. Delightful campus, with architect-designed buildings, tree-lined paths, ocean views, beach and lagoon. Visitor passes and campus maps available at university gate.

Brooks Institute of Photography. 1321 Alameda Padre Serra. Renowned institute of photography. View works of students as well as internationally-acclaimed photographers at the institute gallery. Open Mon.-Fri., 8 a.m. - 5 p.m. (805) 966-3888.

Montecito Village. Located at the northwestern end of Santa Barbara. This is one of America's most luxurious residential communities, with lavish mansions—homes of the rich and famous—tucked away in the hills among age-old palms. Montecito's small shopping district is famous for its antique stores and art galleries, and the Montecito Country Club, just to the south of the village, is also worth viewing, believed to be one of the most exclusive private clubs on the West Coast.

South Coast Railroad Museum. 300 N. Los Carneros Rd., Goleta; (805) 964-3540. Working exhibits of railroad signaling and other communications equipment. Museum and bookshop on premises. The depot also houses the Goleta Chamber of Commerce, and in October each year it provides the setting for the Old Goleta Days Festival. Additionally, miniature train rides are offered Wed. and Fri., 2-3.30 p.m., Sat. and Sun. 1.15-3.45 p.m. The museum is open Wed.-Sun., 1-4 p.m.

Santa Barbara Orchid Estate. 1250 Orchid Drive, Goleta; (805) 967-1284. One-acre outdoor gardens, with an additional acre of greenhouses, dedicated to growing orchids. Open Mon.-Sat. 8 a.m. - 4.30 p.m., Sun. 11 a.m. - 4 p.m.

Channel Islands. Chain of islands lying off the coast of Santa Barbara, 11-40 miles distant, comprising San Miguel, Santa Rosa, Anacapa, and Santa Cruz, the largest. The islands are a designated National Monument—part of the National Parks System—and the surrounding waters a National Marine Sanctuary. Primitive camping facilities are available on one or two of the islands, although these are mostly for day use only. View unique trees and wildflowers, and brown pelicans, sea lions and a variety of sea birds indigenous to the islands. Scheduled excursions to some of the islands depart from the Channel Islands National Park headquarters at Ventura Harbor, 20 miles south of Santa Barbara. The park office is open 8-5 daily; for information and reservations, call (805) 644-8262.

Beaches. Santa Barbara has several good beaches in and around the city. From west to east, these include—*El Capital State Beach,* 15 miles northwest of town, which features camping, picnicking, boat rentals, and boat launching facilities; *Isla Vista Beach,* which adjoins the U.C. Santa Barbara campus; *Goleta Beach County Park,* where there is an excellent, sheltered swimming beach, with good pier fishing and picnicking possibilities; and *Arroyo Burro Beach,* on the western outskirts of Santa Barbara, which offers swimming, surfing and surf-fishing opportunities. *Leadbetter Beach,* situated directly below Santa Barbara's Breakwater, offers some of the best surfing in the area; while *West Beach* and *East Beach,* lying adjacent to Stearns Wharf (one on either side), have swimming, sunbathing, windsurfing and boating, with boat rentals available at West Beach as well. 10 miles southwest of Santa Barbara, off Hwy. 101, is *Carpinteria State Beach,* a gently-sloping sandy beach, with good swimming, camping, picnicking, boating and pier fishing possibilities.

RECREATION

Boating. Boating and water sports are popular recreational activities in Santa Barbara. Several operators offer boat rentals, charters, whale watching and harbor cruises, island excursions, sport fishing trips, and a variety of sailing, cocktail and dinner cruises. Prices usually range from $20.00-$35.00 per hour to $55.00-$150.00 for the whole day. For rentals, charters and cruises, contact any of the following: *Santa Barbara Boat Rental/Santa Barbara Sailing Center,* at the Breakwater, (805) 962-2826; *Hornet Sportfishing,* 125 Harbor Way, (805) 966-2212; *Captain Don's Whale Watching,* at Stearns Wharf, (805) 969-5217/969-0272; *Sea Landing,* Cabrillo at Bath, (805) 963-3564; *Sunset Kidd's,* at the Breakwater, (805) 962-8222; *OceanAdventures,* 10 Breakwater, (805) 682-7501.

Scuba Diving. *Divers Den,* at 22 Anacapa St., has equipment rentals and lessons; phone (805) 963-8917. Diving instruction and equipment rentals are also available at *Underwater Sports,* at the Breakwater, (805) 962-5400; *Anacapa Dive Center,* 22 Anacapa St., (805) 963-8917; *California Watersports/Santa Barbara Scuba School,* 5822 Holister Ave., (805) 964-0830; and *Aquatics,* 5708 Hollister Ave., (805) 967-4456.

Windsurfing. There are several shops in the area offering sailboard rentals and lessons. Rates are generally around $10.00 per hour for equipment rentals, and $10.00 for a lesson. Area shops specializing in sailboard rentals and lessons include *Sundance Ocean Sports,* 809 State St., (805) 966-2474/(805) 963-6969; and *Mountain Air Sports,* 14 State St., (805) 962-0049.

Hang Gliding. *Santa Barbara Hang Gliding Center,* (805) 963-4422. Hang gliding instruction on sand dunes; cost: $59.00 for one-day introduction course, $125.00 for 3-day course. *Hang Glider Emporium,* (805) 965-3733. Lessons given on 200-foot training hill; rates upon request.

Horseback Riding. Riding stables in the Santa Barbara area offer a good selection of trail rides, moonlight and overnight rides, breakfast rides, and picnic and beach rides. Rates usually range from $15.00 to $25.00 per hour; advance bookings are required at most of the stables. Area stables include: *Circle Bar B Riding Stables,* 1800 Refugio Rd., Goleta, (805) 968-3901; *San Ysidro Stables,* 900 San Ysidro Lane, (805) 969-5046; *Rancho Oso Stables,* Paradise Rd., (805) 683-5110.

Polo. *Santa Barbara Polo Club.* 3375 Foothill Rd., Carpenteria; (805) 684-8667. Games held on Sundays, April-Oct.

Bicycling. *Beach Rentals,* 22 State St.; (805) 966-6733. Bicycle rentals; also tandems, mountain bikes and roller skates. Open daily 7.30 a.m.-8.00 p.m. *Bike n Hike,* 1170 Coast Village Rd., Montecito; (805) 969-0719. Bicycle rentals and sales. Hours: 10 a.m.-6 p.m., Mon.-Sat. *Cycles-4-Rent,* 101 State St.; (805) 966-3804. *Isla Vista Bike Boutique,* 880 Embarcadero Del Mar, Goleta, (805) 968-3338.

Golf. There are four public golf courses in the Santa Barbara area. *Sandpiper Golf Course,* 7925 Hollister Ave., Goleta; (805) 968-1541. 18 holes, driving range; green fees (including cart): $80.00 weekdays, $120.00 weekends. *Santa Barbara Community Course,* Las Positas Rd. and McCaw Ave.; (805) 687-7087. 18 holes, driving range; green fees: $25.00 weekdays, $35.00 weekends. *Ocean Meadows Golf Course,* 6925 Whittier St., Goleta; (805) 968-6814. 9 holes, driving range; green fees: $15.00 weekdays, $17.00 weekends. *Twin Lakes Golf Course,* 6034 Hollister Ave., Goleta; (805) 964-1414. 9 holes, driving range; green fees: $8.00 weekdays, $9.00 weekends; senior rates available.

Tours. *Santa Barbara Trolley Co.,* 120 State St., offers regularly scheduled tours of downtown Santa Barbara and the waterfront in restored trolley cars; schedule and information on (805) 965-0353. *Personal Tours, Ltd.* (805) 685-0552. Guided tours of Santa Barbara, wine country and the coast.

RESTAURANTS

(Restaurant prices—based on full course dinner, excluding drinks, tax and tips—are categorized as follows: *Deluxe,* over $30; *Expensive,* $20-$30; *Moderate,* $10-$20; *Inexpensive,* under $10.)

Bistro 11 11. *Expensive-Deluxe.* Housed in the Radisson Hotel, 1111 E. Cabrillo Blvd.; (805) 963-0744. Features California-style cuisine; also pasta, steak, seafood, chicken and roast duck. Open daily for breakfast, lunch and dinner. Reservations recommended. Live entertainment.

The Chart House. *Expensive-Deluxe.* 101 E. Cabrillo Blvd.; (805) 966-2112. Long-standing Santa Barbara institution. Menu features fresh seafood selections, steaks and prime rib, salads, and delicious homemade desserts. Open for dinner nightly. Reservations advised.

China City. *Moderate.* 5688 Calle Real, Goleta; (805) 692-9954. Chinese restaurant, serving Mandarin and Szechuan cuisine. Offers a variety of vegetarian entrees. Open for lunch buffet Mon.-Fri., dinner daily.

China Pavilion. *Moderate.* 1070 Coast Village Rd., Montecito; (805) 565-9380. Chinese cuisine. Heated patio for outdoor dining. Open for lunch and dinner daily.

Citronelle. *Expensive-Deluxe.* At the Santa Barbara Inn, cnr. E. Cabrillo Blvd. and Milpas St.; (805) 963-4717. Charming restaurant atop the Santa Barbara Inn, offering panoramic ocean views. Menu emphasizes French-California cuisine, prepared with the freshest ingredients. Open for breakfast, lunch and dinner daily; brunch on Sundays. Reservations advised.

Eladio's Restaurant. *Expensive.* Cnr. State St. and Cabrillo Blvd.; (805) 963-4466. Continental and Italian cuisine, including veal, pasta dishes, steak, fresh, local seafood, and game. Overlooking Stearns Wharf. Open for breakfast, lunch and dinner, Tues.-Sun. Reservations recommended.

The Harbor Restaurant. *Moderate-Expensive.* On Stearns Wharf; (805) 963-3311. Well-known waterfront restaurant with outdoor deck, offering unobstructed harbor and ocean views. Menu features fresh local and East Coast seafood specialties; also steaks and pasta dishes. Cocktail lounge; live entertainment. Open for lunch, dinner, and Sunday brunch. Reservations advised on weekends.

Harry's. *Moderate-Expensive.* In the Albertson's Shopping Center, Upper State St and Las Positas; (805) 687-9455. Popular restaurant and bar, serving seafood, steaks and prime rib; also sandwiches, and salads and pasta dishes. Open daily for lunch and dinner. Reservations recommended.

Josie's Fourwinds Restaurant & Lounge. *Moderate-Expensive.* 3435 State St.; (805) 682-5174. American cuisine, featuring steak, seafood, pasta, prime rib, veal, salads and sandwiches; also some Mexican entrees. Live music and dancing nightly. Open for breakfast, lunch and dinner.

La Marina. *Deluxe.* At the Santa Barbara Four Seasons Biltmore, 1260 Channel Dr., Montecito; (805) 969-2261. Elegant, ocean-view restaurant, serving California cuisine with a Mediterranean flavor. Open for dinner only. Reservations required. Jackets mandatory for gentlemen.

Mariann's ItalianVilla. *Moderate.* 361 Hitchcock Way; (805) 682-6408. Family-style Italian restaurant, featuring homemade sausage, pizza, gnocchi and pasta; also Steaks and seafood. Open for dinner daily.

The Original Enterprise Fish Co. *Moderate-Expensive.* 225 State St. (cnr. Hwy. 101); (805) 962-3313. Fresh local seafood, prepared over a mesquite grill. Specialties include clam chowder, shrimp, crab salads, and oysters; also some chicken dishes, steaks and burgers. Wharf setting. Lunch and dinner daily.

The Palace Cafe. *Moderate-Expensive.* 8 E. Cota St.; (805) 966-3133. Italian, Cajun and Creole cooking. Dinner nightly, breakfast on weekends.

Paradise Cafe. *Inexpensive-Moderate.* 702 Anacapa St.; (805) 962-4416. Local favorite, featuring oakwood-grilled steaks, fresh seafood and other traditional American fare. The restaurant is housed in an old building, decorated with 40's wall murals and neon signs. Open for lunch and dinner; breakfast on Sundays.

Patio Restaurant. *Moderate-Expensive.* At the Santa Barbara Four Seasons Biltmore Hotel, 1260 Channel Dr., Montecito; (805) 969-2261. Casual atmosphere. Seafood and pasta dishes. Breakfast, lunch and dinner daily.

Petrini's. *Moderate.* 14 W. Calle Laureles; (805) 687-8888. Family-style Italian restaurant, featuring homemade ravioli, lasagna, spaghetti, cannelloni, manicotti, and Italian sausages; also custom pizzas. Lunch and dinner daily.

State Street Cafe. *Moderate.* 3524 State St.; (805) 682-7848. Casual restaurant, serving soups, salads, sandwiches, and home-style meals such as roast turkey, meat loaf, pork ribs, and fish and chips. Open for lunch and dinner daily.

Stonehouse Restaurant. *Expensive-Deluxe.* At San Ysidro Ranch, 900 San Ysidro Lane; (805) 969-4100. Continental cuisine, served in a candlelit atmosphere. Breakfast, lunch and dinner daily; also Sunday brunch. Reservations required; jackets mandatory for gentlemen at dinner.

Woody's BBQ. *Inexpensive-Moderate.* 5112 Holister Ave., Goleta; (805) 967-3775. Casual restaurant, serving chicken, ribs, burgers and sandwiches; also salad bar. Open for lunch and dinner daily.

SANTA CRUZ

"Surf City, USA"

Santa Cruz is of course the original "Surf City," a popular seaside resort noted for its sand, sun, surf and oceanfront amusement park, visited by nearly 2 million tourists each year, mostly during the summer months, and mostly the young. The city has plenty in it to see and do, with more than a dozen beaches, scores of surf shops, and several good accommodations and restaurants. It also boasts a surprisingly large collection of preserved, old Victorian homes, and a university well worth seeing, nestled amid redwoods and pasturelands, and quite possibly among the loveliest campuses in California.

The city of Santa Cruz is located along the northern end of Monterey Bay, roughly 80 miles south of San Francisco by way of either the coastal route, Highway 1, or a combination of Highway 101 (or 280)—south to San Jose—and Route 17, southwestward.

DISCOVERING SANTA CRUZ

Santa Cruz has a prescribed, 29-mile "Tree-Sea" tour of the city and its sights, with posted blue-and-white signs to go by, as well as three or four "Victorian Home" tours, mostly self-guided, with good maps for these available from the local visitors' bureau or one of the city museums. But if you wish to capture the true flavor of Santa Cruz, it is necessary, first of all, to go to the waterfront, where there are four beautiful, white sand beaches, some splendid ocean walks, a municipal wharf which has open-air fish markets and an array of seafood restaurants and gift shops, and—best of all—a vintage boardwalk where there is a Coney Island-type amusement park. This last, of course, is the star attraction of Santa Cruz, originally built in 1907 and believed to be the only such seaside amusement park on the West Coast. Here you will find game arcades, food concessions, souvenir shops, and twenty-five most thrilling rides, including a half-mile-long roller-coaster, the Giant Dipper, which is built entirely from wood, utilizing some 327,000 board feet of lumber (nearly half that required to build a small town!).

Near at hand, adjacent to the Boardwalk, is the grand old Cocoanut Grove Ballroom, the last remaining Victorian-style ballroom in Northern California, where big bands still play to thrill the young-at-heart. The ballroom was built at about the same time as the Boardwalk, in 1907, and in 1983 it underwent a $10-million renovation and conversion to a banquet and convention center. A highlight of the Cocoanut Grove is its dome-topped restaurant, the Sun Room, which features an outsized movable glass roof that can be opened for a unique outdoor dining experience.

The mile-long sandy beach at the Boardwalk is the Santa Cruz Beach, the most popular of them all, stretching from the mouth of the San Lorenzo River—where frolicking rafters can often be seen—to the Municipal Pier farther west, beyond which lies the smaller but equally attractive Cowell Beach. Both beaches have volleyball courts, on-duty lifeguards, and swimming, surfing and sunbathing.

Two other beaches, Natural Bridges State Beach and Twin Lakes State Beach, lie to the west and east of the Santa Cruz Beach, respectively. The Natural Bridges beach, which is about a mile or so from the Boardwalk and where there actually two or three natural, rock bridges, has a bonus. Near to it, at the west end of Delaware Avenue, and also of interest, is the Long Marine Laboratory, part of the research facility of the Santa Cruz university, which has public tours of its aquarium and other marine exhibits, and a display of a skeleton of an 85-foot California blue whale. Also try to see the West Cliff Lighthouse at Lighthouse Point on West Cliff Drive, more or less midway between the Boardwalk and the Natural Bridges beach. It has in it a surfing museum, filled with surfing memorabilia, including old, wooden surfboards and vintage photographs of well-known surfers from previous decades, and on-going video films on surfing.

It is also an excellent idea, we might add, to drive east a little way from the Boardwalk, on East Cliff Drive, which climbs sharply

SANTA CRUZ

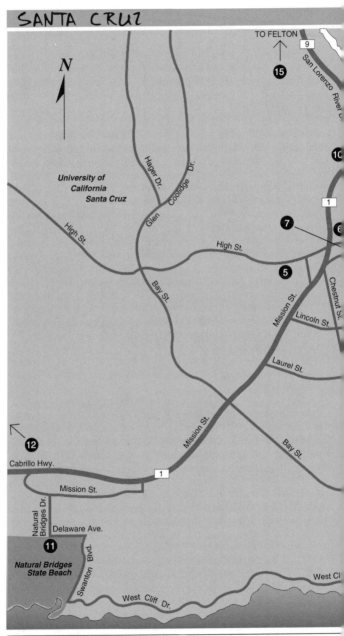

1. Santa Cruz Beach
   Boardwalk
2. Cocoanut Grove
3. Santa Cruz
   Surfing Museum
4. Museum of Natural
   History
5. Mission Hill
6. Mission Santa Cruz
7. Mission State
   Historic Park

SANTA CRUZ

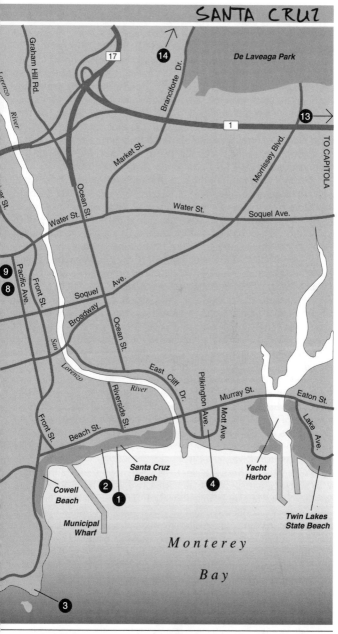

to a point directly above the mouth of the San Lorenzo River, where there is a grassy headland with superb views of the Santa Cruz Beach, boardwalk, Cocoanut Grove, the Municipal Pier, Cowell Beach, and Lighthouse Point. Nearby, at the corner of East Cliff Drive and Pilkington Avenue you can search out the Santa Cruz Museum, which has displays of native birds and fossils and Indian basketry, and a tidepool containing starfish and sea anemones. Farther still are the Santa Cruz Harbor—home to over 800 small craft—and the Twin Lakes State Beach which has a lagoon that is a wildfowl refuge. These last two, however, are not accessible on East Cliff Drive directly; it is necessary to go north a short distance to Murray Street, and east again, passing over the harbor, then southeastward on Lake Avenue and the continuation of East Cliff Drive to the Twin Lake beach.

In any event, north of the waterfront lies downtown Santa Cruz, which also has something in it of interest to the visitor. The place to visit here is of course Pacific Avenue, between Water and Lincoln streets. It is a delightful, newly-redeveloped part of town, tree-lined and with wide sidewalks—built on the site of the old Pacific Garden Mall which was devastated in the 1989 Loma Prieta earthquake—designed essentially for the pedestrian. It not only has good shops, galleries, restaurants, outdoor cafes, and hot-dog stands at intervals, but also 1960s style street entertainers and musicians—guitar in hand, singing for a dime. At the Water Street end of the mall stands an old, restored clock-tower, well worth seeing, and somewhere near the center, just off Pacific Avenue on Cooper Street, you can visit a most unique, eight-sided red-brick building, the Octagon House, dating from 1882. The Octagon House is open to public viewing and features changing art and historic exhibits.

North still is Mission Hill, a good place to view old Victorian homes—some of the city's finest, located mainly on Mission and High streets and Escalona Drive—and where, equally importantly, there is a replica of the Mision la Exaltacion de la Santa Cruz, the twelfth of California's twenty-one missions founded by Franciscan fathers. The old mission was originally built upon the very same site, overlooking the San Lorenzo River, in 1791.

Yet another curiosity to amaze and delight you, some three miles or so northeast of town, off Branciforte Drive, is the frequently famous Mystery Spot. Here, in a circle roughly 150 feet in diameter, balls roll uphill, trees grow sideways, and people are unable to stand upright. It is indeed a strange phenomenon, that completely defies the laws of gravity. Guided tours of the circle are available daily, 10 a.m.-5 p.m.

Before leaving Santa Cruz, take the time also to visit the University of California, Santa Cruz, one of the loveliest in the state, lying at the northwest edge of town, on a wooded hillside, reached primarily on High Street. The university has good programs for the performing and visual arts, as well as social and natural sciences, applied sciences and communications courses. But the great attraction here, for students and visitors alike, has to be the campus itself, with modern, architect-designed buildings tucked away among groves of noble redwoods, and surrounded, quite randomly, by the equally lovely, rolling pasturelands. Detailed maps of the campus can be obtained at the university, together with directions for touring the wooded grounds.

DETOURS

Some three or four miles east of Santa Cruz, also worth visiting, is picturesque Capitola, the oldest seaside village in California, dating from 1880. It has some fine Victorian homes and smaller, brightly colored cottages. It also has abundant opportunities for shopping, dining, and fishing. But much of the action here is centered around the Capitola Beach—which has a freshwater lagoon and an ancient, 150-year-old wharf—and the Esplanade, along which are to be found several well-liked bars and restaurants, including the monstrously popular Margaritaville. Two other beaches, New Brighton and Seacliff, lie just east of Capitola, a mile or two distant. Both have camping facilities, and Seacliff has an added attraction—a unique pier, made up of a 435-foot-long cement ship, the *Palo Alto*.

Felton, 10 miles north on Highway 9, is another favorite tourist haunt. Its claim to fame is of course its historic Roaring Camp, originally founded in the 1880s, and where steam trains now offer rides to visitors through miles of unspoiled redwood forest, with barbecues and frontier music. North of Felton in the San Lorenzo Valley are the tiny, rustic towns of Ben Lomond and Boulder Creek, the latter with a handful of shops strung along its main street (Highway 9), where local artisans display and sell their handicrafts.

For farm visitors, a place of interest is Watsonville, some 18 miles east of Santa Cruz; it has fall apples, and ollalie berries, black-berries and strawberries in summer. There are some good back roads here, meandering through the rolling orchard country surrounding nearby Freedom and Corralitos. Also to be recommended is a journey northeast from Watsonville to Gilroy ("Garlic Capital of the World"), by way of scenic Hecker Pass (Highway 152). There are a dozen or so small, mountain wineries along this route, open to the public for wine tasting and sales.

HOW TO GET THERE

There are several different routes leading from San Francisco to Santa Cruz, which lies approximately 80 miles to the south, at the northern corner of picturesque Monterey Bay. The most commonly used is, of course, *Highway 101*—or *Highway 280*—southeast to Santa Clara (47 miles), then directly south on *Highway 17*, 13 miles, to Santa Cruz.

A more scenic, though somewhat longer, route is by way of *Highway 1*, south along the coast, to Santa Cruz. It is approximately 84 miles by way of the coastal route.

TOURIST INFORMATION

Santa Cruz County Conference & Visitors Council. 701 Front St., Santa Cruz; (831) 425-1234/(800) 833-3494. Variety of tourist brochures and free publications; also maps for walking tours of Victorian homes, and museum guide. Accommodations and restaurants guides, calendar of events.

Capitola Chamber of Commerce. 621B Capitola Ave., Capitola; (831) 475-6522. Maps and tourist literature, including information on the famous Begonia Festival and other annual events.

ACCOMMODATIONS

Bed & Breakfast Inns

Apple Lane Inn. *$95-$150.* 6265 Soquel Dr., Aptos; (831) 475-6868. Beautifully restored Victorian farmhouse, set among vineyards and orchards. 5 rooms, some with private baths. Full breakfast, with homemade muffins, breads, eggs, fresh fruit and juice. No smoking.

Babbling Brook Inn. *$120-$195.* 1025 Laurel St.; (831) 427-2437. 13 guest apartments with balconies and fireplaces; also private baths, TV and phones. Parlor and registration areas date from the early 1900s. Full breakfast.

Chateau Victorian. *$110-$140.* 118 First St.; (831) 458-9458. 7 comfortable rooms in one of Santa Cruz's turn- of-the-century homes. Lovely ocean views; close to beach, wharf and Boardwalk. Continental breakfast, with fresh fruit, croissants and muffins; wine and cheese in the evening. No smoking.

Cliff Crest. *$95-$150.* 407 Cliff St.; (831) 427-2609. 1890s home in garden setting, built by former Lieutenant Governor of California, William Jeter. 5 antique-filled rooms with private baths; complimentary wine and cheese. Central location.

The Darling House. *$95-$225.* 314 West Cliff Dr.; (831) 458-1958. Spanish Revival-style home near Lighthouse Point, with views of wharf and boardwalk areas. 6 rooms, most with fireplaces; also one cottage behind the main house, with accommodations for four. The house dates from 1910.

Davenport Cashstore Bed & Breakfast. *$70-$125*. 31 Davenport Ave., Davenport; (831) 425-1818. 12 rooms, decorated with antiques; private balconies with ocean views. Gift shop and casual restaurant on premises. Buffet breakfast. No smoking.

Mangels House. *$115-$150*. 570 Aptos Creek Rd., Aptos; (831) 688-7982. Beautifully restored 1880s Southern Mansion, former home of industrialist Claus Mangels. Wooded setting. 6 rooms, all with private baths. Full breakfast.

Hotels and Motels

All Suites Inn BestWestern. *$75-$165*. 500 Ocean St.; (831) 426-8333/ (800) 528-1234. 40 units, with TV, phones, refrigerators and microwave ovens; some ocean-view rooms, with fireplaces. Also pool, and jacuzzi. Continental breakfast.

Best Western Inn. *$65-$195*. 126 Plymouth St.; (831) 425-4717/(800) 528-1234. 26 units; TV, phones, hot tub and sauna.

Best Western Torch-Lite Inn. *$559-$149*. 500 Riverside Ave.; (831) 426-7575/(800) 528-1234. 38 units; TV, phones, pool. Also 9-hole putting green.

Candlelite Inn. *$49-$125*. 1101 Ocean St.; (831) 427-1616. 42 units, with TV and phones; non-smoking rooms available. Restaurant; pool.

Carousel Motel. *$49-$159*. 110 Riverside Ave.; (831) 425-7090. Located directly across from the beach and Boardwalk. 34 rooms with balconies; TV and phones.

Casa Blanca Motel. *$78-$300*. 101 Main St.; (831) 423-1570. 34 units, some with fireplaces and private balconies with ocean views. TV, phones; gourmet restaurant on premises.

Comfort Inn. *$49-$129*. 110 Plymouth St.; (831) 426-2664. 52 units; TV, phones, wet bars and refrigerators; some fireplaces. Pool, spa and sauna. Complimentary breakfast.

Edgewater Beach Motel. *$69-$245*. 525 Second St.; (831) 423-0440. 20 units, some with ocean views; also some fireplaces. TV, phones, pool.

Harbor Lights Motel. *$75-$125*. 5000 Cliff Dr., Capitola; (831) 476-0505. 10 units; TV, phones, and private balconies with views of Capitola Beach and Monterey Bay. Also some suites with fireplaces. Centrally located.

Holiday Inn. *$79-$149*. 611 Ocean St.; (831) 426-7100/(800) 241-1555. 170 rooms; TV, phones, pool, jacuzzi, coffee shop, restaurant and cocktail lounge. Non-smoking rooms available.

Holiday Inn Express. *$69-$149*. 600 Riverside Ave.; (831) 458-9660/ (800) 527-3833/(800) 465-4329. 80 units with TV and phones; some balconies. Also pool, and spas. Continental breakfast.

The Inn at Pasatiempo. *$75-$195*. 555 Hwy. 17; (831) 423-5000. 56 units, including 4 suites; TV, phones, pool and restaurant. Complimentary breakfast. Located adjacent to golf course.

Mission Inn. *$65-$100*. 2250 Mission St.; (831) 425-5455. 42 units, including 4 suites; phones, TV, hot tub, sauna. Some non-smoking rooms.

Ocean Echo Motel & Cottages. *$65-$95*. 401 Johans Beach Dr.; (831) 462-4192. 4 units, 5 studios, 6 cottages. Kitchenette units available; also some units with balconies and views. TV, phones; private beach.

Ramada Inn. *$45-$175*. 130 W. Cliff Dr.; (831) 423-7737. Located across from the beach and Boardwalk. 28 rooms, some with ocean views; jacuzzi.

Santa Cruz Travelodge. *$62-139*. 525 Ocean St.; (831) 426-2300/(800) 255-3050. 55 units; phones, TV, pool, non-smoking rooms. Handicapped facilities.

Seacliff Inn-BestWestern. *$75-$135*. 7500 Old Dominion Court, Aptos;

(831) 688-7300/(800) 367-2003. 140 units; TV and phones, restaurant, cocktail lounge, spa, pool, putting green, and fish pond. Non-smoking rooms available.

Travelodge Riviera. *$55-$125.* 619 Riverside Ave.; (831) 423-9515/(800) 255-3050. 62 units, including 20 suites, and some kitchenette units. Phones and TV; hot tub, spa, pool, non-smoking rooms.

West Coast Santa Cruz Hotel. *$129-$309.* 175 W. Cliff Dr.; (831) 426-4330/(800) 662-3838. 163-room beachfront hotel; TV, phones, private balconies with bay views. Jacuzzi, pool, and 2 restaurants. Non-smoking rooms available.

SEASONAL EVENTS

February. *Santa Cruz Baroque Festival.* At the First Congregational Church. Festival runs February through May, and features recitals of baroque music. For a complete schedule, call (831) 426-9693. *Clam Chowder Cook-Off.* Held at the Santa Cruz Beach Boardwalk. Decorated booths and food stalls, featuring Manhattan- and Boston-style clam chowder. More information on (831) 429-3477.

March. *Jazz on the Wharf.* At the Santa Cruz Municipal Pier. Annual event, featuring several local and national jazz performers. For a schedule, call (831) 429-3477.

April. *Spring Wildflower Show.* At the Santa Cruz City Museum, Thursday through Sunday. Display of several hundred wildflowers native to California. (831) 429-3773.

May. *Annual Longboard Club Invitational.* 4th weekend. Surfing competitions, featuring some of the country's best-known surfers; held at Cowell Beach; (831) 429-3477. *Harbor Festival & Boat Show.* At the Santa Cruz Yacht Harbor; 4th week of the month. Boat show and boat parade; dinghy, bathtub, kayak, and sailboat races; also live music, food concessions, booths selling boating equipment, and arts and crafts show. Free admission. *West Coast Antique Fly-In and Air Show.* 4th weekend; Watsonville Airport. Second largest antique fly-in and air show in the nation. View antique planes, military aircraft and experimental craft. Daily airshows and aerobatic displays. Admission: $7.00 adults, $4.00 children. For more information, call (831) 496-9559.

June. *Jose Cuervo Volleyball Tournament.* Santa Cruz Beach. 32 of the world's best 2-man beach volleyball teams compete for $20,000 in prize money. (213) 450-4417. *Strawberry Festival.* At Santa Cruz County Fairgrounds in Watsonville. Two-day festival, celebrating the area's strawberry harvest. Live entertainment, arts and crafts show, 10-kilometer run, and strawberries prepared in every imaginable way. (831) 688-3384.

July. *Fourth of July Celebration.* Harvey West Park; (831) 429-4377. Festivities include a chili cook-off and Firecracker 10-kilometer race. *Aptos 4th of July Parade.* In downtown Aptos. Shortest 4th of July parade in the nation—100 yards. Residents and visitors alike participate, dressed in colorful costumes. Phone (831) 688-2428. *Shakespeare/Santa Cruz Festival.* Performances July through September at the performing arts center at U.C. Santa Cruz. Conventional performances of Shakespearean plays by professional theater groups; outdoor theater settings. Also some workshops. Advance ticket reservations recommended; (831) 429-2121. *Beach Street Revival.* At Beach Street and the Boardwalk; 3rd weekend. 50's and 60's nostalgic festival, with a 50's-style rock 'n roll dance at Cocoanut Grove. Other events include a Miss Beach Street contest, the Soho Soda Grand Cruise Car Parade, and a car show and auction. For a schedule of events, call (831) 438-1957. *Wharf to Wharf Run.* 4th weekend of the month. 10,000 runners take part in a 6-mile run along the coast, from the Santa Cruz Wharf to the Capitola Wharf. Famous beach party with refreshments at the finish. Entry fee: $10.00. For more information, call (831) 475-2196.

August. *Cabrillo Music Festival.* Held at Mission San Juan Bautista; 3rd and 4th weeks. Performances by nationally-known artists; classical, jazz and pop music. Advance reservations advised. Call (831) 426-6966 for reservations and schedule. *International Calamari Festival.* Month-long celebration of the annual migration of the calamari (squid) into Monterey Bay. Variety of entertainment, both at the Municipal Wharf and the India Joze Restaurant at 1001 Center St.; squid inspired food. More information on (831) 427-3554.

September. *National Begonia Festival.* 2nd week of the month; at Capitola Beach. Fun-filled event, with sand sculpture competition, fishing derby and rowboat races, and a nautical parade in which begonia-laden rafts race down the river toward the beach. For a program and more information, call (831) 475-6522/476-3476. *Santa Cruz County Fair.* Also during the 2nd week of the month, at the Santa Cruz County Fairgrounds, Watsonville. Events include a carnival, music, arts and crafts, refreshments, agricultural exhibits, and a wine competition. (831) 688-3384/724-3476. *Northern California Men's Beach Volleyball Tournament.* Held at Capitola Beach; 2nd weekend. Several top teams from Northern California compete for a variety of prizes. For a schedule, call (831) 462-2365.

October. *Brussels Sprout Festival.* Held at the Boardwalk, during the 2nd weekend of the month. Celebration of the area's rich Brussels sprouts harvest. Sprouts prepared in every imaginable way, from sprout chip cookies and sprout soup, to deep fried sprouts and sprout water taffy; also music and live entertainment. For festival information, call (831) 423-5590.

PLACES OF INTEREST

Santa Cruz Beach Boardwalk. Situated along the Santa Cruz Beach, at 400 Beach St. Coney Island-type amusement park, built in 1907 and claimed to be the only seaside amusement park on the West Coast. Features game arcades, refreshment stands, restaurants, gift and souvenir shops, a shooting gallery, and over 250 thrilling rides—including a half-mile-long roller coaster, the "Giant Dipper," built in 1924 employing some 327,000 board-feet of lumber. Free admission; fee for individual rides. Open daily 11 a.m.-10 p.m. (11 a.m.-11 p.m. on Saturdays), May-Sept.; 12-5 weekends rest of the year. For more information, call (831) 426-RIDE/423-5590.

Cocoanut Grove Ballroom. Located adjacent to the Boardwalk, on Beach St. Last remaining Victorian ballroom in Northern California, originally built in 1907. In 1981 the Cocoanut Grove was renovated at a cost of $10 million, and converted into a banquet and convention center. Now contains four unique rooms, including the glass domed *Sun Room* which features a movable glass roof for open-air dining. The Cocoanut Grove still schedules big band concerts and other big name entertainment. For entertainment schedules and information, call (831) 423-2053/423-5590.

Joseph W. Long Marine Laboratory. Located at 100 Shaffer Rd., at the west end of Delaware Ave., near the Natural Bridges State Park. Several marine exhibits on display, including an 85-foot-long skeleton of a blue whale. Also aquarium and tidal and petting pools on premises, open to public tours, Tues.-Sun. 1-4. The laboratory is part of the U.C. Santa Cruz facility. Phone (831) 449-2883/459-4308.

Santa Cruz Municipal Wharf. Off Beach St. Colorful old wharf, lined with open-air fish markets, seafood restaurants and gift and souvenir shops. Originally built in 1914, and expanded in 1980 to accommodate pedestrian walkways and additional shops. A stage at the end of the wharf is used for weekend concerts. The wharf is also the site of the annual Calamari (Squid) Festival, held in August. Fishing charters available.

McPherson Center for Art and History. 705 Front St. (cnr. Cooper St.). The center comprises the *History and Art Museums* of Santa Cruz County. The *History Museum* features ongoing exhibits highlighting the history of the county, while the *Art Museum*, which incorporates the historic *Octagon House* gallery, houses the works of contemporary art. The Art Museum offers lectures, tours and workshops year round. The center is open Tues.-Sun. 11-4. For more information, call (831) 454-0697.

University of California, Santa Cruz. 1156 High St. Picturesque, 2,000-acre campus, with architect-designed buildings nestled among redwoods and other evergreens. Originally opened in 1966, the university is notable for its performing and visual arts programs. There are also some places of visitor interest on the campus, including two art galleries, *Smith Gallery* (831-459-2953) and *Senson Gallery* (831-459-2314), showcasing collections of historic art as well as changing exhibits of contemporary art, both open Tues.-Sun., 12-5 during the academic year; an *arboretum* (831-427-2998), located on the west side of campus, off Empire Grade, and which is essentially a research facility, studying plants from the Pacific Coast, South Pacific and other regions, but which also has on its premises a horticultural library and a gift shop, open Tues.-Sat., 10-4; and the *Institute of Tectonics* (831-459-4137), Earth and Sciences Building, which has exhibits centered around current projects studying earthquakes, the earth's magnetic field, and the earth's mantle. Among others are the *Center for Agroecology and Sustainable Food Systems*, a 25-acre experimental farm, which includes a laboratory and solar greenhouse, located just west of Hagar Drive; and *Chadwick Garden*, a 4-acre garden, located directly below Merrill College. Both the Center for Agroecology and Sustainable Food Systems and Chadwick Garden feature organically grown crops and are open to the public daily, with tours offered on Thursdays at noon and Sundays at 2 p.m.; for more information, call (831) 459-4140. Also, campus maps for self-guided tours are available at the visitors information booth at the entrance. Information can also be obtained by calling the university on (831) 459-0111.

Mision la Exaltacion de la Santa Cruz. Situated on Mission Hill, at 126 High St.; (831) 426-5686. The Santa Cruz mission was the 12th of California's 21 Franciscan missions, founded by Father Junipero Serra in 1791. The present mission building is actually a half-size replica of the original mission, which was destroyed by fire in 1857. The replica dates from 1931. Small mission museum attached to main building, housing early-day mission relics, including books, vestments and other artifacts. Open Tues.-Sat. 10-4, Sun. 10-2.

Santa Cruz Mission State Historic Park. 144 School St. (at Adobe St.). Features a 7-room adobe house, dating from 1822, originally built to house the Indians who worked at the mission. This is the only authentically-restored residence in the California missions chain. Open Thurs.-Sun. 10-4; living history activities offered on Saturdays, 12-3. Park phone, (831) 425-5849.

Mission Hill. Oldest part of Santa Cruz, notable for its rich collection of "gingerbread" Victorians and other historic buildings, with a fair number of them to be seen on High and Mission Streets and Escalona Drive.

Santa Cruz Surfing Museum. Located at Lighthouse Point, off West Cliff Dr. Superb collection of surfing memorabilia, including old surfing photographs, wooden surfboards, and ongoing video films on surfing. Open daily 12-4. Free admission; donations requested. Phone (831) 429-3773.

Santa Cruz Museum of Natural History. Located at the corner of East

Cliff Dr. and Pilkington Ave. Displays of native birds, fossils and Indian basketry, and a tidepool containing starfish and sea anemones. Open Tues.-Sun. 10-5. Admission free; donations requested.

The Mystery Spot. 1953 Branciforte Dr.; (831) 423-8897 The "mystery spot" consists of a most unusual circle, measuring roughly 150 feet in diameter, in which balls roll uphill and trees grow sideways, completely defying the laws of gravity. This strange natural phenomenon was first discovered in 1940. It is now open to public tours, 9.30-4.30 daily; admission $4.00 adults, $2.00 children.

Wilder Ranch State Park. Located on Coast Rd., off Hwy. 1, 2 miles northwest of Santa Cruz. Theme park, centered around 19th-century dairy farm, with a collection of old, restored ranch buildings, including a farmhouse, a bunkhouse and workshop, a horse barn, and a Victorian mansion with original, period furnishings and decor. Also view exhibits of antique farm equipment, such as seed spreaders and road graders, and turn-of-the-century vehicles, among them a Model A Coupe and a 1916 Dodge Touring Sedan. Hiking trails; tours. The park is open daily from 8 a.m. to sunset; visitor center and ranch complex is open Thurs.-Sun. 10-4, with living history activities and ranch tours offered on weekends. Day use fee is $6.00 per car. Park phone, (831) 426-0505.

Ano Nuevo State Park. Situated on New Years Creek Rd., off Hwy. 1, 20 miles north of Santa Cruz. Undeveloped park, notable as a breeding ground for elephant seals—where more than 3,000 of these large marine mammals come ashore to mate and give birth to baby seals. Guided tours offered during breeding season, Dec.-Apr. Also tidepools, and whale-watching in season, usually in November. Open daily 9-3; admission $6.00 per car. Park phone, (415) 879-0595; for tour reservations, call (800) 444-7275.

Forest of Nisene Marks State Park. On Aptos Creek Rd., off Soquel Dr., 2 miles north of Aptos; (831) 335-4598. 10,000-acre park, containing remnants of an old Chinese labor camp. Also hiking trails through redwood forest, including one that leads to the epicenter of the October 17, 1989, Loma Prieta earthquake That caused significant damage in Santa Cruz and San Francisco's Bay Area. Picnic facilities, and campground; camping fee: $4.00 per person.

Capitola. Small, coastal town, situated 3 miles south of Santa Cruz, just off Hwy. 1. This is one of California's oldest seaside resorts, dating from 1880. Features a 150-year-old wharf, a mile-long beach and freshwater lagoon, as well as brightly-colored waterfront cottages. Mediterranean-style bungalows and Victorian homes line the town's narrow streets and perch atop cliffs overlooking the town. Good shops and galleries, craft studios, and several delightful restaurants and bars, many of them strung along the beach-front Esplanade. Capitola also hosts a variety of events throughout the year, including its famous Begonia Festival, held in September.

Roaring Camp & Big Trees Railroad. Located on Graham Hill Rd., at Felton (10 miles north of Santa Cruz). Recreated 1880s railroad camp, with original 19th-century steam locomotives offering rides through miles of redwood forest. The camp was originally founded in 1835, and named for its boisterous community; the railroad arrived some years later, in 1875. The camp is now open to the public daily, with several old-time events scheduled throughout the year, including chuckwagon barbecues, country music, square dancing, and melodrama theater. Cost for train rides is $13.00 adults, $9.50 children. For reservations and information, call (831) 335-4400/335-4484.

Also see **Santa Cruz Beaches**.

RECREATION

Boating. Santa Cruz is a popular boating area, which also offers good fishing opportunities, and whale watching in season. Following are some of the area's charter and cruise boat operators, specializing in fishing charters, moonlight cruises, whale watching excursions, and a variety of boat cruises. *Tom's Fisherman's Supply*, Santa Cruz Yacht Harbor, E. Cliff Dr., Santa Cruz, (831) 476-2648; *Chardonnay Sailing Charters*, 1661 Pine Flat Rd., Santa Cruz, (831) 423-1213; *Pacific Yachting*, Santa Cruz Yacht Harbor, Santa Cruz, (831) 423-7245; *Stagnaro Fishing Trips*, Municipal Wharf, Santa Cruz, (831) 427-2334; *Capitola Boat & Bait*, 1400 Wharf Rd., Capitola, (831) 462-2208; *Pleasure Point Charters*, 2-3665 E. Cliff Dr., Santa Cruz, (831) 475-4657.

Bicycling. *Bicycle Rental & Tour Center*, 131 Center St., Santa Cruz; (831) 426-8687. Daily or hourly rentals; mountain bikes and tandems available; also tours available. *Pacific Avenue Cycles*, 709 Pacific Ave., Santa Cruz; (831) 423-1314. Rentals, service and repairs. *Aptos Bike Trail*, 7514 Soquel Dr., Aptos, (831) 688-8650. Bicycle rentals and repairs; open daily (except Tues.).

Surfing. Santa Cruz is of course one of the most popular places for surfing, on the California coast with scores of surf shops located there, offering a variety of surfboards, boogie boards and wet-suits for both rental and sale, as well as surf and beach reports. Following are some of the area surf shops, most of them located within a block or two of the beaches. *O'Neill's Surf Shop*, 1149 41st Ave., Capitola, (831) 475-4151, and 2222 E. Cliff Dr., Santa Cruz, (831) 476-5200 (surf report on (831) 475-2275); *Arrow Surf and Sport*, 312 Capitola Ave., Capitola, (831) 475-8960, and 2322 Mission St., Santa Cruz, (831) 423-8286; *Full Speed*, 1040 41st Ave., Santa Cruz, (831) 479-7873; *Santa Cruz Surf Shop*, 753 41st Ave., Santa Cruz, (831) 464-3233 (surf report on (831) 475-1616); *Freeline Design*, 861 41st Ave., Santa Cruz, (831) 476-2950.

Golf. For golf enthusiasts, the Santa Cruz area has several notable courses to enjoy, among them—*DeLaveaga Golf Course*, Upper De Laveaga Dr., Santa Cruz, (831) 423-7212; *Pasatiempo Golf Course*, Clubhouse Rd. (off Hwy. 17), Santa Cruz, (831) 459-9155; *Aptos Seascape Golf Course*, 610 Clubhouse Dr., Aptos, (831) 688-3213; *Boulder Creek Golf & Country Club*, Cnr. Hwys. 9 and 236, Boulder Creek, (831) 338-2121; *Pajaro Valley Golf Club*, 967 Salinas Rd., Watsonville, (831) 724-3851; *Spring Hills Golf Course*, 31 Smith Rd., Watsonville, (831) 724-1404; *Valley Gardens Golf Course*, 263 Mt. Hermon Rd., Scotts Valley, (831) 438-3058.

Tennis. *Darby Park*, Woodland Way (next to Natural Bridges School), Santa Cruz; 2 courts, no lights. *Mike Fox Tennis Park*, cnr. Riverside Ave. and San Lorenzo Blvd., Santa Cruz; 4 courts, 2 lighted. *Neary Lagoon Courts*, cnr. Bay St. and California St., Santa Cruz; 3 courts plus 1 practice court. *Cabrillo College*, 6500 Soquel Dr., Aptos, (831) 479-6266; 9 courts, weekends only. *Highlands County Park*, Hwy. 9, Ben Lomond; (831) 336-8551; 3 courts, no lights. *Jade Street Park*, Cnr. Jade St. and 41st Ave., Capitola, (831) 475-5935; 4 courts, with lights.

BEACHES

Capitola Beach. Located at the seaside resort of Capitola, along the Esplanade, some 3 miles south of Santa Cruz. Lovely, sheltered beach, with a freshwater lagoon and beachfront restaurants and bars. Pier fishing; and river rafting down the Soquel Creek.

Cowell Beach. One of Santa Cruz' best-loved beaches, situated adjacent to the Boardwalk. Volleyball courts, lifeguards in summer; swimming and sunbathing. Close to shops and restaurants.

Lighthouse Point. West Cliff Dr. Site of the Santa Cruz Surfing Museum. Spectacular views; a great spot to watch surfers tackle the infamous Steamers Lane.

Lincoln Beach. Quiet, sandy beach at the end of 12th Ave., with a stairway leading down to the beach. No facilities.

Moran Lake Beach. Popular surfing beach, located off East Cliff Dr., at 26th Ave.

Natural Bridges Beach State Park. Situated at the end of West Cliff Dr., near the Long Marine Laboratory. Well-liked rocky beach, named for its natural bridge-like rock formations. Excellent surf fishing and swimming possibilities; some picnicking. The park is also a good place to see Monarch butterflies during their annual migration in October.

New Brighton State Park. Just south of Capitola, off Hwy. 1. Popular sandy beach, with overnight camping facilities.

Pleasure Point. Situated along East Cliff Dr., at 41st Ave., with rocky paths leading down to the beach. Well-known surfing spot.

Red, White & Blue Beach. 6 miles north of Santa Cruz, off Hwy. 1; (831) 423-6332. Swimsuits-optional beach, with volleyball and tetherball courts, picnic facilities, and hot showers. Camping available. Admission: $5.00.

San Lorenzo Point/Castles Beach. Long, sandy beach, situated off East Cliff Dr., between the San Lorenzo River cove and the Santa Cruz Yacht Harbor. Lifeguards in summer; hot dog stands; restrooms.

Santa Cruz Beach. Popular white sand beach, situated off Beach Street, at the front of the Boardwalk. Swimming, surfing, sunbathing, picnicking.

Seacliff State Beach. Located south of Capitola and the New Brighton State Park, off Hwy. 1, at Aptos. Camping and picnicking; also good pier fishing from the unique Seacliff pier, which is actually made up of a 435-foot-long vintage cement ship, the *Palo Alto*.

Sunny Cove. At the end of 17th Ave., off East Cliff Dr. Favorite haunt of bodysurfers.

Twin Lakes Beach State Park. Situated along East Cliff Dr., east of the yacht harbor. Well-liked bonfire beach; features two lagoons, one of which is a wildfowl refuge and the other an 850-berth small-craft harbor. Picnic facilities; fire pits.

RESTAURANTS

(Restaurants prices—based on full course dinner, excluding drinks, tax and tips—are categorized as follows: *Deluxe*, over $30; *Expensive*, $20-$30; *Moderate*, $10-$20; *Inexpensive*, under $10.)

Adolph's. *Moderate.* 525 Water St.; (831) 423-4403. Family-style Italian restaurant, specializing in pasta dinners; also seafood, steaks, and prime rib. Open for lunch and dinner; brunch on Sundays.

Aldos Restaurant. *Moderate.* Located at the Santa Cruz Yacht Harbor, at 616 Atlantic Ave.; (831) 426-3736. Homemade ravioli and Italian fugasa bread, and fresh seafood. Open for breakfast and lunch daily.

Bamboo Restaurant. *Inexpensive.* 1733 Seabright Ave.; (831) 426-6382. Traditional family-style Chinese meals, featuring authentic Cantonese and Szechuan cooking, including steamed rockeye. Lunch and dinner Tues.-Sun.

Bocci's Cellar. *Moderate.* 140 Encinal St.; (831) 427-1795. Specializing in Continental and Italian cuisine; steak, lobster, prime rib, and pasta. Cocktail lounge, and outdoor patio. Open for lunch Mon.-Fri., dinner daily.

Casablanca Restaurant. *Moderate-Expensive.* Cnr. Beach and Main Sts.; (831) 426-9063. Continental cuisine, featuring fresh seafood, steaks and homemade desserts. Extensive wine list. Also Sunday Brunch, comprising seafood, quiche and egg dishes. Dinners from 5 p.m. daily.

Chaminade at Santa Cruz. *Expensive.* One Chaminade Lane; (831) 475-5600. Elegant restaurant, housed in the historic Chaminade Monastery complex which has undergone a $17-million transformation into a corporate meeting place and retreat. Spectacular views of Santa Cruz; Continental cuisine. Open for dinner, and Sunday brunch.

China Szechwan Restaurant. *Inexpensive.* 221 Cathcart St.; (831) 423-1178. Authentic Szechwan cuisine; informal atmosphere. Open for lunch and dinner, 11-3 and 5-9.30, Tues.-Sun.

The Cocoanut Grove Sun Room. *Inexpensive-Moderate.* 400 Beach St.; (831) 423-2053/423-5590. Sunday Champagne Brunch, 9.30-1.30; omelettes, freshly baked blueberry muffins, and other pastries. The Sun Room also features a 4,000-square-foot glass roof which can be retracted for open-air dining. Superb views of the beach and bay.

Compass Grille Bar. *Moderate-Expensive.* At the Dream Inn, 175 W. Cliff Dr.; (831) 426-4330. Specializing in steak, seafood, pasta and chicken preparations; seafood buffet on Fridays. Ocean views. Open for lunch and dinner daily.

The Crow's Nest. *Moderate-Expensive.* Located at the Santa Cruz Yacht Harbor; (831) 476-4560. Waterfront setting; superb views. House specialties include salmon filet and fresh grilled sole with butter sauce; also steaks, and gourmet salad bar. Lunch and dinner daily; brunch on Sundays.

Dolphin Restaurant. *Moderate.* Municipal Wharf; (831) 426-5830. Wharfside setting; ocean views. Offers primarily American fare, including burgers, sandwiches, and lobster and crab. Breakfast, lunch and dinner daily.

El Paisano. *Moderate.* 605 Beach St.; (831) 426-2382. Traditional Mexican food, including burritos and tamales. Garden patio. Open for breakfast, lunch and dinner.

El Palomar. *Inexpensive-Moderate.* Cnr. Front and Washington Sts.; (831) 425-7575. Mexican-seafood restaurant; features daily specials, including several vegetarian and chili dishes. Multi-flavored margaritas; Mariachis on Friday and Sunday nights. Open for lunch and dinner.

The Hindquarter. *Moderate-Expensive.* 303 Soquel Ave.; (831) 426-7770. Fresh seafood, poultry, steaks, lamb chops, prime rib, and pasta. Patio for outdoor dining. Open for lunch Mon.-Fri., dinner daily.

Ideal Fish Restaurant. *Moderate-Expensive.* On the Wharf; (831) 423-5271. Seafood menu, featuring Bouillabaisse, Cioppino, Linguini Calabrese, Monterey Bay Sandabs, and King Salmon. Open for dinner.

India Joze Restaurant. *Moderate-Expensive.* 1001 Center St.; (831) 427-3554. Home of the International Calamari Festival. Wide selection of exotic foods, including Middle Eastern, East Indian, Indonesian and Asian. Delicious baked desserts. Open for breakfast Mon.-Fri., lunch and dinner daily; also Sunday brunch, 10-2.30.

Margaritaville. *Inexpensive-Moderate.* 221 Esplanade, Capitola; (831) 476-2263. Splendid setting, at the Capitola Beach. Enormously popular Mexican restaurant. Exotic drinks, and multi-flavored Margaritas. Open daily 11.30 a.m.-1 a.m.

Polivios. *Moderate.* Cnr. 15th Ave. and East Cliff Dr.; (831) 475-7600. Continental cuisine, including prime rib, steak, veal, spaghetti, ravioli, prawns, and hot and cold sandwiches. Live music on weekends. Open daily for breakfast, lunch and dinner.

Sea Cloud. *Moderate-Expensive.* Municipal Wharf; (831) 458-9393. Menu stresses fresh seafood and nouvelle cuisine sauces. Nautical atmosphere; overlooking the Boardwalk and Steamers Lane. Open for lunch and dinner.

Stagnaro Brothers. *Moderate.* At the end of the Wharf; (831) 423-2180. Fresh seafood specialties, including calamari, seafood Louies, clam chowder, and live crabs and lobster. Casual atmosphere; sweeping ocean views. Lunch and dinner daily.

Sukeroku. *Moderate.* 1701 Mission St.; (831) 426-6660. Japanese restaurant, serving Nigiri, Hosumaki, and Sashimi; also Sushi Bar. Open for lunch Wed.-Fri., dinner Tues.-Sun.

Tampico Kitchen. *Inexpensive.* 822 Pacific Ave.; (831) 423-2240. Informal Mexican restaurant. Late night dining; mariachis on Sundays. Open for breakfast, lunch and dinner.

SOLVANG

"Danish Capital of America"

Solvang is a small, festive town in the Santa Ynez Valley, some 35 miles north of Santa Barbara—or 127 miles north of Los Angeles—famous as the "Danish Capital of America." It is filled with Danish architecture (including real windmills!), Danish bakeries and restaurants, Danish shops and homes—with Danish flags, Danish festivals, and Danish-speaking descendants of real Danes who migrated here from the midwest in 1910, to found a school to educate their children in the Danish traditions. Typical tourist activities here center on shopping, dining—including sampling Danish pastries—and theater, as in season.

Solvang can be reached on Highway 101 from Santa Barbara or Los Angeles, with a small, 3-mile detour east from Buellton on Highway 246. An alternative route from Santa Barbara is by way of the San Marcos Pass, passing by the Lake Cachuma resort and the tiny, cattle-ranching Western town of Santa Ynez.

DISCOVERING SOLVANG

Clearly, Solvang's principal lure is the town itself—a typical Danish village, neatly laid out along a dozen or so small, interconnecting streets, with colorful little shops and bakeries housed in perfectly charming Danish-style buildings, some with real copper roofs, topped with the traditional storks or—as in some cases—with wooden crosses which, according to Scandinavian superstition, are there to ward off evil spirits. Many of the streets, too, have antique gas street lamps—actually imported from Denmark! Besides which there are one or two quite lovely cobblestone and brick-paved walks here, decorated with flowers.

With shopping as the chief pursuit, Copenhagen Drive, quite possibly, is the town's most important street, lively and lined with shade trees and an assortment of shops carrying imported gifts, souvenirs and handicrafts, mostly from Europe. There are also several very attractive malls here, bursting, again, with Danish-theme shops filled with cuckoo clocks, pewter, tiles, music boxes and other such typical Scandinavian gift items. As added interest, at Hamlet Square there is a picturesque blue windmill, at Copenhagen Square a working windmill, and at the Hans Christian Andersen Square there is a splendid fountain pool that, in part, has the makings of a moat. Among other interesting malls are the Petersen Village Square, King Atterdag's Court, Tivoli Square, and Yorick Court which is an outstanding example, architecturally, of a small-town Danish square. Another place of interest, more or less at the center of town, is the Solvang Park, which has in it a bust of Hans Christian Andersen, celebrated Danish storyteller, and a well-rounded rock with an inscription denoting the distance between Solvang and Copenhagen, Denmark—11,270 kilometers. The town also has an outdoor theater, located on Second Street, which schedules some notable theater performances in season; and two Danish festivals, the Danish Days (September) and Fastelavn (February), bring out Danish costumes, music and dance.

North of town on Atterdag Road is the essentially rural Bethania Lutheran Church, also worth a visit. It has in it a lovely, hand- carved wooden pulpit and, in keeping with Danish tradition, a scale model of a fully-rigged ship hanging from its ceiling. A little way to the north of the church are the site of the historic Atterdag College (1914-1974), where there is now a large wind harp, and the state-run Hans Christian Andersen Park, with its wilder scenes. North still, some two or three miles, in an open field just off Fredensborg Canyon Road stands the Wulff Windmill, the oldest and most authentic of them all. It dates from the early 1900s and has been, to some degree, restored. In the early days it was actually used to pump water and grind corn.

Another great glory of Solvang, at the eastern approach to town on Highway 246, is the beautifully preserved Mission Santa Ines, one of California's twenty-one missions founded by Franciscan fathers, dating from 1804. It is, of course, open to public tours, and has a mission museum. Also, if time permits, go to see the Nojoqui Falls, some 7 miles south of Solvang on the Alisal Ranch Road. These

SOLVANG

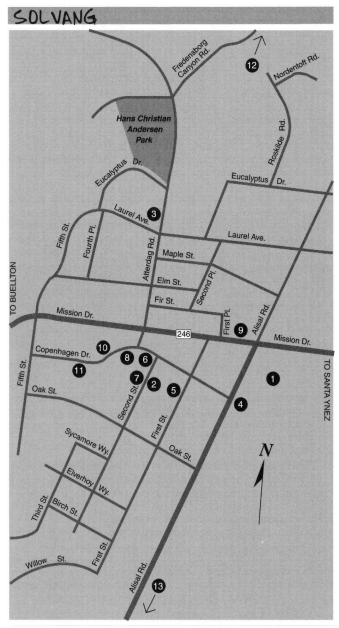

N

1. Mission Santa Ines
2. Theaterfest
3. Bethania Church
4. Copenhagen Square
   (with windmill)
5. Hans Christian
   Andersen Square
6. Hamlet Square
   (with windmill)
7. Yorick's Court
8. King Atterdag's Court
9. Denmarket Square
10. Petersen Village Square
11. Tivoli Square
12. Wulff Windmill
13. Nojoqui Falls

are said to be among the most graceful waterfalls in California, especially lovely in spring. The Nojoqui Falls Park has some good hiking and picnicking possibilities.

DETOURS

There are some other interesting places quite close to Solvang. Santa Ynez, 3 miles east on Highway 246, has an Old West town, a carriage house with antique carriages, and the tourist-alluring Gainey Winery which has public tours, tasting and wine sales. (There are, by the way, a fair number of other wineries in the Santa Ynez Valley, near to Solvang, most with visitor facilities; see *Winery* listings later in this chapter.) Two other old towns in the vicinity are Ballard and Los Olivos, the latter with an historic stage stop dating from the 1800s, now a well-liked tavern.

Buellton, 3 miles west, has modern facilities, including motels and fast food restaurants. It is also the self-proclaimed "Home of the Split Pea Soup"—a specialty of the locally-famous Andersen's Restaurant.

Lompoc, 20 miles or so west on Highway 246, is also well worth a visit. It is, most notably, the "Flower Seed Capital of the World," harvesting, typically, 50-75% of all the flower seeds produced in the world. Most of the flower fields are west of town, on Ocean and Central avenues, between V Street and De Wolfe Avenue; and the flowers are usually in bloom between June and September. In late June the town hosts its annual Flower Festival, with a floral parade, flower shows and flower field tours. Just north of Lompoc is the well-known Vandenberg Air Force Base, which can be toured by appointment; and close to town, northeastward, is to be found the ancient La Purisma Mission, one of California's twenty-one Franciscan missions, originally founded in the 1790s, and rebuilt at its present site in 1813. The mission has some gardens, a corral with animals, and a cemetery containing 1,000 graves of Chumash Indians. Two separate adobes near the mission, add to the interest.

HOW TO GET THERE

Solvang lies roughly 290 miles southeast of San Francisco, just off *Highway 101*. Follow *101* directly to Buellton, then *Highway 246* east some 3 miles to arrive at Solvang.

When approaching from the south, you have a choice of routes. You can take *Highway 101* from Los Angeles directly to Santa Barbara (91 miles), then either continue on *101* to Buellton and so to Solvang, or follow *Highway 154* northwest from Santa Barbara, over the San Marcos Pass, to Solvang. Either way, it is approximately 127 miles from Los Angeles to Solvang.

TOURIST INFORMATION

Solvang Conference & Visitors Bureau. P.O. Box 70, Solvang, CA 93464; (805) 688-6144/(800) 468-6765. Accommodations and restaurants guide, calendar of events, area map pinpointing places of interest.

ACCOMMODATIONS

Alisal Guest Ranch. *$335-$360.* 1054 Alisal Rd.; (805) 688-6411/(800) 425-4725. 10,000 acre ranch, with two 18-hole golf courses, 7 tennis courts, pool, spa, a private lake for boating and fishing, and riding stables. 73 guest units, comprising comfortable, private bungalows. Dining room on premises.

Best Western King Frederik Motel. *$55-$85.* 1617 Copenhagen Dr.; (805) 688-5515/(800) 549-9955. 45 units, with TV and phones. Heated pool, spa; complimentary continental breakfast. Centrally located.

Best Western Kronborg Inn. *$55-$85.* 1440 Mission Dr.; (805) 688-2383/(800) 528-1234. 39 units. TV, phones, heated pool and spa. Complimentary breakfast.

Chimney Sweep Inn. *$75-$275.* 1564 Copenhagen Dr.; (805) 688-2111/(800) 824-6444. 30 individually-decorated units in charming garden setting, with stream and waterfall; and 6 garden cottages with private spas. TV, phones, spa; complimentary continental breakfast.

Danish Country Inn. *$79-$180.* 1455 Mission Dr.; (805) 688-2018/(800) 44-RELAX. 82 units, including some loft units and suites. TV/VCR, phones, refrigerators, heated pool and jacuzzi; complimentary continental breakfast.

Hamlet Motel. *$48-$80.* 1532 Mission Dr.; (805) 688-4413. 14 units, with phones and TV. Continental breakfast.

Inn at Petersen Village. *$125-$235.* 1576 Mission Dr.; (805) 688-3121/(800) 321-8985. 40 rooms with courtyard or garden views, some with fireplaces; TV and phone. Complimentary buffet breakfast, evening wine and dessert.

Quality Inn. *$60-$195.* 1450 Mission Dr.; (805) 688-3210. 75 units, with TV and phones. Also indoor heated pool, jacuzzi, and game room. Complimentary continental breakfast.

Royal Copenhagen Motel. *$80-$110.* 1579 Mission Dr.; (805) 688-

5561/(800) 624-6604. 48 units; TV, phones, heated pool. Complimentary coffee and danish.

Solvang Gaard Lodge. *$43-$58.* 239 Alisal Rd.; (805) 688-4404. 18 units; phones and TV.

Solvang Royal Scandinavian Inn. *$75-$245.* 400 Alisal Rd.; (805) 688-8000/(800) 624-5572. 133 well-appointed rooms. TV, phones, heated pool and spa; also restaurant and cocktail lounge on premises.

Svendsgaard's Danish Lodge. *$50-$85.* 1711 Mission Dr.; (805) 688-3277/(800) 686-8757. 49 units, some with fireplaces and kitchens. TV, phones, heated pool, jacuzzi; complimentary continental breakfast.

Three Crowns Inn. *$40-$150.* 1518 Mission Dr.; (805) 688-4702/(800) 848-8484. 32 units; TV and phones. Complimentary continental breakfast.

Viking Motel. *$42-$80.* 1506 Mission Dr.; (805) 688-1337. 12 units, with phones and TV. Complimentary continental breakfast.

SEASONAL EVENTS

June. *Lompoc Flower Festival.* At Lompoc; held during the 4th week of the month. Well-known annual festival, celebrating Lompoc's rich harvest of flower seeds. Events include a floral parade with multicolored floats, a flower show, and tours of over 1,000 acres of flower fields in full bloom. Also carnival, arts and crafts fair, live entertainment, food concessions, square dancing and marathon. Call (805) 735-8511 for more information. *Theaterfest.* June-Oct. Shakespeare and American classics, including comedy, tragedy and musicals, performed in open-air theater, at 420 Second St. Advance reservations required; for schedule and bookings, call the Theaterfest box office at (805) 922-8313.

September. *Danish Days.* 3rd weekend in September. Celebration of Solvang's Danish heritage; features Danish music and folk dances, with traditional costumes, and variety of Danish foods and entertainment. For more information, call (805) 686-9386.

PLACES OF INTEREST

Mission Santa Ines. Located at 1760 Mission Dr. (Hwy. 246), just east of the business district. This is the 19th of California's 21 Spanish missions, built in 1804. Superb mission museum, with artifacts depicting the history of the mission; original hand-painted murals; lovely gardens. The mission chapel is also open to public viewing. Tours daily, 9 a.m.- 5 p.m. in winter, 9 a.m. - 7 p.m. in summer. Mission phone: (805) 688-4815.

Bethania Lutheran Church. Situated on Atterdag Rd., near the corner of Laurel Ave.; (805) 688-4367. Typical Danish-style church, featuring provincial Danish architecture. The church also has in it a lovely, hand-carved wooden pulpit and, in keeping with Scandinavian tradition, a scale model of a fully-rigged ship hanging from the ceiling. Open to the public.

Solvang Park. Cnr. First St. and Mission Dr. Small, grassy park, located in the center of town; features a bust of Danish storyteller Hans Christian Andersen, and a rock denoting the distance between Solvang and Copenhagen, Denmark—11,270 km. Picnic tables; bandstand. Open to public use.

Theaterfest. 420 Second St.; (805) 922-8313. Timbered, open-air theater, acknowledged as one of the oldest repertory theaters on the West Coast. Scheduled performances during summer, June-Sept. For reservations and program information, call the Theaterfest box office; (805) 922-8313.

Hans Christian Andersen Park. Located just to the north of town, off Atterdag Rd. 50-acre park, with an Old World, Danish-style entrance. Barbecue and picnic facilities, children's play area, tennis courts. Open daily; no admission fee.

Elverhoj Danish Heritage and Fine Arts Museum. Cnr. Atterdag Rd. and Elverhoj Way; (805) 686-1211. Displays include old photographs, furniture, and lithographs, and other items depicting the history of Solvang. Open daily 10-5.

Hans Christian Andersen Museum. 1680 Mission Dr.; (805) 688-2052. Small museum, dedicated to the father of the modern fairy tale. Displays of books, sketches, silhouettes and collages. Open daily 10-5.

Wulff Windmill. Located on Fredensborg Canyon Rd., some 2 miles north of town. Restored, authentic Danish windmill, originally built in 1922 by immigrant Charles Wulff, and used for several years to grind corn and pump water. The windmill is now an historical landmark.

Nojoqui Falls. 6 miles south of town on Alisal Rd. Wooded 84-acre park, featuring a splendid 165-foot waterfall, especially picturesque in spring. Also picnic and barbecue areas, walking trails, athletic field, and children's play area. Open to the public; no admission fee.

Santa Ynez Valley Historical Society Museum and Carriage House. Cnr. Sagunto and Faraday Sts., Santa Ynez; (805) 688-7889. Well-kept 8-room museum, filled with artifacts and mementoes of local historical interest. Open Fri.-Sun. 1-4. The Carriage House features over 30 carriages, wagons, stagecoaches and buggies, and is open Tues.-Sat. 10-4, Sun. 1-4.

Lake Cachuma Recreation Area. Popular, year-round lake resort, situated just 14 miles southeast of Solvang, off Hwy. 154. Facilities include overnight camping, boating, fishing, horseback riding and picnicking. A recreation center at the resort features a swimming pool, miniature golf course and skating rink. Day use fee $5.00; camping fee $12.00-$16.00. For more information, call (805) 686-5054.

Area Farms. There are several unique farms and ranches in and around Solvang, open to the public, including— *Flying V Llama Ranch,* 6615 E. Hwy. 246 (6.5 miles west of Buellton), (805) 735-3577, which offers tours by appointment, and also a gift shop, open daily 10-5; *Ostrich Land,* 610 E. Hwy. 246, Solvang, (805) 686-9696, which is home to hundreds of ostriches and is open to the public daily; and *Quicksilver,* a miniature horse farm, (805) 686-4002/(800) 370-4002, which has public tours daily 10-3.

Lompoc. 20 miles west of Solvang, on Hwy. 246. Famous as the "Flower Seed Capital of the World," Lompoc harvests 50%- 75% of all the flower seeds produced in the world. Tour the multicolored flower fields on Ocean and Central Avenues, between V Street and De Wolfe Avenue; flowers are in bloom May-Sept. In late June, the town hosts its annual *Flower Festival,* with a floral parade, flower shows and flower field tours. Also of interest in downtown Lompoc, is the *Lompoc Murals Project,* with over 40 murals depicting the region's diverse history and industries, most of them completed since 1988; a map of the mural walk is available from the Lompoc Chamber of Commerce, at 111 South I St., (800) 240-0999. Of interest, too, just to the north of Lompoc, is the well-known *Vandenberg Air Force Base,* notable for its space shuttle launch program, and which can also be toured by appointment; call the base on (805) 734-8232, ext. 63595.

Mission La Purisma Concepcion de Maria Santisima. Situated near Lompoc, 15 miles west of Buellton, on Mission Gate Rd. which goes off Hwy.

246. This is one of California's 21 missions built by Franciscan fathers, originally founded in 1797, and rebuilt at its present site in 1813. The mission complex includes two small, adjoining adobes, a cemetery containing 1,000 graves of Indians, and a corral with llamas and other animals. Open to public viewing, 9 a.m.-5 p.m. daily. Mission phone, (805) 733-3713.

Wineries. *Gainey Vineyard,* 3950 E. Hwy. 246, Santa Ynez; (805) 688-0558. Newer, 12,000-square-foot Spanish-style winery, producing primarily varietal wines. Tasting, tours and retail sales, 10-5 daily. *The Firestone Vineyard,* 5017 Zaca Station Rd., Los Olivos; (805) 688-3940. Santa Ynez County's first commercial winery, producing estate varietal wines. Tours, tasting and sales, 10-5 daily. Picnic facilities. *Santa Ynez Valley Winery/LinCourt Winery,* 343 N. Refugio Rd., Santa Ynez; (805) 688-8381. Wine tasting and sales daily 10-5. Picnic area on premises. *Zaca Mesa Winery,* 6905 Foxen Canyon Rd., Los Olivos; (805) 688-3310. Producers of Santa Ynez Valley wines. Tasting and sales 10-4 daily. Picnic facilities available.

RECREATION

Boating. *Lake Cachuma Recreation Area,* 14 miles southeast on Hwy. 154, has motorboat and sailboat rentals; phone (805) 686-5054. Lake Cachuma is open from 6 a.m. - 10 p.m. daily; day use fee $5.00 per car; lake usage fee $5.00. No swimming or water-skiing is permitted. Also, *Gaviota State Park* and *Refugio Beach State Park,* both situated along Hwy. 101, south of Buellton, offer good boating, sailing, surfing and swimming possibilities; park phone, (805) 968-3294/968-1033. Day use fee: $5.00 per car.

Bicycling. *Dr. J's Bicychiatry,* 1661-B Fir Ave.; (805) 688-6263. Bicycle rentals; free Santa Ynez Valley route map.

Golf. *Alisal Guest Ranch,* Alisal Rd. (south of town); (805) 688-6411. Private, two 18-hole courses, open to Alisal Ranch guests and members of other private clubs and SCGA affiliated clubs. *Zaca Creek Course,* Buellton; (805) 688-2575. 9-holes, driving range. Open to the public.

RESTAURANTS

(Restaurant prices—based on full course dinner, excluding drinks, tax and tips—are categorized as follows: *Deluxe,* over $30; *Expensive,* $20-$30; *Moderate,* $10-$20; *Inexpensive,* under $10.)

Bit O'Denmark. *Moderate.* 473 Alisal Rd.; (805) 688-5426. Seafood, and Continental, Danish and American cuisine. Open daily; breakfast, lunch and dinner.

Greenhouse Cafe. *Moderate-Expensive.* Petersen Village Square, cnr. Copenhagen and Atterdag Drs., (805) 688-8408. Traditional Danish and American cuisine, served in an all-glass, flower-filled dining room, or outdoors on patio. Open for breakfast, lunch and dinner daily.

The Little Mermaid. *Moderate.* 1546 Mission Dr.; (805) 688-6141. Small, casual restaurant, featuring Danish and American cuisine; also Smorgasbord, and Danish beer on tap. Breakfast, lunch and dinner daily.

Mandarin Touch. *Moderate.* 1980-C Old Mission Dr.; (805) 688-1538.

Northern Chinese cuisine. House specialties include seafood and homemade soups. Full bar. Open for lunch dinner daily.

Manny's. *Moderate.* 444 Atterdag Rd.; (805) 688-3743. Authentic Mexican cooking; specialties include gourmet soft chicken tacos and homemade tamales. Patio for outdoor dining. Lunch and dinner daily.

Mollekroen Restaurant. *Moderate.* 435 Alisal Rd.; (805) 688-4555. Two-story restaurant, with Danish-style dining room on second floor, and cocktail lounge downstairs. Excellent Smorgasbord, comprising nearly 30 dishes. Open for lunch and dinner daily; live entertainment on Fri. and Sat.

Mortensen's Bakery. *Inexpensive-Moderate.* Petersen Village Square, cnr. Copenhagen and Atterdag Drs., (805) 688-8373. Freshly-baked Danish pastries and cookies. Large patio for outdoor dining. Open 7.30 a.m. - 6 p.m. daily.

Olsen's. *Inexpensive-Moderate.* 1529 Mission Dr.; (805) 688-6314. Bakery and coffee shop, serving Danish pastries, cakes, cookies, breads, petit fours and kranskage. Open Mon.-Fri. 7.30 a.m. - 6 p.m., Sat.-Sun. 7.30 a.m. - 7 p.m.

Paula's Pancake House. *Inexpensive-Moderate.* 1531 Mission Dr.; (805) 688-2867. Menu features Danish thin pancakes, buttermilk pancakes, waffles, omelettes, sandwiches, burgers, soups and salads, and daily lunch specials. Open for breakfast and lunch.

The Red Viking. *Inexpensive-Moderate.* 1684 Copenhagen Dr.; (805) 688-6610. Family-style restaurant, featuring primarily Danish and American food, including a variety of sandwiches, as well as a smorgasbord with a wide selection of hot and cold entrees. Full bar. Breakfast, lunch and dinner daily.

Royal Scandia. *Moderate-Deluxe.* At the Sheraton, 400 Alisal Rd.; (805) 688-8000. Traditional Danish cooking; specialties include fresh fish, beef, and fowl prepared in several different styles. Danish atmosphere; live entertainment. Open for breakfast, lunch and dinner daily; brunch on Sundays. Reservations recommended.

Solvang Bakery. *Inexpensive-Moderate.* 460 Alisal Rd.; (805) 688-4939. Bakery and cafe, serving delicious homemade pastries and breads. Open daily, 7 a.m. - 5.30 p.m.

The Viking Garden. *Inexpensive-Moderate.* 466 C Alisal Rd.; (805) 688-1250. Popular local restaurant, featuring Danish, German and American fare. House specialties include Danish thin pancakes and Aebleskiver, potato pancakes, variety of sandwiches, hamburgers, thick pea soup and other homemade soups, chili, fish and chips, and chicken; also daily lunch specials. Open 8 a.m.-8 p.m. daily.

SONOMA

Wine, Cheese and California History

Sonoma is a delightful little California town, lying in the fertile Sonoma Valley (popularized by novelist Jack London as the "Valley of the Moon"). The town is famous for its wine, cheese, dairies, fruit and bread, and superb mild climate, epitomizing, in many ways, the "good life of California." It is also rich in California history—it is the birthplace of California's Bear Flag Republic, and of California's wine industry, with several old vineyards and wine estates in and around town, as well as many ancient Mexican-colonial adobes strung around a lovely Spanish plaza. There are, in addition, good restaurants, shops and bed and breakfast accommodations here.

Sonoma is situated roughly 45 miles northeast of San Francisco, reached on Highway 101 north and routes 116 and 12 east and north, respectively. An alternative route is by way of Santa Rosa—Highway 101 north and 12 southeast.

DISCOVERING SONOMA

We suggest you begin your tour of Sonoma where Sonoma itself began—at the Sonoma Plaza. It is the focal center of town and the largest and most picturesque Spanish plaza in California. It is also, equally importantly, the site of the famous Bear Flag Revolt of 1846—a well-remembered historic event in which a group of thirty American frontiersmen rode into town, took captive the Mexican commandante, General Mariano Vallejo, and declared here an independent Bear Flag Republic, raising a handmade, and somewhat crude, "Bear Flag," which remains today the official flag of the State of California. There is a large bronze statue commemorating the revolt located in a park in the center of the plaza, where, by the way, there are also several picnic tables, a children's play area, an open-air theater, a duck pond, a rose garden, and an abundance of splendid shade trees.

The plaza itself is a delightful place to wander around, leisurely exploring the old adobes and other historic and lovely buildings. Here, for instance, you can search out the Mission San Francisco de Solano at the northwest end of the plaza, originally built in 1823 as the last and northernmost of the twenty-one California missions founded by Franciscan fathers. The mission now houses a museum with early day relics from the mission and a series of paintings of all twenty-one California missions. It is open to the public daily.

Across from the mission are the Sonoma Barracks, another beautifully restored adobe, originally built in 1836 to house General Vallejo's Mexican army garrison. It now contains exhibits from Sonoma's three most important eras: Indian, Mexican and early American. The last of these includes a replica of the original, handmade "Bear Flag," which, reportedly, was destroyed in the 1906 earthquake. There is also a second floor balcony open to the public here, with superb, all-round views of the plaza and the park.

Adjoining the barracks, still on Spain Street, is the venerable old Toscano Hotel, also an adobe, notable mainly for its colorful display of the seven flags that have flown over Sonoma, at one time or another; Russian, British, Spanish, Mexican Empire, Mexican Republic, Bear Flag, and Stars and Stripes. Farther still, just west of the Toscano Hotel, are the site of the Casa Grande, General Vallejo's first home; the Casa Grande Servants' Quarters, where Vallejo's Indian servants were housed; and finally the Sonoma Cheese Factory, home of Sonoma Jack Cheese—famous all over California. The cheese factory was originally established in 1914 and is still operated by the same family. It now also has a fully stocked deli—quite popular for picnic lunches—and an audio-visual program, with views of its plant, explaining the cheese-making process, quite interesting to first time visitors.

Farther along on Spain Street and West First Street are the so-called Swiss Hotel, the Sonoma Hotel and the El Dorado Hotel, all dating from the 1830s and 1840s, and now restored to their former elegance. The El Dorado Hotel incorporates in it part of the old adobe home of Captain Salvador Vallejo, brother of General Mariano Vallejo. The Vallejo home is notable as one of the oldest adobes in Sonoma.

Along the east side of the plaza is another ancient adobe (Blue Wing Inn) built by Salvador Vallejo, dating from the 1840s, and the El Paseo de Sonoma, a charming little Spanish-style courtyard mall with a handful of small, interesting shops. The Place des Pyrenees, a few doors down, is another interesting courtyard-style mall, filled with shops and restaurants. There are several other very interesting historic buildings along here, now containing fine shops, restaurants and delis; among them the Sonoma French Bakery, with its Sourdough French Bread and baguettes claimed to be among the best in the Bay Area.

At the center of the plaza, in the park, are two other most notable buildings, well worth seeing. One, the south-facing Sonoma City Hall, characteristic in its native stone and brick construction, dates from 1905 and is quite possibly the most attractive building in town. The other, also quite attractive and dating from the early 1900s, is nestled along East First Street, and now houses the Sonoma Valley Visitors Bureau. (Good "walking tour" maps of Sonoma are available from the Visitors Bureau of Commerce office for a nominal charge.)

Among other places of interest, a little way from the plaza, just off Spain and West Third streets, is the enchanting Lachryma Montis (meaning "mountain tears"), the later home of General Vallejo, named for the natural springs on the estate. The home was originally built in about 1851, and remained the residence of Vallejo until his death in 1890. It is now maintained by the State Parks Department and is open to the public for viewing. Most of the rooms have been remarkably well preserved in their original state, with antique furnishings and fixtures, besides which there are also beautifully kept grounds here, with age-old shade trees and flower beds overflowing with seasonal color.

Also try to visit the Depot Park on East First Street, just north of the plaza, which has in it a lovely children's play area and a most interesting railroad museum, open to the public daily. Another place of interest to railroad buffs—as well as children—is Train Town, at the south end of town, on Broadway. Open on weekends during summer, Train Town offers steam train rides around a 10-acre landscaped park, journeying through tunnels, over bridges, and around small, artificially created lakes. South still, eight miles or so from Sonoma, is the Sears Point Raceway, where motor racing events are scheduled throughout the year, frequently featuring such celebrity race drivers as Paul Newman.

Before leaving Sonoma, try to also find the time to visit the town's famous old wineries, most of them lying just at the edge of town. Sebastiani Vineyards, for one, lies within easy distance of the Sonoma Plaza, on Fourth and East First streets. It dates from 1904, originally founded by Samuele Sebastiani, and is still owned and operated by the same family. It has wine tasting, in a well-appointed, comfortable tasting room, and scheduled public tours through its barrel room, where one can view a fine collection of hand-carved redwood casks, believed to be the largest such collection in North America.

The Buena Vista Winery, a little farther on the Old Winery Road, is another historic gem. It is housed in a fabulous old stone cellar,

SONOMA

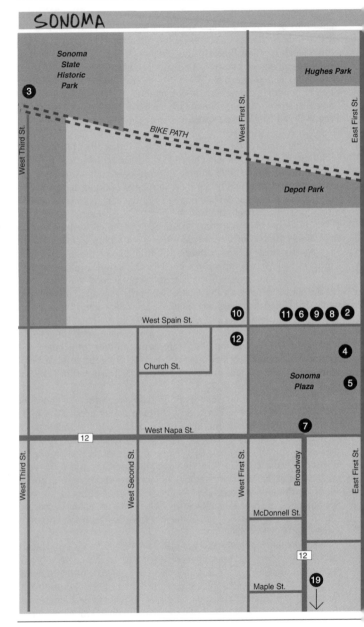

1. Sonoma Mission
2. Sonoma Barracks
3. Vallejo Home
4. Bear Flag Revolt Statue
5. Visitors Bureau
6. Sonoma Cheese Factory
7. City Hall
8. Toscano Hotel
9. Casa Grande

SONOMA

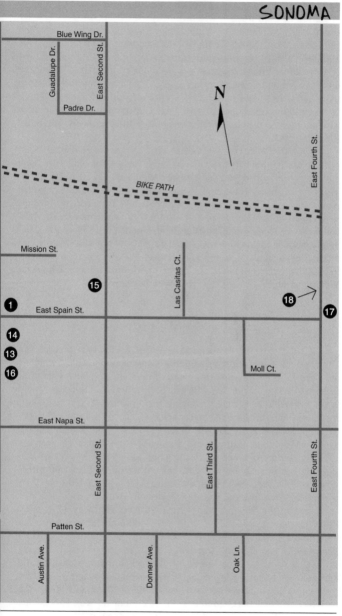

10. Sonoma Hotel
11. Swiss Hotel
12. El Dorado Hotel
13. Place des Pyrenees
14. El Paseo de Sonoma
15. Vella Cheese Factory
16. Sonoma French Bakery
17. Sebastiani Vineyards
18. Buena Vista Winery
19. Train Town

dating from 1857, and is claimed to be the oldest winery still in operation in California. It was originally established in the 1850s by Count Agoston Haraszthy, acknowledged, also, as the founder of the California wine industry, who in 1861 imported into California over 100,000 cuttings of some 300 grape varieties from Europe's famed wine regions, giving the state's wine industry its start. The winery now has a superb tasting room, a large, shaded picnic area, nature trail, and self-guided tours of its wine museum and ancient ageing caves, where cream sherry is still aged in oak barrels. During the summer months the winery features outdoor music concerts and other special events.

Two other wineries, well worth visiting, are the Hacienda Wine Cellars and Gundlach-Bundschu Winery, located on Vineyard Lane and Thornberry Road (southeast of the Sonoma township), respectively. The first of these, Hacienda, is especially notable for its delightful picnic area, which overlooks the ancient, 50- acre Buena Vista Vineyard —now part of the Hacienda estate—originally established by Agoston Haraszthy in 1862. Gundlach-Bundschu, founded in 1858, is also quite lovely, housed in an old, native-stone building. It has wine tasting and retail sales, a picnic area, and a small reservoir adjacent to the winery. Yet another winery of interest is Ravenswood, situated in the Chamizal Valley just north of town, and also open to the public.

DETOURS

If time permits, we suggest a detour north from Sonoma on Highway 12, some 7 or 8 miles, to the scenic Sonoma Valley, which is adjoined to its east by the Mayacamas Mountains, beyond which lies the Napa Valley, celebrated winegrowing region. The Sonoma Valley is itself notable as a wine producing region too, with a dozen or so reputable wineries located there, including the well-known Chateau St. Jean, historic Kenwood, St. Francis, Valley of the Moon, and the Smothers Brothers' tasting room. Kenwood and Chateau St. Jean are of course the best known of all, the latter housed in a lovely chateau-style building, with a tower that has commanding views of valley vineyards. St. Jean also offers an educational, self-guided tour of its winemaking facility, and has superb grounds, with a picnic area.

Also in the Sonoma Valley, just west off Highway 12 is Glen Ellen, a small, historic town, with associations to famous American writer Jack London—author of *The Call of the Wild* (1903), *White Fang* (1906) and *Burning Daylight* (1910), among others. The town, in fact, is adjoined to its north by the Jack London State Historic Park, site of London's legendary "Beauty Ranch," where the author lived and worked during his final years, until his death in 1916. In the park one can view the charred remains of London's "Wolf House," his grave, and "The House of Happy Walls," a splendid stone mansion built in the early 1900s by the author's wife, Charmain, and where several of London's possessions are now on display. There are some good walking trails and picnic areas in the park, as well as horseback riding possibilities.

The Glen Ellen area also has two or three wineries of interest; among them Grand Cru Vineyards—which is built upon the site of a 100-year-old stone cellar—and the Glen Ellen Winery, situated directly below the Jack London park, and originally part of the ancient Rancho Petaluma, Mexican governor General Vallejo's estate. There are, besides, some good dining places in Glen Ellen, and one or two well-appointed bed and breakfast inns.

HOW TO GET THERE

Sonoma lies 45 miles northeast of San Francisco. The best and easiest way to reach it is by way of *Highway 101* north from San Francisco to Novato (26 miles), then a combination of *Highways 37, 121* and *12* directly northeast to Sonoma. A slightly longer route from San Francisco is by way of *Interstate 80* east to Vallejo (31 miles), then northwest some 25 miles on *Highways 29, 37, 121* and *12* to Sonoma.

TOURIST INFORMATION

Sonoma Valley Chamber of Commerce. 651 Broadway, Sonoma; (707) 996-1033. Visitor information brochures, visitor guides; also calendar of events and information on area wineries, cheese factories and art galleries.

Sonoma Valley Visitors Bureau. 453 First Street East, Sonoma; (707) 996-1090. Information on accommodations, restaurants, seasonal events and wineries; also walking tour maps and visitor guides.

ACCOMMODATIONS

Bed & Breakfast Inns

Magliulo's Pensione. *$95-$150.* 691 Broadway; (707) 996-1031. Splendid Victorian bed and breakfast inn, located just south of the plaza. 5 well-appointed guest rooms, decorated with fine antiques and fresh flowers; some private baths. Gourmet restaurant on premises.

Trojan Horse Inn. *$135-$165.* 19455 Sonoma Hwy.; (707) 996-2430. 7 antique-decorated rooms in historic, rural mansion, built in 1887. Creekside setting; gardens, patio, spa, and bicycles for guests' use. Gourmet breakfast.

Victorian Garden Inn. *$95-$175.* 316 E. Napa St.; (707) 996-5339/(800) 543-5339. Quiet, 1860s farmhouse-style inn near the Plaza. 4 guest rooms; creekside gardens, pool. Hearty country breakfast.

Vineyard Inn. *$75-$185.* 23000 Arnold Dr.; (707) 938-2350. 12 guest rooms with private baths. Phones, TV; continental breakfast.

Hotels and Motels

Best Western Sonoma Valley Inn. *$80-$125.* 550 Second St. West; (707) 938-9200/(800) 334-5784. 75 units. TV, phones, pool, spa, complimentary continental breakfast. Located close to downtown Sonoma.

El Dorado Hotel. *$120-$150.* 405 First St. West; (707) 996-3030. Beautifully restored adobe inn, situated on the plaza. 29 rooms, private baths; excellent Italian restaurant, saloon, fireplace lounge, heated pool. Continental breakfast.

El Pueblo Motel. *$60-$85.* 896 W. Napa St.; (707) 996-3651. 39 motel units; TV, phones, pool.

Sonoma Hotel. *$155-$220.* 110 W. Spain St.; (707) 996-2996. Historic hotel on the plaza. 4 suites and 12 rooms, all with private baths and air conditioning. Garden patio, restaurant and bar. Continental breakfast.

Sonoma Mission Inn & Spa. *$149-$349.* 18140 Sonoma Hwy., Boyes Hot Springs; (707) 938-9000/(800) 862-4945. Luxury resort, located 2 miles out of Sonoma. 160 guest rooms, many with fireplaces and balconies. Facilities include restaurants, pools, tennis courts, and a European-style spa with a bathhouse, whirlpool, aerobics classes, exercise equipment, heated pool, beauty salon and massage room.

SEASONAL EVENTS

June. *Sonoma Valley Shakespeare Festival.* Held at the Gundlach-Bundschu Winery, Sonoma; (707) 775-3854. Performances take place through September. *Bear Flag Day Celebration.* Also at the Sonoma Plaza; (707) 996-2337. Celebration of Bear Flag Revolt. Events include a flag raising ceremony, barbecue, and entertainment.

July. *Midsummer Mozart Concert.* Open-air concert at historic Buena Vista Winery, with performances by some of Northern California's top musicians. For a program, call the winery at (707) 938-1266. Concerts begin during the 3rd week of July and continue into late August. *Salute to the Arts.* Sonoma Plaza, Sonoma. Celebration of visual and performing arts, winemaking and culinary arts. For schedule, call (707) 938-1133.

August. *Annual Wine Showcase and Auction.* Held at the Sonoma Mission Inn & Spa, usually during the third week of the month. Some of Sonoma County's finest wineries offer their wines for auction. For more information, call (707) 579-0577. *Dixieland Jazz Festival.* At the Red Lion/Doubletree Hotel, Santa Rosa; 4th week. Performances by several fine jazz musicians and bands. Call (707) 539-3494 for a schedule.

September. *Shakespeare at Buena Vista.* Buena Vista Winery; (707) 938-1266. Shakespeare performances by the Sonoma Vintage Theatre; first three weeks of the month. *Valley of the Moon Vintage Festival.* Held at the Sonoma Plaza; (707) 996-2109. Festivities include a flower show, gem show, arts and crafts show, and a parade and ball.

October. *Sonoma County Harvest Fair.* At the Sonoma County Fairgrounds, Santa Rosa; 1st week of the month. Annual fair featuring a variety of events, including an art show, wine competition, jazz festival, 10-kilometer run, and grape stomp. For more information, call (707) 543-4200.

November. *Nouveau Beaujolais Festival.* Hosted by Sebastiani Vineyards, generally around the middle of the month. Celebration of the first wine of the year's harvest. Wine tasting and music. For a schedule of events, call the winery at (707) 938-5532.

December. *Holiday Candlelight Tour of Inns.* Bus tours of selected Sonoma County Bed & Breakfast Inns, offered during the 2nd and 3rd weeks of month; music and refreshments along the way. Sponsored by the Sonoma County Museum; (707) 579-1500.

PLACES OF INTEREST

Sonoma Plaza. Delightful Spanish-style plaza, dating from the Mexican era. Visit old adobes and other historic buildings; among them the *Sonoma Barracks, Sonoma Mission, Toscano Hotel, Swiss Hotel, Sonoma Hotel, El Dorado Hotel*, and the remains of General Vallejo's *Casa Grande*. Most of these old buildings now house charming little shops and restaurants; of particular interest are the famous *Somona Cheese Factory*, home of California's Sonoma Jack cheese, and the *Sonoma French Bakery*. There is also a lovely, tree-shaded park at the center of the plaza, with picnic tables, children's play area, flower bushes, footpaths, a duck pond, and a large bronze statue commemorating the 1846 Bear Flag Revolt. The picture-perfect *Sonoma City Hall*, dating from 1910, is at the southern end of the plaza park, and the *Sonoma Valley Visitors Bureau*, also housed in a splendid old building, along its east side. (Maps pinpointing Sonoma's historical sites and other places of interest are available from the Visitors Bureau for a nominal fee.)

Sonoma Mission. Cnr. Spain St. and First St. East. Last and northernmost of California's 21 missions founded by Franciscan fathers, established in 1823. Mission museum has displays of local historical interest, and a splendid collection of paintings of all 21 California missions. Open daily 10-5. An admission fee of $3.00 adults/$2.00 children (ages 6-12) allows entry to the Sonoma Mission, Sonoma Barracks and the Vallejo Home. Phone (707) 938-1519.

Sonoma Barracks. Spain St. Picturesque old adobe, dating from the 1840s, formerly used to house the troops of General Mariano Vallejo, Mexican Governor of California. The Barracks now contain historic artifacts from Sonoma's three most important eras—Indian, Mexican, and early American. The last of these includes a replica of the original, handmade "Bear Flag" raised at Sonoma in 1846. Lovely courtyard, and balcony with plaza views. Open daily 10-5.

Vallejo Home (Lachryma Montis). Located 3 blocks west of the Mission, off Spain Street. Beautiful redwood house on landscaped grounds, formerly the home of General Mariano Vallejo, built in the early 1850s. Vallejo lived here with his family until his death in 1890. Most of the rooms have been superbly restored to their original state, with the original, antique furnishings and fixtures. Also on display here are Vallejo's 19th century carriage and several old, historical photographs. The home is now part of the Sonoma State Historic Park which also contains in it the Sonoma Mission and Sonoma Barracks. An admission fee of $3.00 adults/$2.00 children allows entry to all three historic buildings. Open daily 10-5. Park phone, (707) 938-1519.

Depot Park. 270 First St. West. Grassy park with picnic and barbecue facilities, children's playground and a well-kept railroad museum. Park open daily; museum hours, Wed.-Sun. 1-4.30.

Sonoma Cheese Factory. 2 Spain St.; (707) 996-1000. Makers of famous Sonoma Jack Cheese. Watch the cheese being made in the factory, with pre-taped commentary to explain the process. Fully-stocked deli on premises, offering excellent picnic fare. Open daily 9-6.

Vella Cheese Factory. 315 Second St. East; (707) 938-3232. Another good place to observe the cheese-making process. Also variety of cheeses for sale. Open Mon.-Sat. 9-6, Sun. 9-5.

Train Town. 10-acre theme park just south of town on Broadway, featuring short, 20-minute train rides around its premises, passing through tunnels and over bridges. Petting farm for children. Cost of train ride: $4.00 adults, $3.00 children and seniors. Open 10.30-5 daily, June-Sept.; 11-5 Fri.-Sun. the rest of the year. For more information, call (707) 938-3912.

Jack London State Historic Park. London Ranch Rd., Glen Ellen; (707) 938-5216. 800-acre park, comprising novelist Jack London's famous "Beauty Ranch," where the author lived and worked during his latter years, until his death in 1916. Chief attractions in the park are the stone ruins of London's *Wolf House*, and *The House of Happy Walls*—built in 1919 by the author's wife, Charmain London, and now housing a museum with displays of furnishings and other items from London's original study as well as from the Wolf House, and the author's collection of South Pacific art. The park also has good hiking, picnicking, and horseback riding possibilities. Park open daily, 8 a.m. until sunset; museum hours, 10-5. Admission: $5.00 per car.

Sugarloaf Ridge State Park. 2605 Adobe Canyon Rd., Kenwood. Park in Sonoma Valley setting, with camping, picnicking, hiking and horseback riding. Campsites $16.00 per day; day use $5.00 per car. Open daily, sunrise to sunset. For campsite reservations and information, call (707) 833-5712.

WINERIES

Arrowood Vineyards & Winery. 14347 Sonoma Hwy., Glen Ellen; (707) 938-5170. Situated on a knoll overlooking Sonoma Valley, Arrowood produces primarily varietal Chardonnay and Cabernet Sauvignon. Open for tours, tasting and sales, Mon.-Sat. 10-4.30.

Benziger Family Winery. 1883 London Ranch Road, Glen Ellen; (707) 935-3000. Historic winery, located adjacent to Jack London State Historic Park, and housed in an old barn dating from the 1860s. The winery offers estate-grown Sauvignon Blanc, Chardonnay and Cabernet Sauvignon. Shaded picnic area on premises. Open for tasting and sales daily 10-4.30; tours on weekends.

Buena Vista Winery. 18000 Old Winery Rd., Sonoma; (707) 938-1266. California's oldest winery in operation, founded in 1857 by Count Agoston Haraszthy, father of the California wine industry. Visit original three-story stone winery building, with its ancient ageing caves, now a State Historical Landmark; also wine museum, art gallery, and tasting room. Large picnic area; some nature trails. Open to the public daily 10-5.

Carmenet Vineyard. 1700 Moon Mountain Rd., Sonoma; (707) 996-5870. 450-acre hillside ranch in the Mayacamus Mountains. Produces primarily Bordeaux-style wines, including a Cabernet Sauvignon blend and Sauvignon Blanc Semillon. Open for tours, tasting and sales by appointment.

Chateau St. Jean. 8555 Sonoma Hwy., Kenwood; (707) 833-4134. Housed in a splendid chateau-style building, with a tower and colonnade, and surrounded by estate vineyards. Highly regarded, white varietal wine producer. Self-guided tours, wine tasting, sales. Picnic area on premises. Open daily 10-4.30.

Cline Cellars. 24737 Arnold Dr., Sonoma; (707) 935-4310. Producer of Rhine varietal wines. The tasting room is situated in historic farmhouse, with sweeping views of the Carneros region. Picnic area on premises. Open for tasting and sales daily 10-6, tours by appointment.

Gloria Ferrer Champagne Caves. 23555 Hwy. 121, Sonoma; (707) 996-7256. Large, newly-built Spanish-style winery, specializing in *methode champenoise* sparkling wine. Guided tours of winery and its recently-excavated limestone ageing cellars. Tasting patio, overlooking estate vineyards. Hours: 10.30-5.30 daily.

Grand Cru Vineyards. 1 Vintage Lane, Glen Ellen; (707) 996-8100/833-2325. Producer of premium varietal wines, established in 1970. Utilizes state-of-the-art winemaking equipment and techniques, and century-old stone and concrete fermentation tanks. The winery is built on the site of a 100-year-old wine cellar. Tasting room located at 8860 Sonoma Hwy., Kenwood; tasting and sales 10-4.30 daily; winery tours by prior appointment.

Gundlach-Bundschu Winery. 2000 Denmark St., Sonoma; (707) 938-5277. Historic Sonoma winery lying just to the south of town, founded in 1858 by pioneer vintner Jacob Gundlach. Picnic area on premises, overlooking small reservoir. Varietal and sparkling wines offered under winery label. Open 11-4.30 daily for tours, tasting and sales.

Hacienda Wine Cellars. 1000 Vineyard Lane, Sonoma; (707) 938-3220. Delightful Spanish-style winery, situated on the historic, 50-acre Buena Vista Vineyard estate, on the outskirts of Sonoma township. Shaded picnic area, adjacent to vineyards. Wine tasting and sales 10-5 daily; tours by appointment.

Kenwood Vineyards. 9592 Sonoma Hwy., Kenwood; (707) 833-5891. Well-known, medium-sized winery, established in the Sonoma Valley in 1906. Offers a full line of vintage-dated varietal wines. Rustic tasting room; picnic area. Wine tasting and sales 10-4.30 daily; tours by appointment.

Ravenswood Winery. 18701 Gehricke Rd., Sonoma; (707) 938-1960. Producer of Sonoma County varietal wines, situated just above the town of Sonoma. Picnic area on premises. Open for tours, tasting and sales, 10-4.30 daily.

St. Francis Winery. 8450 Sonoma Hwy., Kenwood; (707) 833-4666. Housed in contemporary wood-frame building, surrounded by estate vineyards. Producer of vintage-dated varietal wines. Open for tasting and sales 10-4.30 daily; tours by appointment only.

Schug Carneros Estate. 602 Bonneau Rd., Sonoma; (707) 939-9363. State-of-the-art winery producing Pinot Noir, Chardonnay, and Rouge de Noir, a sparkling wine made from Pinot Noir grapes. Open for tasting and sales daily 10-5, tours by appointment.

Sebastiani Vineyards. 389 Fourth St. East, Sonoma; (707) 938-5532. Founded in 1904 by Italian immigrant Samuele Sebastiani, and still owned and operated by the same, Sebastiani family. Daily winery tours, highlighting Sebastiani's fascinating collection of hand-carved redwood casks. Also at the winery are an Indian Artifact Museum and outdoor displays of a small, antique crusher and basket press with which Samuele Sebastiani made his first wine, in 1895. Tasting and sales. Winery open 10-5, daily.

Smothers Winery (Tasting Room). 9575 Hwy. 12, Kenwood; (707) 833-1010. The famous Smothers brothers, Dick and Tom, offer varietal wines from grapes grown in both the Santa Cruz Mountains and Sonoma County. Tasting room open daily 10-4.30.

Valley of the Moon Winery. 777 Madrone Rd., Glen Ellen; (707) 996-6941. Historic Sonoma Valley winery, established in 1857. Previously owned by General "Fighting Joe Hooker," of Civil War fame; Eli Shepard, American Consul to China; and U.S. Senator, George Hearst, among others. Estate-grown varietal wines. Tasting and sales 10-5 daily.

ViansaWinery. 25200 Arnold Dr., Sonoma; (707) 935-4700. Italian-style winery situated on a knoll just south of Sonoma. Produces primarily Cabernet Sauvignon, Chardonnay and Sauvignon Blanc. Wine and gift shop on premises. Open for tours, tasting and sales daily 10-5.

RECREATION

Tours. The following tour companies offer tours of Sonoma and the surrounding wine country, some of them including visits to specific wineries. *Linda Viviani Touring Company,* 500 Michael Drive, Sonoma, (707) 938-2100; *Sonoma Charter & Tours,* 22455 Broadway, Sonoma, (707) 938-4248/(800) 232-7260; *HMS Tours,* 707 Fourth St., Santa Rosa, (707) 526-2922.

Ballooning. *Sonoma Thunder Wine Country Balloon Safaris,* (707) 829-9850. One-hour balloon flights over the Sonoma Valley, followed by a champagne brunch. Cost is around $175.00 per person. *Air Flambuoyant,* 250 Pleasant Ave., Santa Rosa; (707) 838-8500/(800) 456-4711. Flights over the Sonoma wine country, followed by a champagne brunch. flight cost is $175.00 per person.

Scenic Flights. *Biplane Rides,* 23982 Arnold Dr. (at Schellville Airport), Sonoma; (707) 938-2449. Offers unique scenic flights over the Sonoma Valley in a vintage biplane.

Golf. *Sonoma Golf Club,* 17700 Arnold Dr., Sonoma; (707) 996-0300. 18-hole championship course; par 72. Green fees: $45.00 Mon.-Thurs., $50.00 Fri., $70.00 weekends; rates include cart rental. Pro shop, lessons. *Oakmont Golf Club,* 7025 Oakmont Dr. (off Hwy. 12), Oakmont; (707) 538-5524. Two 18-hole championship courses; par 72 and par 63. Green fees: $24.00-$29.00 Mon.-Fri., $32.00-$39.00 Sat.-Sun. Cart rental $24.00. Lessons, and pro shop.

Horseback Riding. *Sonoma Cattle Company,* (707) 996-8566. Guided trail rides in Jack London State Historic Park and Sugarloaf Ridge State Park. Rates: $40.00 for 1½ hours, $45.00 for 2 hours, and $55.00 for 3 hours.

Spas and Hot Springs. *The Spa at Sonoma Mission Inn,* Hwy. 12, Boyes Hot Springs; (707) 938-9000/ext. 427. Luxury resort, with full line of spa treatments. Reservations required. *Agua Caliente Mineral Springs,* 17350 Vailetti Dr., Agua Caliente; (707) 996-6822. Facilities include spa, mineral water swimming pool, diving pool, and picnic area. *Morton's Warm Springs,* 1651 Warm Springs Rd., Kenwood; (707) 833-5511. Heated pools, picnic area, and snack bar.

RESTAURANTS

(Restaurant prices—based on full course dinner, excluding drinks, tax and tips—are categorized as follows: *Deluxe,* over $30; *Expensive,* $20-$30; *Moderate,* $10-$20; *Inexpensive,* under $10.)

Depot 1870 Restaurant. *Moderate.* 241 First St. West; (707) 938-2980. Housed in historic stone building near the Sonoma Plaza. Offers Northern Italian cuisine, with emphasis on fresh ingredients and locally-grown Sonoma County produce. Delightful brick patio for outdoor dining. Open for lunch Wed.-Fri., dinner Wed.-Sun. Reservations suggested.

The Grille. *Moderate-Expensive.* At the Sonoma Mission Inn, Hwy. 12, Boyes Hot Springs; (707) 938-9000. Features pasta specialties, and items from the mesquite grill. Open for lunch and dinner daily; brunch on Sundays. Reservations advised.

La Casa. *Inexpensive-Moderate.* 121 E. Spain St.; (707) 996-3406. Mexican restaurant, emphasizing traditional Mexican foods. Homemade specialties; multi-flavored margaritas and Mexican beer. Open daily.

L'Esperance. *Expensive-Deluxe.* 464 First St. East (behind the French Bakery); (707) 996-2757. Fine French dining; elegant setting. Lunch and dinner daily; brunch on Sundays. Reservations required.

Magliulo's Restaurant. *Expensive.* 691 Broadway; (707) 996-1031. Established Sonoma restaurant, housed in a charming, antique-decorated cottage. Features Italian-American cuisine primarily. Brick patio for outdoor dining. Lunch and dinner daily. Reservations advised.

Marioni's. *Expensive.* 8 W. Spain St.; (707) 996-6866. Menu emphasizes steaks and seafood. Contemporary Southwestern decor; multi-level dining rooms. Open for lunch and dinner, Tues.-Sun. Reservations suggested.

Ranch House. *Moderate.* 20872 Broadway; (707) 938-0454. Authentic Mexican cooking, with emphasis on foods from the Yucatan region. Casual atmosphere. Lunch and dinner daily.

Sonoma Cheese Factory. *Inexpensive-Moderate.* Located on the Plaza on Spain St.; (707) 996-1000/996-1931. Popular deli-cum-cafe; home of the famous Sonoma Jack cheese. Large variety of sandwiches and salads, cheeses and Sonoma County wines. Excellent picnic lunches. Outdoor patio. Open daily 9.30 a.m.-5.30 p.m.

Sonoma Hotel. *Moderate.* 110 Spain St. (on the Plaza); (707) 996- 2996. Historic hotel-restaurant, with delightful garden patio and antique mahogany bar. House specialties include fresh pasta and seafood, and homemade desserts. Menu changes weekly. Open for lunch and dinner Fri.- Tues.; brunch on Sundays.

Swiss Hotel. *Moderate.* 19 W. Spain St.; (707) 938-2884. Restored historic hotel, located on the Plaza. Features Italian, Chinese and American fare; informal setting. Open daily.

SOUTH LAKE TAHOE

"America's All-Year Playground"

South Lake Tahoe is a popular, all-season resort town, picturesquely situated at the southern end of Lake Tahoe—one of America's largest and most beautiful lakes—at an elevation of around 6,250 feet. It offers vacationers a wealth of summertime recreational pursuits, including wilderness hiking, bicycling, horseback riding, golf, swimming and boating, as well as snow skiing in winter, boasting one of the country's largest alpine ski resorts. It also has in it a dazzling, Las Vegas-type casino district, with bright lights, multi-storied casinos, big name entertainment, and all-night gambling action. Besides which, the town is abundant in motel accommodations and fine, European-style restaurants.

The best and most direct route from San Francisco to South Lake Tahoe—which lies approximately 190 miles distant, eastward—is by way of Interstate 80 east to Sacramento, then Highway 50 more or less directly into South Lake Tahoe.

DISCOVERING SOUTH LAKE TAHOE

It must be right to say that South Lake Tahoe is one of the most spectacular mountain towns in the West, nestled along Lake Tahoe's splendid shoreline, amid towering pines and firs, and backed by the dramatic Sierra Nevada mountains, which rise some 9,000-10,000 feet. This is also, we might add, a town that has been largely built around the tourist, with more than 9,000 hotel rooms and as many as 100 fine restaurants packed into a 10-square-mile area, and with plenty in it for the holiday-maker to see and do.

The great glory of South Lake Tahoe, however, is its famed casino district—a half-mile glitter strip lying along the east side of the California-Nevada stateline, with some of the lake's finest highrise hotel-casinos situated there, featuring star- studded live entertainment and thrilling, non-stop gambling action—with a variety that ranges from slot machines to craps, keno, blackjack, roulette and even betting on horse races and ball games. There are, in fact, four well-known hotel-casinos in the district, and two or three smaller clubs; among them Harrah's Tahoe, Harvey's Resort Hotel, Caesar's Tahoe (part of the Caesar's, Las Vegas chain) and the Horizon Casino Resort. Harvey's —which is propped right up against the stateline, with barely inches to spare between its west wall and the State of California (where gambling, as practiced in Reno and Las Vegas, is illegal)—is of course the oldest casino at the lake, dating from 1946, and which has the added distinction of being the first highrise at Lake Tahoe, and now, also, the tallest building at the lake—22 stories high. It has over 600 well-appointed guest rooms, three or four delightful restaurants, and a glass elevator that offers panoramic views of the lake and mountains as it climbs to the top floor of the hotel, where there is a superb restaurant-lounge, Llewellyn's. Harrah's, directly across the street from Harvey's, has an 18-story hotel with plush decor and 540 rooms, and over 70,000 square feet of casino space; it also has a small shopping arcade, and a well-liked restaurant, The Summit, with expansive, all-round views of the lake and the Sierras. Just east of Harrah's and Harvey's are Caesar's and the Horizon, fifteen and fourteen stories high, respectively; both have good in-house restaurants, and Caesar's also has a mini-arcade, with fine gift and clothing stores and one or two art galleries.

Adjoining to the northeast of the casino district is the splendid Edgewood Golf Course, the site of professional golf tournaments, and rated by *Golf Digest* as one of the top ten courses in the country. It has a spacious clubhouse and a mile or so of lake frontage. Just to the southeast of there, and also of interest, is the historic Kingsbury Grade which climbs sharply to over 7,300 feet, offering good views of the lake, then plunges into the Carson Valley, down the eastern slopes of the Sierra, to achieve a descent of some 3,000 feet in just 6 miles. Another place worth visiting, a little way to the north of Edgewood, is Zephyr Cove, which has a beach, marina, lodge and campground. Zephyr Cove is also the home port of the *M.S. Dixie*, Tahoe's oldest cruise boat in service, which made its debut on the

Lake *Tahoe*

TO EMERALD BAY

N

16

17

1

2

10

89

Kiva Beach Rd.

15

Pope Beach Rd.

TAHOE KEYS

3

San N
Los

A

Fallen

Leaf

Lake

Fallen Leaf Rd.

Emerald Bay Rd.

13th St

Tata Ln.

Julie Ln.

D St.

89

Dunlap

Lake Tahoe Blvd.

Tahoe Keys Blvd.

4th St.

8

50

Lake Tahoe Airport

Lake Tahoe Blvd.

Emerald Bay Rd.

Truckee

Upper Truckee Rd.

50

Pioneer

Trail

**TAHOE PARA
(MEYERS)**

TO SACRAMENTO

1. Visitors Center	4. Timber Cove Marina
2. Camp Richardson	5. Ski Run Marina
Marina	6. Lakeside Marina
3. Tahoe Keys Marina	7. Heavenly Valley Tram

8. South Y Center	
9. Crescent V Center	
10. Camp Richardson	
11. Visitors Bureau	

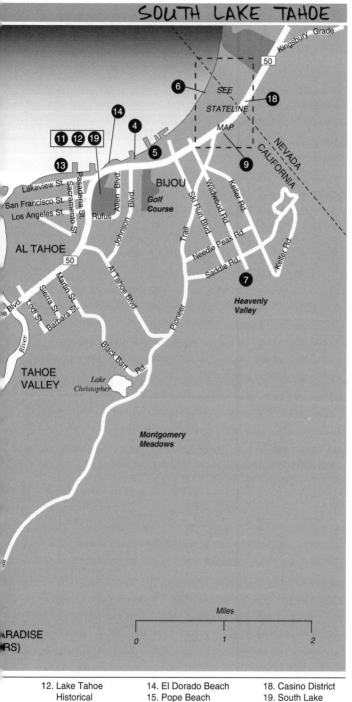

SOUTH LAKE TAHOE

Kingsbury Grade

50

6

SEE

STATELINE

18

MAP

14

4

11 **12** **19**

5

9

13

Lakeview St.

San Francisco St.

Los Angeles St.

Pasadena St.

Sacramento St.

Rufus

Allen Blvd.

Johnson Blvd.

BIJOU

Golf Course

Ski Run Blvd.

Wildwood Rd.

Keller Rd.

NEVADA

CALIFORNIA

AL TAHOE

50

Martin St.

Sierra St.

Lodi St.

Barbara St.

e Blvd.

Al Tahoe Blvd.

Pioneer

Trail

Needle Peak Rd.

Saddle Rd.

Keller Rd.

7

Heavenly Valley

River

TAHOE VALLEY

Black Bart Rd.

Lake Christopher

Montgomery Meadows

Miles

RADISE
RS)

0   1   2

lake in 1947. The *Dixie* has daily lake cruises in summer.

West of the casino district and stateline lies the essential "city" of South Lake Tahoe, with a host of shops, restaurants and motels. The tract immediately adjacent to the stateline, on the lake side of the highway (50)—which here is known as Lake Tahoe Boulevard, and which is the main street of the city—is Tahoe's "motel country," with at least three dozen motels jockeying for position along a handful of small side streets. This, too, is a good place to stay, due to its proximity to the casinos.

Not far from the stateline, on the south side of Lake Tahoe Boulevard, is the world-famous Heavenly Valley Ski Resort, encompassing over 20,000 acres of skiable terrain—including nine mountains—with a third of it lying in the State of California and two thirds in Nevada. The resort has three base lodges, two of which are on the Nevada side—reached on small side roads that branch off the Kingsbury Grade —and one in California, situated just off Ski Run Boulevard. The California base lodge, of course, has an added attraction; Heavenly's tourist-alluring aerial tram—which climbs to over 1,400 feet above lake level, to the delightful Top of the Tram Restaurant, offering panoramic views much of the way—is located here. Heavenly also, we might add, is notable as the site for the prestigious 1985 World Cup Skiing.

South of Heavenly Valley, at the lake end of Ski Run Boulevard is the Ski Run Marina, home port of the *Tahoe Queen*, another Mississippi riverboat-style paddlewheeler, which has the distinction of being Lake Tahoe's largest cruise boat. The *Tahoe Queen* has daily lake cruises, with dinner, dancing and live music on board.

The center of the city is of course an urban sprawl, with shopping centers, steakhouses and a half-dozen or so wedding chapels. There is, however, an in-city golf course here too, on Lake Tahoe and Johnson boulevards; and two sandy beaches, Regan and El Dorado, lie just off Lakeview Street. Both beaches have picnicking and sunbathing possibilities, and are good places from which to view the lake.

At the northwest end of the city, a mile or two above the South Tahoe "Y" (intersection of Highways 50 and 89), is Camp Richardson, a well-wooded, picture-postcard village, with stables, a marina, a beach, a lodge, and a 230-site campground. Camp Richardson is adjoined to its north by the historic Tallac Estates, where you can walk among some of Tahoe's finest stands of virgin pine, and tour two or three fabulous, turn-of-the-century homes—including the Pope, Tevis and McGonagle estates. Here also is to be found the site of the famous Tallac Hotel, once billed as the "Saratoga of the Pacific." Two beautiful sandy beaches, Kiva and Pope, lie to the north and south of the estates, respectively, and just to the north, also worth a visit, is the Lake Tahoe Visitor Center, which has a "stream profile chamber," from where you can view native Kokanee Salmon and other lake fish in their natural habitat.

North of Camp Richardson and the Tallac Estates, the highway (89) winds madly along one of the most scenic stretches of Lake Tahoe, until some two or three miles farther it passes over a ridge that has commanding views of two spectacularly beautiful bodies of water,

Cascade Lake and Emerald Bay. Emerald Bay, of course, is one of the most photographed sights of Tahoe. It has at the center of it an island with a stone "tea house," dating from the 1930s, and above the bay are the magnificent Eagle Falls, which cascade in three successive falls down into the bay. The chief attraction at the bay, however, is without doubt the splendid Vikingsholm, a masterful replica of a 1,200-year-old Viking castle, nestled along the northwest end of the bay and reached by way of a mile-long walking trail. The Vikingsholm has been described as "the finest example of Scandinavian architecture in North America," and it may well be. Open to public viewing on weekends in summer, it features a wealth of fine treasures, including antique Scandinavian furniture, hand-carved beams, Norwegian weavings, and all sorts of other ornate decor from the Viking era. Vikingsholm dates from 1929.

HOW TO GET THERE

The most direct route from San Francisco and Sacramento to South Lake Tahoe is by way of *Interstate 80* and *Highway 50,* more or less directly northeast. From San Francisco, the city is 190 miles distant, and from Sacramento, approximately 103 miles.

Also, *American Airlines* (800-433-7300) and *American Eagle* (530-541-8360/800-433-7300) have regular flights to South Lake Tahoe from Los Angeles and San Francisco. The South Lake Tahoe Airport is located just to the south of the city.

TOURIST INFORMATION

South Lake Tahoe Chamber of Commerce. 3066 Lake Tahoe Blvd., South Lake Tahoe; (530) 541-5255. Tourist information brochures, including lodging and restaurant listings, and show information; also calendar of events. Accommodation referrals and tourist information can also be obtained through *Lake Tahoe Visitors Authority,* 1156 Ski Run Blvd. (cnr. Tamarack St.), South Lake Tahoe; (530) 544-5050/(800) 288-2463.

ACCOMMODATIONS

Hotels and Motels

Best Western Station House Inn. *$108-$128.* 901 Park Ave.; (530) 542-1101/(800) 528-1234. 100 rooms; TV, phones, pool, beach, spa, restaurant.
Best Western Lake Tahoe Inn. *$79-$129.* 4110 Lake Tahoe Blvd. (Hwy. 50); (530) 541-2010/(800) 528-1234. TV, phones. Close to casinos.

Casino Area Travelodge. *$89-$109.* 4003 Hwy. 50; (530) 541-5000. 66 rooms; TV, phones, pool.

Embassy Suites Resort. *$99-$199.* 901 Ski Run Blvd.; (530) 541-6122/ (800) 362-2779. Suites with full kitchens; some lake and marina views. Indoor and outdoor pools, exercise room. Complimentary continental breakfast, and evening wine and cheese reception.

Holiday Lodge. *$65-$90.* 4095 Laurel St.; (530) 544-4101. 148 rooms, TV, phones, pool, sauna.

Mark Twain Motel. *$48-$70.* 947 Park Ave.; (530) 544-5733. 34 rooms; TV, phone, pool, spa; close to beach and casinos.

Royal Valhalla Motor Lodge. *$60-$129.* 4104 Lakeshore Blvd.; (530) 544-2233. 79 units, many with private balconies overlooking the lake; some kitchen units. TV, phones, heated pool and spa; private beach.

Tahoe Marina Inn. *$89-$180.* Hwy. 50, at the Bijou Shopping Center; (530) 541-2180/(800) 448-4577. 76 units, with TV and phones; some fireplaces and lakeside balconies. Heated pool, sauna, private beach.

Tahoe Beach & Ski Resort. *$105-$175.* 3601 Hwy. 50; (530) 541-6220. 120 units, with TV and phones. Pool, spa, hot tub, restaurant.

Tahoe Seasons Resort. *$110+.* Keller & Saddle Rds.; (530) 541-6010. 160 units; TV, phones, pool, hot tub, restaurant.

Tradewinds Motel. *$48-$75.* 944 Friday St.; (530) 544-6459. 68 rooms, TV, phones, pool, hot tub.

Viking Motor Lodge. *$49-$65.* 4083 Cedar St.; (530) 541-5155. 58 rooms, TV, phones, pool, spa, beach.

Hotel-Casinos

Caesar's Tahoe. *$135-$250.* Lake Tahoe Blvd., Stateline; (775) 588-3515/ (800) 648-3353. 15-story, five star hotel, part of the Caesar's Palace-Las Vegas chain, situated 100 yards or so east of Harrah's. 446 luxury hotel rooms, most with lake views. Casino and shopping arcade on premises; also 6 restaurants, tennis and racquetball courts, indoor pool, jacuzzis and weight room. Live entertainment.

Harrah's Tahoe. *$129-$189.* Lake Tahoe Blvd., Stateline; (775) 588-6611/ (800) 648-3773 from California. 540-room, 18-story luxury hotel, located directly across from Harvey's. 70,000-square-foot casino floor, 5 superb restaurants, indoor swimming pool, sauna and spas, nautilus center, shopping arcade. Big name entertainment.

Harvey's Resort Hotel. *$145-$190.* Lake Tahoe Blvd., Stateline; (775) 588-2411. 547-room, 22-story resort hotel. Casino, arcade, 7 restaurants, live entertainment. For show information and reservations, call (800) 648-3361.

Horizon Casino Resort. *$109-$159.* Lake Tahoe Blvd., Stateline; (775) 588-6211/(800) 648-3322. 14-story hotel-casino, located directly across from Caesar's. Three notable restaurants, live entertainment and dancing. Full casino.

SEASONAL EVENTS

January. *South Lake Tahoe Winter Celebration.* At Heavenly Ski Resort, usually during the last week of the month. Week-long event, featuring ski races, ice-sculpting, fireworks, and a variety of other festivities. For more information, call (775) 586-7000.

June. *The Wagon Train Festival.* A wagon train comprising 30 authentic 19th-century wagons rolls through town, along Highway 50, enroute to Placerville. The wagons make an overnight stop in South Lake Tahoe; celebrations include street dancing and other festivities. For schedule and information, call (530) 626-2344. *Valhalla Summer Arts Music Festival.* Tallac Historic Site. Events continue through August, and include World Music Festival, Festival of Native American Fine Arts, theatrical performances, a classic film series, and a jazz series. For a complete schedule of events, call (530) 541-4975.

July. *Star Spangled Fourth,* South Lake Tahoe. Firework displays, acrobatic air show and a variety of Independence Day celebrations. For more information, call the South Lake Tahoe Chamber of Commerce; (530) 541-5255. *Lake Tahoe Celebrity Golf Invitational.* Held at the Edgewood Golf Course, Stateline. Long-running, annual Pro-Am invitational tournament. For exact dates, call the South Lake Tahoe Visitors Bureau at (530) 544-5050.

August. *Great Gatsby Festival.* Held at the Tahoe Keys Marina and the Tallac Historic Site, in South Lake Tahoe. Events include living history days, antique boat show and barbecue. Also Dixieland music, games, and arts and crafts show. (530) 541-5227.

PLACES OF INTEREST

Historical Society Museum. 3058 Lake Tahoe Blvd. (Hwy. 50), South Lake Tahoe, (530) 541-5458. Artifacts from Lake Valley's early days, some of Indian origin; also several old photographs depicting Lake Tahoe's history. Worth viewing too is a 1920s bobsled and two or three pieces of 19th-century farm machinery. Open Tues.-Sat. 11-4.

Heavenly Valley Aerial Tram. Located at Heavenly's California Base Lodge (follow signs from Ski Run Blvd., south off Hwy. 50, to the ski resort); (530) 541-1330. A 50-passenger tram car takes you to the *Top of the Tram* restaurant, some 2,000 feet above lake level, offering spectacular views of the lake and surrounding mountains. The tram operates year-round. Also visit the ski area, "America's largest alpine ski resort," sprawled over 20 square miles, nine mountains and two states.

Casino District. At the Stateline, on the Nevada side. Half-mile strip, where some of Lake Tahoe's finest hotel-casinos—*Harrah's, Harvey's, Caesar's* and the *Horizon Casino Resort*—are located, offering round-the-clock non-stop gambling action and Las Vegas-style shows, featuring some of the best in big name entertainment. The district is much to be recommended to first-time visitors to the area.

Kingsbury Grade. Southeast of the Stateline casinos, off Hwy. 50; the grade actually forms part of Nevada Route 207. Drive up the grade to Daggett Summit (elev. 7,375 feet), then down the Haines Canyon in a more less vertical drop, and into the Carson Valley; the descent is approximately 3,000 feet, achieved in just over 6 miles. This is one of the most spectacular drives at the lake, with great views of both the Carson Valley and Lake Tahoe.

Zephyr Cove. 4 miles north of Stateline, on Hwy.50 east. Well-liked summer resort, with a marina, a sandy beach, and stables. Also home port of *M.S. Dixie*, a glass-bottomed Mississippi river boat, which also has the distinction of being Lake Tahoe's oldest cruise boat. The resort is open May-Oct.

Historic Tallac Estates. Situated between Camp Richardson and *Kiva Beach Recreation Area*, off Hwy. 89; reached via Kiva Beach Rd. Park at Kiva and explore on foot. Tour some splendid 1920s homes, including the *Pope-Tevis*

Estate, the *McGonagles Estate*, and the *Baldwin Estate*. Visit also the *Tallac Museum* and *Tallac* site. Special events during summer. Open June-Sept. For more information on events held at the site, and for museum hours, call (530) 541-5227.

Visitors Center. Also off Hwy. 89; look for the turnoff 300 feet past Kiva Beach turnoff. Visit the *Stream Profile Chamber*, an enclosed viewing area at stream level, which shows off native fish in their natural habitat; in fall, usually in October, you can watch Kokanee Salmon as they swim upstream to spawn. Some worthwhile walking trails can also be enjoyed here, starting out from near the center. Open June-Oct.

Emerald Bay State Park. Approximately 8 miles north of South Lake Tahoe, on Hwy. 89. The park contains in it the magnificent Emerald Bay, billed as "the most beautiful inland harbor in the world." Also splendid walking trails, campgrounds, picnic areas and waterfalls. A highlight of the park is the fabled *Vikingsholm*, situated in the cradle of the bay, and reached by way of a mile-long hike from the parking area on the northwest corner. *Vikingsholm* is a masterful replica of a 1,200-year-old Viking castle, acknowledged as "the finest example of Scandinavian architecture in North America." Tours of the 38-room castle are conducted by park rangers during the summer months. Some lovely Scandinavian antiques and furniture can be viewed within, as well as Norwegian weavings, a Swedish wood-carving, and several ornate fixtures. Open July-Aug. 10-4.

Fallen Leaf Lake. Self-contained summer resort, 5 miles west of South Tahoe; reached via Fallen Leaf Road, the turnoff for which lies just past Camp Richardson, off Hwy. 89. View Fallen Leaf Lodge, built in 1913. Also camping, hiking, fishing, boating and horseback riding possibilities. Open May-Sept.

RECREATION

Tours. *Lake Tahoe Tours* offers regularly scheduled, narrated minibus tours of Lake Tahoe and Emerald Bay. For reservations, call (530) 544-8687/(800) 458-9743.

Lake Cruises. South Lake Tahoe has two large Mississippi river-boat type cruise boats: the *Tahoe Queen/Hornblower Cruises*, berthed at the Ski Run Marina on Lake Tahoe Blvd., (530) 541-3364/541-4652; and the *M.S. Dixie*, berthed at the Zephyr Cove Marina on Hwy. 50 east, (775) 588-3508/882-0786. Both offer year-round Emerald Bay and lake cruises; prices usually range from around $14.00-$16.00 for a day cruise to $38.00-$40.00 for a dinner and dance cruise (including dinner). Also berthed at Zephyr Cove is the trimaran *Woodwind*, offering cruises about one of the largest sailing vessels at the lake; (775) 588-3000.

Bicycling. Many miles of bike trails can be enjoyed in and around South Lake Tahoe, with bicycle rentals available from *Sierra Cycle Works,* 3430 Hwy. 50, (530) 541-7505; *Lakeview Sports,* 3131 Highway 50, (530) 544-7160; *Anderson's Bicycle Rental,* 645 Emerald Bay Rd., (530) 541-0500; *Tahoe Sports Ltd.,* Crescent V Center, Stateline, (530) 542-4000; and *Richardson's Resort Bicycle Rentals,* Camp Richardson, (530) 541-7522.

Beaches and Picnic Areas. There are several good, sandy beaches in the area. Among them, the *Regan* and *El Dorado* beaches, situated adjacent to one another along Lake Tahoe Blvd. (Hwy. 50) in the center of town; both have swimming and picnic areas, on-duty lifeguards, and restrooms. Regan Beach also has windsurfing and sailboard rentals. Another small in-city beach, *Connolly Beach*, is located behind the Timber Cove Lodge, at the end of Bal Bijou Rd.; it has swimming and picnicking possibilities, on-duty lifeguard, food stand, and restrooms. Other good beaches in the area include *Kiva Beach* and *Pope Beach,* just to the northwest of town, off Emerald Bay Road (Hwy. 89); and *Baldwin Beach,* also off Hwy. 89, just to the north of Kiva Beach. All three have good picnicking possibilities.

Boating. Boat rentals, buoys, and launching facilities are available at the following South Lake Tahoe marinas: *Richardson's Marina,* on Jameson Beach Rd. (off Hwy. 89), at Camp Richardson, (530) 541-1777; *Tahoe Keys Marina,* on Venice Dr. (off Tahoe Keys Blvd.), (530) 541-2155; *Timber Cove Marina,* on Wagon Rd. (off Hwy. 50), (530) 544-2942; *Ski Run Marina,* at the lake end of Ski Run Blvd., (530) 544-0200; *Lakeside Marina,* 828 Park Ave., (530) 541-6626; *Zephyr Cove Marina,* off Hwy. 50 east (4 miles northeast of Stateline), (775) 588-3833.

Golf. *Edgewood Tahoe Golf Course.* On Loop Rd., behind the Horizon Casino Resort; (775) 588-3566. 18 holes, 7563 yards, par 72; green fee: $150.00/ with cart (cart mandatory). Pro shop, driving range, restaurant, bar. *Tahoe Paradise Golf Course.* Off Hwy. 50, at Tahoe Paradise (4 miles south of the South Lake Tahoe Y); (530) 577-2121. 18 holes, 4119 yards, par 66; green fee: $30.00/18 holes, $20.00/9 holes. Pro shop, driving range, coffee shop. *Lake Tahoe Country Club.* On Hwy. 50 (1 mile south of Lake Tahoe Airport); (530) 577-0788. 18 holes, 6588 yards, par 71; green fee: $42.00. Pro shop, driving range, cocktail lounge and snack bar. *Glenbrook Golf Course.* On the east shore of Lake Tahoe, off Hwy. 50 (8 miles north of the Stateline); (775) 749-5201. 9 holes, 2591 yards, par 34; green fee: $39.00. Carts, pro shop, driving range, bar and snack bar.

Horseback Riding. Several different area stables offer horse rentals, trail rides, hay rides, breakfast and sunset rides, and a variety of other scenic rides. For rates and more information, contact any of the following stables: *Camp Richardson's Corral,* Emerald Bay Rd., Camp Richardson, (530) 541-3113; *Cascade Stables,* Hwy. 89, South Lake Tahoe, (530) 541-2055; *Sunset Ranch,* Hwy. 50 (just west of Lake Tahoe Airport), (530) 541-9001; *Zephyr Cove Stables,* Hwy. 50, Zephyr Cove (4 miles north of Stateline), (775) 588-5664.

Hiking. The South Lake Tahoe area also offers abundant opportunities for hiking, with at least 20 different trails leading through the adjoining 63,469-acre Desolation Wilderness and parts of the El Dorado and Tahoe National Forests. For maps and wilderness permits, contact the *Lake Tahoe Basin Management Unit,* South Lake Tahoe, at (530) 573-2600.

WINTER SPORTS

Downhill Ski Areas

Heavenly Valley. This 20-square-mile expanse, America's largest alpine ski area, straddles the California-Nevada stateline a couple of miles to the south of South Lake Tahoe's "casino district"; West Heavenly lies in California, and Heavenly North in Nevada. In California, approach via Ski Run Blvd., off Hwy. 50; in Nevada, Benjamin Drive, off the Kingsbury Grade, leads straight to the base of the mountain. Heavenly's elevations: top 10,167 feet, base 6,100 feet; vertical drop 3,600 feet. Facilities available: 31 lifts, tram, helicopter skiing, NASTAR races, lessons, rentals, restaurant and bar, and shuttle bus. Lift prices: $52.00/adults, $38.00/youth (ages 13-15), $24.00/children (ages 6-12); half day: $38.00 adults, $28.00/youth, $14.00/children. Phone (530) 541-1330/541-7544.

Kirkwood Ski Resort. Take Hwy. 89 south to Pickett's Junction; at the junction take Hwy. 88 west to Kirkwood. Although slightly out of the way, this ski area enjoys some of the heaviest snowfall in the region, and remains open until the Fourth of July. Elevations: top 9,800 feet, base 7,800 feet; vertical drop 2,000 feet. Facilities include 12 lifts, NASTAR races, lessons, rentals, bar, snack bar, restaurant, store, and shuttle bus. Lift prices: $45.00/adults, $35.00/youth (ages 13-18), $23.00/seniors, $7.00/children; half day: $36.00/adults, $26.00/youth, $17.00/seniors, $7.00/children. Phone (209) 258-3000/258-6000.

Sierra-at-Tahoe Ski Area. Just off Hwy. 50, approximately 12 miles southwest of South Lake Tahoe. Elevations: top 8,852 feet, base 6,640 feet; vertical drop 2,212 feet. Facilities: 10 lifts, lessons, rentals, day lodges, snack bar, mountain top restaurant, and shuttle bus. Lift prices: $45.00/adults, $35.00/young adults (ages 13-22), $24.00/seniors, $7.00/children; half day: $32.00/adults, $25.00/young acults (ages 13-22), $24.00/seniors, $7.00/children. Phone (530) 659-7475/659-7453.

Nordic Ski Areas

Kirkwood Cross Country. At the Kirkwood Ski Area on Hwy. 88, 28 miles south of South Lake Tahoe. 80 kilometers of trails; tours, lessons, rentals, restaurant, lodge, child care, and shuttle bus. Trail fee: $15.00/adults, $5.00/children (7-12); half day: $12.00/adults, $3.00/children. Phone (209) 258-6000.

RESTAURANTS

(Restaurant prices—based on full course dinner, excluding drinks, tax and tips—are categorized as follows: *Deluxe*, over $30; *Expensive*, $20-$30; *Moderate*, $10-$20; *Inexpensive*, under $10.)

The Beacon. *Expensive.* Hwy. 89, Camp Richardson; (530) 541-0630. Beachfront restaurant, serving primarily seafood and continental dishes. Live jazz music. Lunch and dinner; brunch on weekends. Reservations advised.

Cantina Bar and Grill. *Inexpensive-Moderate.* 765 Emerald Bay Rd.; (530) 544-1233. Authentic Mexican cooking. Cocktail lounge. Lunch and dinner daily.

Christiania Inn. *Deluxe.* Across from Heavenly Valley ski area; (530) 544-7337. Delightful alpine inn, with large stone fireplace. Gourmet continental cuisine; creative desserts. Dining room featured in *Bon Appetit* magazine. Dinner daily; reservations required.

The Dory's Oar. *Expensive.* 1041 Fremont Ave.; (530) 541-6603. Well-known seafood restaurant, established in 1975. House specialties include live Maine lobster and Maryland soft shell crabs. New England atmosphere. Open for dinner daily, lunch Mon.-Fri. Reservations recommended.

Fresh Ketch. *Expensive.* 2435 Venice Dr. East (at the Tahoe Keys Marina); (530) 541-5683. Spectacular views of the lake, and an enchanting waterfall featured inside the restaurant. Long Island oysters are the favorite here; also some poultry. Lunch and dinner daily; brunch on weekends. Reservations suggested.

Friday's Station. *Expensive.* At Harrah's, Stateline; (775) 588-6611. Notable Tahoe steakhouse, located on the 18th floor of the hotel, with good all-round views. Open dinner daily.

Llewellyn's. *Deluxe.* At Harvey's Resort Hotel; (775) 588-2411. Superb restaurant on the top floor of the hotel, with panoramic views of the lake and

Sierras. Contemporary cuisine. Piano bar. Lunch and dinner daily; Sunday brunch. Reservations required.

Paul Kennedy's Steak House. *Moderate-Expensive.* 4114 Hwy. 50; (530) 541-5077. Popular steakhouse, located adjacent to Stateline casinos. Excellent selection of steaks; also seafood. Extensive wine list. Open for dinner. Reservations suggested.

Primavera. *Expensive.* At Caesar's Tahoe; (775) 588-3515. Delightful poolside restaurant, specializing in Italian cuisine. House specialties include veal, calamari and linguini. Lunch and dinner daily; European-style brunch on weekends.

Scusa. *Moderate.* 1142 Ski Run Blvd., South Lake Tahoe; (530) 542-0100. Traditional Italian dishes, including a variety of fresh, homemade pasta, and gourmet pizza. Also offers seafood. Open for lunch and dinner.

The Sage Room. *Expensive.* Housed in Harvey's Resort Hotel; (775) 588-2411. Exceptional dining, with several dishes prepared at the tableside. Steak specialties; Western atmosphere. Open for dinner daily; reservations required.

The Summit. *Deluxe.* At Harrah's Hotel-Casino; (775) 588-6606. Gourmet restaurant on 16th floor. Superb Continental cuisine. Live music. Some lake and mountain views. Open for dinner. Reservations required.

Swiss Chalet Restaurant. *Expensive.* Hwy. 50, 4 miles west of Stateline; (530) 544-3304. Owned and operated by the chef for over 30 years, the restaurant serves excellent steaks and European cuisine; also homemade Swiss pastries. Delightful alpine atmosphere. Cocktail lounge. Dinners daily; reservations recommended.

Tep's Villa Roma. *Moderate.* 3450 Hwy. 50; (530) 541-8227. Traditional Italian dishes, and freshly-baked Italian breads and garlic sticks. Also seafood specialties, and all-you-can-eat antipasto bar. Open for dinner daily.

The Waterwheel. *Moderate.* Crescent V Shopping Center, cnr. Hwy. 50 and Park Ave.; (530) 544-4158. Authentic Mandarin and Szechwan cuisine. Open for dinner daily.

Zachary's Restaurant. *Expensive.* Behind Roundhill Mall, 2 miles north of Stateline; (775) 588-2108. Established, well-known restaurant, serving seafood, steaks, chicken, veal and lamb. Also homemade desserts. Dinner from 6 p.m.; reservations recommended.

TAHOE CITY

A Mecca for Skiers

Tahoe City is a small, well-wooded resort town, situated at an elevation of around 6,300 feet, at the northwest corner of Lake Tahoe, America's most celebrated alpine lake. The town, in fact, is at the center of an important ski area, with a score or more alpine and nordic ski resorts lying within a 25-mile radius of it. It is also quite popular with summer vacationers, with typical summertime activities centering on boating, lake cruising, rafting, wind-surfing, swimming, bicycling, hiking and golf. There are, in addition, dozens of fine European and seafood restaurants in and around town, and an abundance of well-stocked ski shops and specialty stores.

Tahoe City lies approximately 200 miles east of San Francisco, reached on Interstate 80—which leads directly to the town of Truckee, to the northwest—and a small, 15-mile detour southward on Highway 89.

DISCOVERING TAHOE CITY

Tahoe City, it must be fair to say, is one of California's most charming small towns, dotted quite splendidly with knotty-pine stores and a handful of wood-frame shopping centers, and with only a dozen or so enchanting little streets meandering through it. The town, of course, has much of tourist value, but its chief interest lies in its abounding ski areas—20 in all! Here, for instance, just one-quarter mile south of town, off Highway 89, is Granlibakken, the smallest and oldest ski resort at Lake Tahoe, originally established in 1926, and with its old ski hill still in operation. Another, Lakeview Cross Country Center, with its 65 kilometers of groomed cross-country trails journeying through scenic wooded terrain, lies at the eastern edge of town, a half-mile or so, off Highway 28.

Northeast of Tahoe City, some miles, are other notable ski areas, among them Mount Rose and Diamond Peak at Ski Incline—both lying on the Nevada side of the lake—and Northstar-at-Tahoe, the greatest of all. This last, situated near the Brockway Summit (Highway 267), approximately 15 miles distant, is in fact one of the "Big Five" ski areas of Lake Tahoe (the others being Squaw Valley, Heavenly Valley, Alpine Meadows and Kirkwood), described as "an intermediate skier's paradise." Northstar also, we might add, is a superb, self-contained resort, encompassing 2,500 acres, and with a full range of visitor facilities, including condominiums, restaurants, horse stables, an Olympic-size swimming pool, and an 18-hole golf course. It also offers good hiking and fishing possibilities in summer.

The gem of Tahoe City's ski areas, however, it has to be admitted, is Squaw Valley USA, located some 4 miles to the northwest, just off Highway 89. Squaw Valley was the site of the 1960 Winter Olympic Games, and is now one of the most prestigious ski resorts in the world. The valley, as such, is surrounded by a series of picturesque, 9,000-foot-high mountains, cut into which are over 100 ski trails, with such striking names as Headwall, Red Dog and K-2. There is also a well-known restaurant here, Granite Chief, perched on a mountain of the same name, at an elevation of over 8,000 feet, and reached by way of an aerial tram which offers panoramic, all-round views. Squaw Valley, besides, has good lodging and skier facilities, and over Christmas-New Year and during "Snowfest"—a local winter festival held in early March—the valley features some spectacular torchlight parades in which skiers carrying lighted torches descend the slopes in formation, creating a scene to behold.

Immediately south of Squaw Valley, and reached on a side road that goes off Highway 89 a mile or so to the south, is Alpine Meadows, the other big ski area of Tahoe City, and also with national fame. The resort boasts over 2,000 acres of skiable terrain, and more than 100 different ski runs, including one that is 2 miles long. Alpine also enjoys an annual snowfall of some 450 inches, and one of the longest ski seasons at the lake, remaining open well into spring, often until the Fourth of July.

North and northwest of Alpine Meadows and Squaw Valley are

TAHOE CITY

TO KINGS BEACH

N

TO TRUCKEE

Bunker Rd.

Fairway Dr.

Skylark St.

Grove St.

Pioneer St.

Jackpine St.

Tahoe St.

North Lake Blvd.

Bliss St.

Tahoe Recreation Area

Tahoe City Golf Course

28

River Rd.

River

89   89

Truckee

West Lake Blvd.

Tavern Rd.

League Dr.

Lake Tahoe

Kimberly St.

Tonopah Rd.

Rawhide

Virginia

Goldfield

Silverado

Bonanza St.

Cathedral Rd.

Tavern Rd.

Olympic

St.

Tonopah Rd.

Chapel Rd.

Feet

0   1000   2000

89

TO HOMEWOOD

1. Lake Tahoe Dam
2. Gatekeeper's Cabin
3. Fanny Bridge
4. Tahoe City Y
5. Watson's Log Cabin

6. Tahoe Commons Beach
7. Tahoe City Boatworks
8. Cobblestone Mall
9. Roundhouse Mall

10. Lighthouse Center
11. Granlibakken Lodge and Tennis Courts
12. Stone Chapel

yet other ski areas, including Tahoe-Donner, Soda Springs, Sugar Bowl, Donner Ski Ranch, Boreal Ridge, and Royal Gorge, the most famous. The Royal Gorge is in fact the largest nordic ski resort in North America, encompassing more than 9,000 acres of terrain, with roughly 320 kilometers of groomed trails, 10 warming huts and three full-service cafes.

Apart from the ski scene, Tahoe City itself has something of interest, too. Here, for instance, you can search out the celebrated Fanny Bridge, located just to the south of the Tahoe City "Y" (intersection of Highways 89 and 28) and built across the mouth of the Truckee River, Lake Tahoe's sole outlet. The bridge overlooks the ancient Lake Tahoe Dam, originally built in 1870, and rebuilt in 1910, to regulate the flow of water from the lake. Just south of Fanny Bridge and the dam, and also worth visiting, is the picturesque Gatekeeper's Cabin, a splendid, late 19th-century log cabin, which now houses the North Lake Tahoe Historical Society Museum, with displays of items of local historical interest.

Among other places of interest, more or less in the center of town, is the small but lovely Watson's Log Cabin, originally built in 1880 as the honeymoon cottage of pioneer settlers Robert and Stella Watson, and now a living museum, completely restored with original, period furnishings, and also maintained by the North Tahoe Historical Society. South, also of interest, is the Tahoe City Commons Beach — a good place for picnicking, swimming and sunbathing.

Try to also find the time to visit Tahoe City's Cobblestone Mall— a charming replica of a Bavarian alpine village—and the Boatworks and Roundhouse malls, the latter housed in the old, turn-of-the-century Southern Pacific Railroad roundhouse building. The Boatworks Mall, of course, is notable for its art galleries and waterfront restaurants, besides which it has at the front of it the Tahoe Boat Company Marina.

HOW TO GET THERE

Tahoe City lies approximately 200 miles northeast of San Francisco, or 115 miles from Sacramento. The best and most direct way to reach it is by way of *Interstate 80*, which leads directly to the town of Truckee, then *Highway 89* south, some 14 miles, directly into Tahoe City.

The nearest commercial airport to Tahoe City, the Reno International Airport, lies approximately 50 miles to the northeast. Several different commercial airlines service this airport, including *American Airlines* (800) 433-7300/(775) 329-9217, *United Airlines* (800) 241-6522/(775) 329-1020, *Delta* (800) 221-1212/(775) 323-1661, *American West* (800) 247-5692/(775) 348-2777, *Continental* (800) 525-0280/(775) 322-9075, *Northwest* (800) 225-2525, *US Air* (800) 428-4322/(775) 329-9365.

TOURIST INFORMATION

North Lake Tahoe Chamber of Commerce. 245 North Lake Blvd., Tahoe City; (530) 581-6900. Tourist information brochures, including listings of accommodations and restaurants; maps, calendar of events.

North Tahoe Resort Association. 950 North Lake Blvd., Tahoe City, CA 96145; (530) 583-3494/(800) 822-5959 in California/(800) 824-8557 from outside California. Tourist information, ski packages. The Bureau also offers an accommodations reservation service; for reservations and information, call the toll-free numbers.

ACCOMMODATIONS

Bed & Breakfast Inns

Cottage Inn. *$140-$210.* 1690 West Lake Blvd.; (530) 581-4073. Bed and breakfast inn with 8 duplex units and 6 individual rooms. Full breakfast, served in dining room or in bed. Also sauna. Close to beach.

Mayfield House. *$85-$150.* 236 Grove St.; (530) 583-1001. Established Old Tahoe bed and breakfast inn, housed in historic stone cottage. 6 rooms, some private baths. Full breakfast, with homemade pastries. Centrally located.

Rockwood Lodge. *$100-$200.* 5295 West Lake Blvd., Homewood (6 miles south of Tahoe City); (530) 525-5273. Delightful, 50-year-old stone lodge, with 5 guest rooms. Antique decorated; feather beds, down comforters, Laura Ashley fabrics. Breakfast includes homemade croissants and freshly squeezed fruit juices. No smoking.

Hotels and Motels

Lake of the Sky Motor Inn. *$79-$109.* 955 North Lake Blvd.; (530) 583-3305. 22 rooms, TV, phones, pool.

Pepper Tree Inn. *$55-$90.* 645 North Lake Blvd.; (530) 583-3711. 51 rooms, several with lakeviews; TV, phones, pool and sun deck.

River Ranch. *$59-$110.* Cnr. Hwy. 89 and Alpine Meadows Rd.; (530) 583-4264. Refurbished Old Tahoe lodge on the banks of the Truckee River. 22 rooms, with TV and phones; restaurant and patio, overlooking river.

Sunnyside Lodge. *$90-$175.* 1850 West Lake Blvd., Sunnyside (2 miles south of Tahoe City); (530) 583-7200. Luxury resort in lakeside setting; completely remodeled. 23 rooms, individually decorated; private balconies overlooking lake. Excellent restaurant on premises, serving breakfast, lunch and dinner.

Tahoe City Inn. *$50-$120.* 790 North Lake Blvd.; (530) 581-3333. 33 rooms; in-room spas, waterbeds. Some lake views.

Tahoe City Travelodge. *$75-$100.* 455 North Lake Blvd.; (530) 583-3766. 47 rooms, TV, phones, pool and hot tub.

SEASONAL EVENTS

March. *Snowfest.* Held during the first and second weeks of the month. 10-day winter carnival, featuring a variety of ski races, fireworks, torchlight parade at Squaw Valley, crowning of a Snowfest Queen, ice sculpture competition, and several other gala happenings. For schedule of events and information, call (530) 583-7625. *Great Ski Race.* Hosted by the Lakeview Cross-country Ski Area, usually scheduled for the first weekend in March. 30-kilometer ski race from Tahoe City to Truckee, claimed to be the largest race of its kind in the West, with nearly 800 participants. For more information, call (530) 583-9353.

June. *Truckee-Tahoe Airshow.* Last weekend of the month. Well-known Northern California airshow; events include aerobatics, historic war games, and air races; also display of vintage planes. More information on (530) 582-9068.

July. *Fourth of July.* Fireworks at the Tahoe City Commons Beach, in the center of town. *Lake Tahoe Summer Music Festival.* Second and third weeks. A variety of classical and popular music performances at several locations in North Lake Tahoe. For a complete schedule, call (530) 583-3101. *Sand Harbor Music Festival.* Held at Sand Harbor (just south of Incline Village); fourth week. Music concerts, featuring jazz, pop and blues. Beach setting. For a schedule and more information, contact the North Tahoe Fine Arts Council, (775) 831-7267.

August. *Concours d'Elegance.* First weekend of the month. Antique boat show, featuring pre-war wooden boats; hosted by the Sierra Boat Company, Carnelian Bay; (530) 546-2551. *Shakespeare at Sand Harbor.* Annual, two-week event; series of Shakespeare plays, performed by members of professional theater companies. Beach setting. For schedule and reservations, call the North Tahoe Fine Arts Council at (775) 831-7267.

PLACES OF INTEREST

Squaw Valley. 4 miles northwest of Tahoe City, off Hwy. 89. World-renowned ski resort; site of the 1960 Winter Olympic Games. Ride the *Squaw Valley Aerial Tram* to High Camp, perched at 8,200 feet, where there is a swimming lagoon, spa, poolside cafe and ice-skating rink, open to the public. Also bungee jumping. Spectacular view enroute. Tram operates year-round. Cost of tram ride $14.00 adults, $12.00 seniors, $5.00 children. For more information, call (530) 583-6985.

Fanny Bridge and Outlet Gates. Located at the Tahoe City "Y" (intersection of Hwys. 89 and 28). The bridge is a summertime favorite; watch Rainbow trout in pool beneath the bridge. The dam at the Outlet Gates was built in 1910. This is also the lake's only outlet.

Gatekeeper's Log Cabin Museum. Just south of Outlet Gates, reached via a small side road off West Lake Blvd. (between Truckee River Bank and Bridgetender restaurant). Restored log cabin situated in park-like setting, now a museum operated by North Lake Tahoe Historical Society. View artifacts and old Tahoe photographs. The museum also houses the Marion Steinbach Indian Basket Collection. The museum is open May-Oct., daily 11-5. (530) 583-1762.

Watson's Log Cabin. In the heart of Tahoe City, on North Lake Blvd. Oldest building in the area, built in the 1880s as the honeymoon cottage of Robert and Stella Watson. Now houses a North Lake Tahoe Historical Society Museum, with exhibits of local historic interest. Open during summer. Call (530) 583-8717 for hours.

Tahoe City Commons Beach. Popular beach area situated in the center of town. Site of annual Fourth of July fireworks display. Swimming and picnic areas, children's playground, fire pits, restrooms. Open to the public year-round.

Fleur du Lac. 4 miles south of Tahoe City on Hwy. 89. This is the former Henry J. Kaiser Estate, where "Godfather II" was filmed. Great big stone wall encircles the estate, and it is generally not open to public. It is best viewed from the lake; take a cruise on board North Lake Tahoe Cruises' *Sunrunner,* for this pauses before the estate, with commentary on its history.

Chamber's Landing. Just past Homewood, reached via a small side road off Hwy. 89. Restored 1870s over-water clubhouse, now housing a cocktail bar and lounge; offers superb, all-round views of the lake. The clubhouse is open during summer. There is also a sandy public beach here.

Sugar Pine Point State Park. Nearly 8 miles south of Tahoe City. 2,000-acre park with several enchanting walks through it. Visit the fabulous *Ehrman Mansion*, located at the end of a small side road, east off the highway (the turnoff is marked with a "picnic area" sign). The mansion is a magnificent, gabled and turreted three-story edifice, built in 1903 and billed as "the finest High Sierra summer home in California." Splendid grounds, open to the public year-round. The mansion itself is open during summer, with State Park personnel offering guided tours through it. Park fee: $6.00 per car. Phone, (530) 525-7982.

Northstar-at-Tahoe. Just over the Brockway Summit (north of Kings Beach), off Hwy. 267. 2,500-acre "model development," dating from the early 1970s. There are alpine and nordic ski areas here, as well as an 18-hole golf course; and accommodations and restaurants. Also features an arts and crafts fair, and several live performances in summer. For information on events and visitor facilities, call (530) 562-1010.

Ponderosa Ranch. Situated at the southeast corner of Incline Village, off Hwy. 28. Rambling western theme park; site of the TV series, "Bonanza." Visit the *Cartwright Home, Mystery Mine Shaft, Ponderosa Church, petting farm,* and several western shops and museums with interesting displays of ancient firearms, carriages, wagons, and farm machinery. Also visit stables for scenic horseback rides through the Ponderosa back country. Open May-Oct., 10-6; admission $9.50 adults, $5.50 children. For information, call (775) 831-0691.

Art Galleries. *Sierra Galleries,* Boatworks Mall, Tahoe City, (530) 581-5111; bronze sculptures and paintings. *High Sierra Silver Works,* 600 N. Lake Blvd., Tahoe City, (530) 583-1600; variety of artists, material and mediums represented, with an operating jewelry studio. *Pogan Gallery,* 255 North Lake Blvd., Tahoe City, (530) 583-0553; original works of regional artists.

RECREATION

Lake Cruises. *Tahoe Gal*, operated by North Tahoe Cruises, offers daily scenic and historic cruises along the west shore on board a Mississippi-riverboat-style paddlewheeler, May-Oct. The Tahoe Gal departs from the marina at the Lighthouse Center—off North Lake Boulevard— in Tahoe City. Cruise cost is $15.00-$20.00 for adults, $5.00-$8.00 for children. For reservations and information, call (530) 583-0141.

Rafting. River rafting is a favorite summertime recreational activity in the Tahoe City area, with the 4-mile stretch of the Truckee River, between Tahoe City and River Ranch, especially well-liked. Raft rentals are available from *Mountain Air Sports*, (530) 583-5606, *Fanny Bridge Raft Rentals,* (530) 583-

3021, and *Truckee River Rafting Center*, (530) 583-0123, all situated just near the Tahoe City Y, on River Road (Hwy. 89) or West Lake Boulevard.

Bicycling. Bicycling is also quite popular in and around Tahoe City, with several miles of bike paths to enjoy. For bicycle rentals, contact any of the following: *Cyclepaths Mountain Bike,* 1785 West Lake Blvd., (530) 581-1171; *Tahoe Gear,* 5095 West Lake Blvd., Homewood, (530) 525-5233; *Olympic Bike Shop,* 620 North Lake Blvd., (530) 581-2500; *Porter's Ski & Sport,* 501 North Lake Blvd., (530) 583-2314.

Boating. Boat rentals, jet ski rentals, and launching facilities are available at several marinas in the area. Among them, the *Tahoe Boat Company Marina* at the Boatworks Mall, (530) 583-5567; *Sunnyside Resort & Marina,* off Hwy. 89 (2 miles south of Tahoe City), (530) 583-7201; *Obexer's Marina,* Hwy. 89, Homewood (6 miles south of Tahoe City), (530) 525-7962; *High & Dry Marina,* Hwy. 89, Homewood, (530) 525-5966.

Golf. *Tahoe City Golf Course.* In Tahoe City (behind the Bank of America); (530) 583-1516. 9 holes, 2700 yards, par 33; green fees: $26.00/9 holes, $40.00/ 18 holes. Pro shop, driving range, restaurant. *Northstar-at-Tahoe Golf Course.* Off Highway 267, approximately 15 miles northeast of Tahoe City; (530) 587-0290. 18 holes, 6897 yards, par 72; green fees: $67.00/all day, $25.00/twilight. Pro shop, driving range, restaurant. *Old Brockway Golf Course.* Cnr. Hwys. 28 and 267, Kings Beach (approximately 8 miles northeast of Tahoe City); (530) 546-9922. 9 holes, 3237 yards, par 35; green fees: $25.00/9 holes, $45.00/18 holes. Squaw *Creek Golf Course,* at the Resort at Squaw Creek, Squaw Valley; (800) 327-3353/(530) 583-6300. 18-hole, Robert Trent-Jones-designed golf course, 6931 yards, par 71; green fees $110.00 (including cart). Pro shop, driving range, practice putting green, club rentals.

Horseback Riding. Horse rentals, trail rides and scenic rides are available at the following stables in the area: *Alpine Meadows Stables,* 2600 Alpine Meadows Rd. (4 miles north of Tahoe City, off Highway 89), (530) 583-3905; *Squaw Valley Stables,* 1525 Squaw Valley Rd., (530) 583-7433; *Northstar Stables,* 910 Northstar Dr., Northstar (off Highway 267), (530) 562-1230.

Tours. *Cal-Vada Aircraft* at the Tahoe City Marina offers scenic flights over the lake; phone (530) 583-0673/546-3984.

WINTER SPORTS

Downhill Ski Areas

Alpine Meadows. 7 miles northwest of Tahoe City, at the end of Alpine Meadows Rd. (off Hwy. 89). Elevations: top 8,700 feet, base 6,840 feet; vertical drop 1,730 feet. Facilities: 12 lifts, NASTAR races, lessons, rentals, child care, snack bar, restaurant, bar, and shuttle bus. Lift prices: $48.00/adults,$36.00/ juniors (13-18), $26.00/seniors, $10.00/children (7-12), $6.00/children (6 and under); half day: $36.00/adults, $26.00/seniors, $10.00/children (7-12), $6.00/ children (6 and under). Phone (530) 583-4232/583-6914.

Boreal Ridge. 10 miles west of Truckee, just off I-80 (take Castle Peak exit). Elevations: top 7,800 feet, base 7,200 feet, vertical drop 600 feet. Facilities: 9 lifts, night skiing, lessons, rentals, snack bar and restaurant. Lift prices: $28.00/ adults, $14.00/seniors, $10.00/children (5-12); night skiing: $19.00/adults, $10.00/seniors and children. Phone (530) 426-3666/426-3663.

Diamond Peak. Ski Way, off Country Club Dr., Incline Village. Elevations: top 8,540 feet, base 6,720, vertical drop 1,840 feet. Facilities: 6 lifts, lessons, rentals, snack bar, restaurant. Lift prices: $38.00/adults, $14.00/children; half day: $28.00/adults, $11.00/children. Special family packages available. Phone: (775) 831-3211/832-1177.

Donner Ski Ranch. West of Truckee; take Soda Springs exit off I-80, then 3½ miles down old Hwy. 40. Elevations: top 7,960 feet, base 7,135 feet, vertical drop 825 feet. Facilities: 6 lifts, night skiing, lessons, rentals, snack bar and restaurant. Lift prices: $23.00/adults, $10.00/juniors (6-12), 5.00/seniors and children; half day: $17.00/adults, $10.00/juniors, $5.00/seniors and children. Phone (530) 426-3635.

Granlibakken. Just south of Tahoe City, at the end of Tonopah Dr. (off Hwy. 89). Elevations: top 6,610 feet, base 6,330 feet, vertical drop 280 feet. Facilities: 2 lifts, lessons, rentals, snack bar, snow play area. Lift prices: $15.00/adults, $8.00/children; half day: $10.00/adults, $6.00/children. Phone (530) 583-9896.

Homewood Ski Area. On Hwy. 89, 6 miles south of Tahoe City. Elevations: top 7,880 feet, base 6,230 feet, vertical drop 1,650 feet. Facilities: 10 lifts, lessons, rentals, restaurant and snack bar. Lift prices: $36.00/adults, $25.00/juniors (ages 13-18), $11.00 youth (ages 9-12), $12.00 seniors; half day: $26.00/adults, $9.00/children (9-12), children 8 and under are free. Phone (530) 525-7256.

Mount Rose. 10 miles north of Incline Village, on Mount Rose Highway (Route 431). Elevations: top 9,700 feet, base 8,250 feet, vertical drop 1,450 feet. Facilities: 5 lifts, lessons, rentals, bar, snack bar and restaurant. Lift prices: $38.00/adults, $14.00/children, $19.00/seniors; half day: $26.00/adults, $8.00/children, $13.00/seniors. Phone (775) 849-0704/849-0706.

Northstar-at-Tahoe. Just off Hwy. 267, 6½ miles southeast of Truckee. Elevations: top 8,600 feet, base 6,400 feet, vertical drop 2,200 feet. Facilities: 11 lifts, NASTAR races, lessons, rentals, day lodge, store, snack bar, restaurant, and shuttle bus. Lift prices $48.00/adults, $38.00/young adults (ages 13-22), $23.00/seniors, $10.00/children; half day: $34.00/adults, $32.00/young adults, $23.00 / seniors, $10.00/children. Phone (530) 562-1010/562-1330.

Soda Springs. West of Truckee; on old Hwy. 40, near Soda Springs exit off I-80. Elevations: top 7,352 feet, base 6,700 feet, vertical drop 652 feet. Facilities: 3 lifts, night skiing, snowboarding, lessons and rentals; also snow tubing. Lift prices: $15.00/adults, $15.00/children (ages 7-12); half day: $15.00/adults, $15.00/children. Phone (530) 426-3666.

Squaw Valley U.S.A. 8 miles northwest of Tahoe City, at the end of Squaw Valley Road (off Hwy. 89). Elevations: top 8,900 feet, base 6,200 feet, vertical drop 2,700 feet. Facilities: 27 lifts and 2 gondolas. NASTAR races, night skiing, lessons, rentals, snack bar, restaurants, and shuttle bus; also snow tubing. Lift prices: $49.00/adults, $24.00/juniors (ages 13-15), $5.00/children (12 and under); half day: $33.00/adults, $24.00/juniors, $5.00/children. Phone (530) 583-6985/583-6955.

Sugar Bowl. West of Truckee, take Soda Springs exit off I-80, then onto old Hwy. 40. Elevations: top 8,383 feet, base 6,881 feet, vertical drop 1,502 feet. Facilities: 8 lifts and 1 gondola, night skiing, lessons, rentals, snack bar and restaurant. Lift prices: $45.00/adults, $39.00/juniors (ages 13-21), $20.00/seniors, $10.00/children; half day: $30.00/adults, $20.00/seniors, $10.00/children. Phone (530) 426-3651/426-3847.

Tahoe Donner. 2½ miles northwest of Truckee, off Donner Pass Road. Elevations: top 7,350 feet, base 6,750 feet, vertical drop 600 feet. Facilities: 3 lifts, lessons, rentals, snack bar and restaurant. Lift prices: $26.00/adults, $12.00/children and seniors; half day: $15.00/adults, $7.00/children and seniors. Phone (530) 587-6028.

Nordic Ski Areas

Clair Tappan. Old Hwy. 40, Soda Springs. 10 kilometers of trails; lodge. Trail fee: $7.00/adults, $3.50/children. Phone (530) 426-3632.

Diamond Peak Cross Country. 1210 Ski Way, Incline Village. 35 kilometers of trails; tours, lodge. Trail fee: $14.00/adults, $8.00/children; half day: $11.00/adults, $6.00/children; dog pass/ $3.00. Phone (775) 832-1177.

Eagle Mountain Cross Country. 20 miles west of Donner Summit, take Yuba Gap exit off I-80. 75 kilometers of trails, warming huts, day lodge, snack bar, lessons and rentals. Trail fee: $16.50/adults, $10.00/children (ages 7-12), $10.00/seniors; half day: $13.50/adults, $10.00/seniors and children. Phone (530) 389-2254.

Lakeview Cross Country Ski Center. Off Hwy. 28, 2½ miles northeast of Tahoe City. 30 miles of trails; tours, warming huts, day lodge, snack bar. Trail fee: $15.00/adults, $12.00/seniors and juniors (ages 13-17), $6.00/children (7-12); half day: $12.00/adults, $9.00/seniors and juniors, $6.00/children; twilight special (after 3 p.m.) $5.00/adults, $4.00/seniors and juniors, $3.00/children. Phone (530) 583-0484/583-9858.

Northstar Cross Country. Off Hwy. 267, 6 miles south of Truckee. 65 kilometers of trails; tours, lodge, restaurant, child care. Trail fee: $17.00/adults, $10.00/children; half day: $13.00/adults, $8.00/children. Phone (530) 562-2475.

Royal Gorge. A mile from I-80, at the Soda Springs exit. 320 kilometers of trails; tours, warming huts, lodge, restaurant. Trail fee: $21.50/adults, $9.50/children (ages 12-16); half day: $14.50/adults, $9.50/children . Phone (530) 426-3871.

Squaw Creek Cross Country. Off Squaw Valley Rd. (which goes off Hwy. 89), Squaw Valley. 30 kilometers of trails. Trail fee: $13.00/adults, $10.00/children; half day: $11.00/adults, $8.00/children. Phone (530) 583-6300.

Spooner Lake Cross Country. 1 mile north of junction of Hwys. 50 and 28. 101 kilometers of trails; lodge, snack bar. Trail fee: $15.00/adults, $3.00/children; half day: $11.00/adults, $3.00/children. Phone (775) 749-5349.

Tahoe Donner Cross Country. West of Truckee; off Northwoods Blvd. 65 kilometers of trails; tours, lodge. Trail fee: $16.00/adults, $14.00/seniors and youth (ages 13-17), $9.00/children; half day: $13.00/adults, $11.00/seniors and youth, $7.00/children. Phone (530) 587-9484.

RESTAURANTS

(Restaurant prices—based on full course dinner, excluding drinks, tax and tips—are categorized as follows: *Deluxe,* over $30; *Expensive,* $20-$30; *Moderate,* $10-$20; *Inexpensive,* under $10.)

Bacchi's Inn. *Moderate.* 2905 Lake Forest Rd.; (530) 583-3324. Established Italian restaurant, owned and operated by the same family for three generations. Great family- style dinners, generous portions. Bacchi's Minestrone Soup is famous the world over, featured in several gourmet magazines. Dinners daily. Reservations recommended.

Captain Jon's. *Deluxe.* Located at the Tahoe Vista Marina, Hwy. 28, Tahoe Vista; (530) 546-4819. French- country seafood, in lakeside setting. Among the favorites are Poached Salmon and Roast Duck with Blueberry or Oyster Sauce; also worthwhile are the seafood salads and fresh fruit daiquiris. Daily specials; extensive wine list. Dinners from 6 p.m., Tues.-Sun. Reservations required.

Christy Hill. *Expensive-Deluxe.* 115 Grove St.; (530) 583-8551. Long-standing Tahoe institution, specializing in California cuisine. Homemade chocolate mousse desserts. Lakefront setting. Open for lunch and dinner. Reservations required.

Hacienda Del Lago. *Inexpensive-Moderate.* Boatworks Mall (upstairs), 760 North Lake Blvd.; (530) 583-0358. Popular Mexican restaurant, with cocktail lounge and deck overlooking lake. Multi-flavored margaritas. Dinner daily.

Jake's on the Lake. *Expensive.* Boatworks Mall, 760 North Lake Blvd.; (530) 583-0188. Lakefront restaurant, featuring fine, fresh seafood. Daily specials. Open for dinner; reservations advised.

Le Petit Pier. *Deluxe.* 7252 North Lake Blvd., Tahoe Vista; (530) 546-4464. Acknowledged as one of the finest French restaurants in California, and with a splendid lakefront setting. Specialties are lamb and pheasant dishes. Open for dinner. Reservations required.

Pfeifer House. *Moderate-Expensive.* Hwy. 89, ½ mile west of Tahoe City; (530) 583-3102. Excellent European dishes; large portions. House specialty is Roast Duckling in Orange Sauce. Dinners from 6 p.m. daily (except Tues.). Reservations recommended.

River Ranch. *Moderate-Expensive.* Hwy. 89 at Alpine Meadows; (530) 583-4264. Historic lodge in lovely, on-the-river setting. Roast Duck Montmorency specialty; also seafood and veal preparations. Vintage wines by the glass. Open for dinner daily; reservations recommended.

Sunnyside Restaurant. *Expensive.* At the Sunnyside Lodge, 1850 West Lake Blvd., Sunnyside (2 miles south of Tahoe City); (530) 583-7200. Well-regarded Tahoe City restaurant, housed in delightful, rebuilt lodge. Serves primarily seafood and salads; also sushi bar. Lakeside deck for outdoor dining. Open for lunch and dinner daily, brunch on weekends.

Swiss Lakewood Restaurant. *Expensive.* 5055 West Lake Blvd., Homewood (6 miles south of Tahoe City); (530) 525-5211. Charming European lodge, serving fine Swiss and Continental cuisine. Open for dinner, Tues.-Sun.; reservations recommended.

Tahoe House. *Expensive.* 625 West Lake Blvd. (½ mile south of Tahoe City); (530) 583-1377. Swiss and California cuisine; seafood entrees, homemade pastas, freshly- baked bread and pastry desserts. Warm, knotty-pine decor. Dinners from 5 p.m. daily. Reservations advised.

Wolfdale's. *Expensive.* 640 North Lake Blvd.; (530) 583-5700. Creative California seafood. Lake views. Open for dinner daily; lunch in summer. Reservations suggested.

INDEX